BEFORE HIS FACE

BEFORE HIS FACE

MEDITATIONS
FOR PRIESTS AND RELIGIOUS

GASTON COURTOIS

VOLUME II

HERDER AND HERDER

1962

HERDER AND HERDER NEW YORK
232 Madison Ave., New York 16, N. Y.

Original edition
"Face au Seigneur, Récollections Sacerdotales",
Fleurus, Paris. Translated by Sister Helen Madeleine, S.N.D.

The Catholic Truth Society, London, are thanked for their kind permission
to use extracts from the C.T.S. English translation
of the Encyclical, *Menti Nostrae*

Nihil Obstat: Daniel Duivesteijn, S.T.D. Censor deputatus
Imprimatur: E. Morrogh Bernard. Vic. Gen.
Westmonasterii, die 29. Novembris, 1961.

The Nihil Obstat and Imprimatur are a declaration that a book or pamphlet
is considered to be free from doctrinal or moral error.
It is not implied that those who have granted the Nihil Obstat and Imprimatur agree
with the contents, opinions or statements expressed.

Library of Congress Catalog Card Number: 61-8837
First published in West Germany © 1962 Herder KG
Printed in West Germany by Herder

CONTENTS

PREFACE

A book of meditations for priests must fulfil certain exacting requirements. It must be readable, it must be practical and down to earth, it must present age-old truths in a new and challenging way, it must suggest a plan which different temperaments can adapt to their own inclinations and needs. *Before His Face* seems to meet all these conditions. Its short, penetrating reflections are easy to read and to reflect upon. Its subject matter embraces considerations which all priests will find related to their needs and to the shortcomings which issue from the human weakness which the great High Priest has deigned to strengthen and to sanctify. The book says nothing which every priest has not heard or read about over and over again, yet its manner of approach is fresh and buoyant, and its insight into the principles of the spiritual life is incisive and engaging. Its plan is flexible and spontaneous, suggesting more the vivacity and the resourcefulness of the preacher facing his audience than the impersonal formality of the writer at his desk.

I feel certain that this book will help greatly to meet a need that cannot be sufficiently provided for: that of affording incentive and direction for the priest's daily meditation and for his occasional day of recollection. In one of the chapters of the book, reference is made to the great reward merited by the priest who comes to the assistance of his fellow priests, and thus brings blessings to the thousands of souls to whom the priest in turn will transmit the benefits which he has gained. Every priest who uses this book in accordance with the authors' instructions will experience its transforming effects within his own soul, and will thus become a light to all who look to him for inspiration and for guidance. We cannot be sanctified independently of our efforts; but when we undertake seriously the work of our spiritual renewal, it helps us inestimably to have at our disposal a plan that has been worked out by a master of the spiritual life.

I am grateful to Sister Helen Madeleine for her painstaking efforts in preparing this English translation of the inspiring work by the Abbé Courtois. I invite all priests who come upon this book to put it to the test, not merely by reading it, but by meditating upon it, chapter by chapter, by submitting to the searching examinations of conscience which it suggests, and by adapting to their own circumstances the constructive resolutions which it enjoins.

† RICHARD CARDINAL CUSHING
Archbishop of Boston

THE PRIEST AND THE CHILD

Meditation

At the beginning of this meditation let us adore our Lord who, to save men, became a child. "For a child is born to us, and a son is given to us." (Isa. 9:6) Besides, is he not the Child of the Father, and did he not become incarnate so that men might recover, in him, their understanding and appreciation of that divine sonship?

According to the teaching which Saint Paul has handed down to us, every created thing must renew itself in Christ, under the influence of the Holy Spirit, for Christ is essentially the Son, and it is with the heart of a child that he gives himself unreservedly to his Father. Let us hear what our Lord himself says to us about childhood.

"Suffer the little children to come unto me, and forbid them not." (Mark 10:14)

"Whosoever shall not receive the Kingdom of God as a little child shall not enter into it." (Mark 10:15)

"Rather than he should scandalize one of these little ones it were better for him that a millstone were hanged about his neck and he cast into the sea." (Luke 17:2)

"Whosoever shall receive one such child as this in my name, receiveth me." (Mark 9:36)

Indeed, it seems, as we read the Gospel, that this attitude of our Lord towards children was far from being understood, not merely by the Pharisees, but even by the apostles. In William's *Life of our Lord* we read: "Why should he loiter with children?

There are more important things to do than waste time with them."

Children themselves understood that the divine Master was their friend. They gathered around him eagerly. Was it not a child in the front of the crowd who gave Jesus the loaves and fishes? Was it not the children who surrounded our Lord and welcomed him each time he entered Jerusalem? Indeed, chief priests became indignant, and asked him to keep the children quiet. But Jesus, defending the children, replied: "Have you never read; 'Out of the mouth of infants and sucklings thou hast perfected praise'?" (Matt. 21:15, 16)

In silence, we should ask our Lord to make us share his love for children, and to help us understand better what, as priests, our attitude towards these little souls should be.

To stimulate our prayer and our zeal, we should meditate on the following points. Firstly, why should we concern ourselves with children, and secondly, how should we manifest our concern for them?

The priest, as an extension of Christ, must have a very special affection for children. This was the point upon which Pope Pius XI insisted in his Encyclical, *Divini Illius Magistri*. A priest must be concerned with the whole world without any exceptions but, like our Lord, he must demonstrate particular concern for children.

In his Lenten Pastoral Letter in 1933, Cardinal Suhard, then Archbishop of Rheims, recalled the following words of Pope Pius XI: "The Christian education of children is the concern of all the faithful. If parents must devote all their attention to it, so all active Catholics must concentrate the major part of their efforts on it, and priests and nuns sacrifice their life for it. It is even proper that contemplatives should make it the principal object of their intentions, and apply their prayers and sacrifices to them."

This idea is stressed by Pope Pius XII at many points in his Encyclical, *Quemadmodum,* of January 6, 1946. "It is relevant here to comment that the Church, in all ages, has been full of concern for youth, and has seen the young as her special responsibility and in special need of her love. On account of what that concern has moved her to do, and what she continues to do,

2

she undoubtedly walks in the footsteps of her divine founder, and follows the teaching of the one who drew little children to him by his gentleness and who said to the apostles when they chided the childrens' mothers: 'Suffer the little children to come unto me, and forbid them not, for of such is the Kingdom of God.' For Christ loves that childhood which he himself assumed in mind as well as body. Christ loves childhood which is the mistress of humility, the guide of innocence, the ideal of meekness. Christ loves childhood, which he prescribes as a standard for the behaviour of the greatest men, to which he leads old age back, and which he urges those whom he destines for his eternal kingdom to imitate."

Canon Law (Canon 467; cf. 1330, 1331, 1332), moreover, places an obligation on parish priests to see that children have a Catholic education. The priest's mission is one of spiritual fatherhood. Saint Paul says: "My dear children, of whom I am in labour again, until Christ be formed in you." (Gal. 4:19) He must be deeply concerned about this spiritual birth in all those souls for which he is responsible, especially children, since childhood is normally the time when the seeds deposited at baptism fructify, and the time when the conscience and moral habits are formed.

In this awakening and growth of the religious sense, the family, the school, and institutions generally have their part to play and their responsibilities.

The role of the priest is twofold. Firstly, his influence over those who contribute to the education of the child, legally or naturally. Secondly, his direct influence on the child, for there are graces which are transmitted only by the priest, for the awakening and the growth of religious awareness, the moral sense, and the understanding of the Church. By his behaviour, by his words, by his testimony, the priest who is by profession the man of religion, the man of God, the man of conscience, the man of the Church, has a unique part to play. And that is why special authority and a special grace are attached to his intervention, whether it be in the confessional or outside.

Childhood is the appropriate age for Christian formation. The early years are of supreme importance for the shaping of the whole life. Even on the natural level, all psychologists agree that first sensations, first impressions, have a preponderant influence, generally unsuspected. That is still more true from the supernatural point of view. The newly baptized baby, with all the gifts of the Holy Ghost freshly bestowed on it, is, as it were, living on the supernatural plane.

Pope Pius XI, in his address at the canonization of the Little Flower, seems to have adopted this thesis of the child's identification with grace. We know the importance of this compact and living malleability of childhood, which did not escape the notice of Saint Thérèse of Lisieux. "When I considered these new-born souls, I compared them to soft wax on which one can etch any impression; that which is evil, just as well as that which is good. I understood the word of Jesus, that it would be better to be thrown into the sea than to scandalize one of these little ones. How many souls would achieve deep sanctity if they had been well directed from the beginning."

Nature takes special account of periods of acquisition, development, and growth. In his book on education, Henri Wallon writes: "For certain song-birds the genius of the breed only displays itself once. If the propitious moment passes without its being stimulated to sing by others of its kind, it is too late, the bird will never sing. The genius of childhood, too, must perhaps also be given its stimulus at a particular moment."

To repeat a phrase dear to Maria Montessori, childhood is the age of impressionable periods, and if we neglect these it will be difficult to recover what we have lost.

Childhood is the period when flexibility of thought is developed, when habits and reflexes are acquired. A medical inspector of schools in Paris reached the conclusion after much research that moral habits are three times easier to acquire before puberty than after.

Even if a child does not persevere because of social pressure the impression religion has made will be ingrained in him and will remain below the surface throughout his life. The memory of the holy priest who gave him a real knowledge of Christ will never be effaced. In the last years of life when childhood memories return vividly to the old or at the hour of death when the final choice is made, souls whose childhood were permeated

4

with a knowledge of Christ, are more likely to receive our Lord's pardon.

Finally, do not forget that childhood is humanity in flower. The humanity of tomorrow will be largely what childhood is today.

If we neglect this Christian formation, the child will be the victim of injurious influences which may well poison his entire life. Many children today are exposed to evil influences and are victims of pseudo-education. Physically and morally, modern life leads in many cases to a real massacre of the innocents. The failure of parents to supervise their children's education – and this applies to all classes of society – and the psychological errors of many "educationalists", lead to distortions of conscience of which children are the first victims.

We can be certain that if, on one pretext or another, priests and active Catholics cease to make Christian education for children the main object of their efforts, others will make themselves responsible for the care of the children in order to neutralize them, that is to say, in practice, to shut them off from God.

These thoughts should make us appreciate the grave danger if priests, in their desire to emphasize certain aspects of their ministry which are admittedly too often misunderstood, think they are achieving something, even though they pay too little attention to or even neglect the care of youth. "These things you ought to have done, and not to leave those undone." (Matt. 23:23)

How should we apply ourselves to the care of children? If the apostolate of youth has, in many cases, ended in at least outward and relative defeat, it is not because we have displayed too much concern about it, but too often because we have failed to allow for all the individual problems of each child in particular and of youth in general. If, in our mission, we want to succeed with children we must adopt suitable methods, and work in association with others.

What makes the apostolate of children particularly delicate and even difficult is, primarily, the fundamental difference between the psychology of the adult and the psychology of the child, and secondly the almost universal illusion that we understand children and that children understand us.

One educational writer has said: "The child is a being apart; his logic, his physiology are as unlike those of an adult as a tadpole is unlike a frog." And another wrote: "The discovery of a child calls to mind the venture of Columbus in discovering the New World. It is reaching into the unknown, beyond the barriers which our adult memory set up, into the language and thought of the child."

We can cure this ignorance by studying the laws of child psychology, by carefully observing children – and that is why there is no substitute for experience – but above all by an immense supernatural love for those little souls. There is, in truth, an intuitive knowledge, engendered only by love, an intuition which so marvellously takes possession of a mother's heart.

This psychological knowledge, which should extend not only to children in general but to each child in particular, will finally make us understand a certain number of mistakes which we are accustomed to make without paying attention to them. Our vocabulary may be too learned, our sentences too long, our sermons too abstract, our logic too deductive and too rational. Our sermons and ceremonies make no provision for children to play an active part and we ignore the hidden resources which a child's soul enjoys. There is ample matter there for meditation and good resolutions.

It is a fact that social environment exercises considerable pressure on the child and affects him profoundly. That is why the priest should know of all the influences which are exercised on the child, for good or bad, and seek to support, to neutralize, or to fight, these various influences. "To be efficacious, action to help youth should form part of a general plan dealing with the whole milieu and its customs. In other words, to work effectively for children the state and the spiritual community must work together." That is why action based on the conditions in which the children live must end in concerted action.

It is an elementary psychological law that the child is always "frustrated" when his various teachers appear to contradict each other. That is one of the reasons why our priestly care should strive for the combination of those forces serving the child. In the interest of these little ones, a priest must try to enlist the support of all those who, in one way or another, can have an influence on their souls: their teachers in school, the municipal authorities, even cinema owners, librarians, newsagents, militant Christians in Catholic Action, but above all, their families.

It is essential to take account of family conditions and to base what we do on them. The family receives its mission and consequently its right to give the child its education directly from God. This is an inalienable right.

The child, we must remember, is the surest way to the heart of adults. Often the best way to help the parents to make progress is to teach them how to bring up their children. The ideal is not only to do nothing without the family, but to do everything with the family, and as much as possible through the family. The same is true of the school when it is capable of carrying out its mission. But that does not in any way lessen the importance of the priest's work, which must be superimposed on the rest.

If so much of our devotion to duty is unrewarded, is it not because we lack the spirit of prayer and so come to forget the essential purpose? We dissipate our energies and waste our time on by-ways which lead us astray and exhaust us. Our essential purpose, to which all others are subordinate, is to make the life of Christ grow in the souls for which we are responsible. We can pave the way for this by solving any problems which poison the child's environment. Respect for the psychology of the child is a prerequisite. But only supernatural means can achieve results which are essentially of a supernatural order.

This elementary truth, which is valid over the whole field of the priest's work, is particularly important where children are concerned, since they possess a deeper intuition and a keener perception of spiritual truths than is commonly supposed.

The priest who is concerned with children ought to have a radiant faith. Children should feel in dealing with him that for him Jesus is not something, but someone; not an abstract and distant being, but the great friend to whom the priest is

7

happy to have consecrated his life. It is largely the inspiration of their priest's faith that will determine the extent to which religious feeling will influence their whole adult life.

A priest must never appear blasé or peevish when he speaks of Jesus. Nor must he appear listless or simply perfunctory when he speaks to Jesus. If a priest should reveal the supernatural world to the child by his faith he should inspire him to get into contact with that supernatural world by his example. As he educates the child to believe, he should educate him to pray at the same time.

The priest who is concerned with children must also radiate something of God's great charity. Are we always mindful of the responsibilities which our title of God's representative confers upon us? "I have seen God in a man!" cried a pilgrim returning from Ars. That is what all children should say when they think of us: "In Father I see the good God."

To help in the growth of Christ in the child the priest should appeal to all the supernatural forces which were deposited in the soul of the child at baptism. All those with experience of children's souls appreciate that the most elaborate techniques are ineffective if grace is not active, and that the ascendancy which an outstandingly skilful and persuasive teacher appears to have achieved on the human plane can prove illusory.

The depths of the child's soul, where the drama of his eternity is enacted, does not belong to us. The secret of our spiritual effectiveness lies in our alliance with the interior Master who already dwells, at least as a seed, in the heart of the child. We must not be afraid to call upon Jesus who is there in the little child, and asks only to grow in him. We must not be afraid to adore him there, to pray to him, and to unite ourselves to him, to be on the alert for what he particularly expects of the little child with whom we are dealing.

Jesus does not ask the same thing from each person but he wants each of us to achieve the most we can: what this will represent will vary according to the plan of his Providence.

In any case, there is a certain form of love and of service which each individual alone can give to God, and which no one else can give in his place. Far from wishing to lead all souls along the same path, or to form them in the same mould, the

8

priest concerns himself with the soul of each child with supreme respect and with an attentive submission to the Holy Spirit.

In general, we err more through excess of timidity than through excess of boldness. We do not believe sufficiently in the supernatural possibilities of the child: whether it be on the level of silent prayer, on the plane of sacrifice, or that of fraternal charity, the child, even in what may be a hostile environment, has an astonishing capacity. Most of us have had experience of this, and have had the opportunity of testing the extraordinary power of a child's prayer – when he has had the good fortune to meet teachers who have known how to stimulate and direct his efforts!

That is why work among children is so rewarding, though it is at the same time a terribly exacting apostolate. One priest has summed it up by saying: "Children – our masters." They are our masters in the sense that nothing escapes their observation. But, they are even more our masters because we cannot honestly require of them what we do not give ourselves.

In truth, they force us to raise, or better to renew our soul until it is like those of whom our Lord spoke when he said: "I confess to thee, O Father, Lord of heaven and earth: because thou hast hid these things from the wise and prudent, and hast revealed them to little ones." (Matt. 11:25)

Christ speaks to his Priest

Always treat children with the greatest kindness. Read in the Gospel how I ignored current conventions and displayed tremendous interest in them. It would be playing into Satan's hands to neglect children, whatever the excuses with which we try to disguise our neglect. Those who help to discredit this form of priestly work or even to cause it to be underestimated, will incur a heavy burden of guilt in my eyes. Look on the apostolate of youth as one of the most important which can be entrusted to you.

The power which the pure soul of a child has over my heart is inconceivable. It is your mission to develop this marvellous power. Children have every potentiality for good as well as for evil. They are eager but unstable, generous but frail, simple yet malleable. If we do not take the trouble to guide them, direct them, stimulate them, and even on occasion to reprove them paternally, they will be the victims of harmful influences. If we do not help them to develop the seeds planted in them at baptism and all the hidden riches which they have inherited from their forebears, it will be their evil tendencies that sweep them away. And then there will be wasted lives, or at least lives which do not provide the support for the redemption of the world which I have a right to expect.

Devotion towards children based on faith, intelligence, and love is never fruitless. If we are devoted to them we must never be discouraged; even if the results are not always visible or apparently lasting, something permanent survives which will facilitate the return of the prodigal unexpectedly. But often the seed falls on good ground. Do we appreciate what a crime it would be to deprive this good ground of the divine seed!

Nothing saddens me more than the loss of the supernatural which so many little ones suffer without realizing it. "The little children asked for bread, and there was no one to give it to them." (Lam. 4:4) In order to grow, they need an atmosphere that is healthy, joyous, and invigorating. To neutralize them is often unfortunately to make them spiritually anaemic or even to suffocate them. Woe to them who destroy children's souls, woe to them who destroy me in children's souls. Blessed, on the other hand, are those who help to make children grow in my love, and to make me develop in their hearts!

If it is true that I consider as done to myself whatever one man does to another, how much more is that so when a child is involved. "Whatsoever you do to the least of my little ones you do to me." Let the little ones come to me. Let the path be made smooth for them to come. Let me be presented to them as I am, tender and kind, and do not, as false devotion often does, misrepresent me in their eyes.

I need priests for them, true teachers, priests with faith. What a grace is the influence of such at a time when impressions are so easily made. My Son, be such a priest to all the children whom you meet!

Examination of Conscience

1. What are my reactions to working with children – fear – timidity – irritation – a natural attraction – profound concern – supernatural devotion?

2. Do I guard myself against the dangers of dictatorship, of seeing my ministry as nothing but the "Apostolate of Youth"; and against the danger of negligence – regarding my work with children as secondary and unimportant?

3. Am I convinced both of the unique character of my role as a priest – handing on the faith, sacramental action, formation of conscience, bearing witness as a "Man of God" to the excellence that a priest ought to display – and the importance of the family and educational environment? Am I particularly careful, not so much to take the parents' place but to instruct them and help them to fulfil their mission to educate their children by visiting their homes, running courses for parents, giving them to read what is adapted to their needs?

4. Have I not noticed that the child is often the shortest path to the heart of the adult?

5. In my dealings with children do I pay particular attention to their psychology? Have I studied the child's psychology? Is there a risk of my deceiving myself by too great a trust in my experience? May this delusion not be a hidden cause of some of my failures and mistakes? What kind of mistakes? Speaking to children as if they were adults. Preaching them sermons which require them to sit still for longer than a quarter of an hour. Crowding them behind the altar or in side aisles where they can see nothing and do nothing during the whole of Mass. Preaching a retreat to a congregation ranging from children in the sixth form to those in the lowest class. Inflicting punishments that are humiliating. Asking children to serve three or four Masses or making them assist at funerals or weddings during school hours.

6. When I speak to an audience of children am I careful to awaken their interest, to come down to their level, to give them time in which to reflect and to apply my remarks, to end with a practical suggestion which they can assimilate and implement in their own lives?

11

7. Am I careful to teach them how to pray, not only with their lips, but with their hearts? So many children are capable of a personal, deep prayer!

8. Have I been zealous in teaching children how to make a meditation in keeping with their age?

9. While trying to give all of them the minimum essential for a Christian, do I try to give and ask of each individually the maximum compatible with his education and the graces he has received? Remember the parable of the talents. It is our duty, without neglecting our general responsibilities, to give particular attention to the souls of whom God is asking more. How many remain mediocre because no one encouraged them and taught them to rise higher!

10. Do I take care that the children's confessions are regular and serious? It is often difficult, but this is what ensures the formation of their conscience and regular Holy Communion.

11. Am I careful to prepare my catechism lessons painstakingly? Do I combine clear and comprehensible teaching with a living education in faith and charity?

12. Do I allow for the various elements which can influence a child towards Christianity or towards indifference? His environment, the books he reads, the cinema, clubs, holidays, etc.?

13. Do I fight against the current abuse of paying children for their services in choir, when there are so many better means of rewarding them: subscriptions to magazines, book tokens, outings, pilgrimages, picnics?

14. Have I a truly moral authority over children, an authority which combines kindness without weakness, firmness without harshness?

15. Am I scrupulously just with children? Do I avoid giving even the impression of having special favourites? There is only one form of favoured treatment children will readily understand – our singling out the most abandoned children and the sick.

16. Do I devote proper care to the sick children in my parish, and to those who are in hospitals? Too many children are morally abandoned.

17. Do I guard my heart in dealings with children, loving them all with the heart of the Master, and never permitting myself any marks of affection which, even if given with pure intentions,

are always liable to be misunderstood either at the time or later?

18. Do I show deep concern about children who do not come to church, whether by praying for them, or by bringing the influence of active Catholics to bear on them?

19. Can I bear witness that in me the children can easily discover the man of God, interested in their souls because it is my job, yet at the same time because I am filled with supernatural love for them?

Resolutions

1. Without neglecting my other duties, to give to the Christian training of children the place it deserves.

2. Often to ask the divine Master who showed such predilection for children when on earth, to draw them to him now.

3. To ask his blessing for all the children in my parish, especially when I pass by a school or when I meet them in the street.

4. To watch with more attentive care the preparation of my catechism classes, the regularity of the confessions of the children, and to give to each child sufficient time to train his conscience, to rouse his contrition, and to incite him to greater efforts.

5. To be as much concerned about those who are being instructed as for the instruction.

6. To train children in personal prayer. As long as the children have not acquired the habit and the taste for contact with Jesus, "the seed of faith" will be in danger, and their perseverance uncertain.

7. To observe the conditions in which the children live. I must not think that I know everything. Some loyal efforts in making inquiries will make me understand many things, and will suggest points which call for concerted action.

8. To make more opportunities for meeting parents. To neglect no effort, not only to interest them in my own educational efforts, but to help them to become better teachers themselves.

13

9. To study humbly some books on psychology, on the spiritual direction of children, on youth movements. Not to limit myself to my own experience.

10. To seek for directors of children among mothers, young men and women and catechists. To attach great importance to their spiritual training and to their technique.

Spiritual Reading

Certain priests make a complete failure of their ministry with children. They feel that they are absolutely powerless to penetrate these young minds, and sometimes they even display a hostility which shows itself in conduct utterly lacking in courtesy and graciousness. Someone has said that we are living in a pitiless age. That is true, especially when there is question of demonstrating to a school-master, a catechist, or a confessor that he is not liked. In these circumstances the child has not the art of camouflaging his feelings, but shows a cold cruelty which makes one feel that he is heartless. We can appreciate that, under these conditions, the life of the teacher is not all roses. But it is only right to share the responsibility equitably. The child is not always the principal culprit when this happens.

I pass over the fact that there are certain characteristics and qualities which naturally antagonize children and which fully account for the unhappiness of many teachers. It is on a more general plane that I want to base my argument. To those who express their complaints so bitterly I put this simple question: "Do you really love these children about whom you complain?" Take care: children have a marvellous instinct, almost a gift of divination, for recognizing those who love them. If you deal with them in a prejudiced spirit, it will be useless for you to hide your true feelings under a forced amiability: they will size you up, see through you and make you understand without beating about the bush that you have not taken them in. Let us be honest enough to admit it: the most frequent cause of our failure with children is that we do not love them enough. This is the explanation of the majority of our failures.

14

I have noticed a similarity between a priest's work for children and piety. A very moderate amount of piety puts our conscience in order before God; but is it sufficient to make our relations with him sweet and pleasing? No; it only produces this effect when it is demonstrated lavishly. So it is in our apostolate. It brings us consolation and pleasure only when we spend ourselves completely for children. They have a keen appreciation of what is done for them, and a delicate way of showing their gratitude. They work generously to control themselves, to reform their characters and to achieve the advance to perfection which we have planned for them.

Monsignor Lejeune

Subjects for Discussion

1. Why is the Church always so anxious about the souls of children?
2. What danger lies in underestimating the priestly apostolate for children?
3. What problems do children's confessions and the direction of their souls pose for the conscience of a priest?

Prayer

Lord Jesus, who said: "Let little children come to me", teach me to love them, and grant me the gift of knowing how to attract them to you. Let me understand the problems which concern them and the means of contributing effectively to their solution.

I offer for your blessing all the little ones who live in my parish. Preserve them from Satan, and keep their hearts pure. Increase vocations to the priesthood and religious life among them. May they learn to know you, to love you, and make you loved.

O Lord, hear my prayer of loving confidence. May each of those whom I approach not fail to reach you in heaven. Amen.

Thought

The ideal of the Christian teacher is to make the child accept the primacy of the spirit in all things, not as an imposed discipline, but as a source of life, joy, and light.

Mother Connolly

THE PRIEST AND THE SICK

Meditation

Even if our duties do not call us to serve the sick directly, it would seriously detract from our vocation if we were not concerned about the suffering members of Jesus Christ. Which of us does not from time to time have to visit some sick person, a neighbour or a friend? Which of us may not be called, at any moment, to prepare a dying person – perhaps a relative or colleague – for death?

After adoring the Sacred Heart of our Lord, always so kind to the sick and suffering, let us try to appreciate properly some of the reasons we have for increasing our love and zeal for the sick.

We can group these reasons as follows. As priests we should continue the work of our Lord in the exercise of his charity towards the sick. The sick are the suffering members of Christ. Our devotion to them is one of the most effective means of showing our gratitude and our love to our Lord. The Church recommends the sick very specially to our care and to our prayers, to comfort them in their sufferings, to sustain them in their struggles, and to prepare them for their last journey. Our zeal for the sick is a source of grace.

Let us consider the attitude of Jesus towards the sick. It would seem almost that he came only for them. We would be justified in asking if we are to take in a purely spiritual sense the statement: "I have not come for those in health, but for the sick." In any case, Saint Matthew does not hesitate to interpret the Prophet Isaias in a material sense: "And when evening was come, they brought to him many that were possessed with devils: and he cast out the spirits with his word: and all that were sick he healed: that it might be fulfilled, which was spoken by the prophet Isaias, saying: He took our infirmities, and bore our diseases." (Matt. 8:16, 17)

See him surrounded, beset on all sides. No infirmity repels him, no importunity wearies him. Where they are concerned, fatigue does not count with him. He interrupts his discourses, as at the cure of the paralytic at Capharnaum and at the cure of the blind man at Jericho. He is not indifferent to any appeal. Leaving any matter at hand, he turns to help the sick. He even makes a long journey, as in the case of the daughter of Jairus, or the raising of Lazarus. He acts at a distance, if need be, as for the servant of the Centurion. He breaks rules which he has made himself, as in the case of the Caananite woman. Tactful and scrupulous as he was in order not to transgress traditions, even though he himself stood above them, he disobeys the Law, and unhesitatingly effects a cure on the Sabbath Day.

Where the sick are concerned he does not reject anyone; rich or poor, child or old man, pure or impure. He makes himself their servant, to a point that he forgets to eat or drink. It is not in order to astound everyone that he is interested in them and cures them. It is solely out of compassion, and his words "I have compassion on the multitude", refer primarily to physical distress. The anxiety to bring comfort to those who suffer physically is a divine reflex with him. Even at the very hour when they arrest and ill-treat him he cures Malchus, whose ear had been cut off by Peter.

Speaking to the disciples of John the Baptist he puts the care of the sick first. "The poor have the Gospel preached to them", comes only sixth on the list.

He attaches so much importance to visiting the sick that he gives his disciples the express command: "Heal the sick", "cast out devils". All this done for love, of course; there is no question of money. "Freely have you received, freely give." (Matt. 10:8)

For some moments let us try to share this divine tenderness for all those who suffer. Let us read again slowly all the Gospel texts which show this astonishing preference for those whose lives have been injured. "And Jesus went about all Galilee, teaching in their synagogues, and preaching the gospel of the kingdom, and healing all manner of sickness and every infirmity among the people." (Matt. 4:23)

"And there came to him great multitudes, having with them the dumb, the blind, the lame, the maimed, and many others: and they cast them down at his feet, and he healed them: so that the multitude marvelled seeing the dumb speak, the lame walk, the blind see: and they glorified the God of Israel." (Matt. 15:30, 31)

"For he healed many, so that they pressed upon him for to touch him, as many as had evils." (Mark 3:10)

"And all the multitude sought to touch him, for virtue went out from him, and healed all." (Luke 6:19)

Does it not seem that beyond them he saw all that incessant procession of human misery which would spread over the world until the end of time, as a result of the sins of humanity? With anguish in his heart he took advantage of his months of public life to cure and to comfort as many as possible, wishing thereby to encourage those who would follow him to put care and zeal for the sick foremost in their apostolic duties.

Not only did our Lord show a preference for the sick, but he wished to identify himself with them; they are in a special way an integral part of himself. "I was sick and you visited me." (Matt. 25:36)

In fact, from the twenty-fifth chapter of Saint Matthew's Gospel it would seem that what will finally separate the elect from the rejected, is the way in which they performed the works of mercy. The most important factor will be the way in which they will have visited him in his sick members. To the question of the charitable man: "When did we see thee sick . . . and came to thee?" (Matt. 25:39), the reply is decisive: "Amen, I say to you, as long as you did it to one of these my least brethren, you did it to me." (Matt. 25:40)

Moreover, the saints have all had the common characteristic of recognizing Christ intuitively in the sick as in the poor. Sometimes our Lord himself encouraged the faith and the charity of his saints by revealing himself in his suffering members. At other times he renewed the great law of identification, by applying it to particular cases. Thus, we read that, during an illness, Saint Mechtilde, grieving and complaining to Jesus of all the care she was receiving, and fearing to receive too much relief, received this reply: "Fear nothing, be troubled about nothing, because it is I who endure all that you suffer, and for that reason the care shown to you is given to me; and so I shall reward these people as if they had laboured for me."

When priests reflect on all the marks of love which we have had showered upon us through the generosity of the Lord, we sometimes feel almost crushed by it and do not know how to repay him love for love; the most ardent sentiments, the most sincere words are very little in the end. Certainly we spend ourselves and tire ourselves out in the service of the Lord. By trying to accomplish his divine will in everything, we can prove the intense gratitude we feel towards him, but fundamentally it is nothing compared to what we have received from him. And yet how can we compensate him who is infinite goodness in any way? Listen to the reply given to Saint Catherine of Genoa, a reply which echoes well known passages from the epistles of Saint James and Saint John.

"He who loves me must love what I love; consequently he must love his neighbour next to God, work with his whole heart and soul to procure his salvation, and never avoid occasions, even painful and dangerous ones, to bring help to him. The love of the neighbour is an infallible sign of the love that the creatures bear to God, since the Lord is the Creator, the Father, and the Preserver of all men. It is by love of his neighbour that the creature will show his gratitude for the great love which God has for him. As he is unable to do good to the divine Majesty, who has no need of it, it will procure help for the suffering members of Jesus Christ."

"At the end of our life", declares Saint John of the Cross, "we shall be judged on our love". Sometimes we run the risk of deceiving ourselves about the quality of our love for God. There is nothing like devotion to the sick, above all if this devotion seems burdensome to our poor nature, to intensify our charity and to prove to him who has given us so much, the sincerity of our response.

Canon 468 shows us with what spirit and with what sentiments the priest should dedicate himself to the sick. "The priest, with zealous care and extreme charity, ought to help the sick in his parish, especially those who are close to death, by preparing them carefully for the Sacraments and by commending their souls to God."

Under the heading "Concerning the visitation and the care of the sick", the Ritual deals with every point in detail. The priest must remember in the first place that the service of the sick must not be the last of his duties: "The priest should remember that he must consider the care of the sick among the first, not among the last of his duties." That is why, as soon as he learns that one of his parishioners is ill, he should not wait to be called but go immediately to visit the patient, not only once, but as often as may be necessary. The Ritual even suggests the use of a register of the sick. "It will be helpful, especially in large parishes, to have a list or register of the sick, so that he knows their circumstances and condition and remembers them more easily and can help them at the right time." This detail shows the importance the Church attaches to the organization of this essential part of the ministry.

The sick whom we have to visit are of different types. There are those who are more or less crippled; there are the permanent invalids suffering from some lengthy illness, which in certain cases is incurable; there are the surgical cases; there are the accident cases; there are those whom sickness keeps away from work for a time; there are those who are incapacitated by an unforeseen illness with the risk of serious complications; finally, there are the dying, whose last sign may come at any moment.

We should be seen often visiting the sick, even those whose condition does not cause serious concern, so that our visits are not interpreted as a sign of approaching death. Our presence should bring them true comfort. In this connection it is important that we should overcome a certain professional weakness which, from force of habit, makes us more or less insensible

21

to the sufferings of others. We must have been ill ourselves to understand from experience the interior conflict which sickness causes. "Sickness is the stage on which two great dramas are enacted. In the one – the more tragic perhaps – we are struggling with ourselves, certain elements of our being dissociated from and engaged in war against one another so that the intrusion of the illness shatters the habitual framework of existence. The other drama unfolds between the patient and those who deal with him."

Those who are in good health always find it difficult to understand that. Mauriac wrote, with sharp and realistic insight into the human soul: "The best of sons finds it difficult to live with his dying mother." In any case, the patient, whose sensitivity is often more intense, whose receptivity is deeper, needs to feel that he is understood and loved just for himself. He must feel an immense kindness, a devotion which is not demonstrated by mere words, a patience, a tact, a gentleness which nothing discourages.

It will be easy if we begin, before visiting someone who is sick, by commending him to the tender and strong love of Jesus, who loves him so much. There are occasions when, in the presence of certain forms of distress, words do not come. Then the smiling kindness of a priestly soul, a truly loving soul, finds the way into hearts. Moreover the priest who knows quite simply that he is the extension of Jesus, and who tries to live under the influence of his Spirit, soon perceives that our Lord blesses very simple words, and infuses them with his grace.

Even if we are not received as we would like, we must never be discouraged. The incumbent of a suburban parish in Paris tells this story.

"For about four months I went to visit a young man suffering from intestinal tuberculosis. He was in great pain. Faith seemed dead in him. He escaped by banter from every attempt at serious conversation. Towards the end I went to see him twice a week, but always to no purpose. When I ventured the remark: 'It is a long time since you made your Easter duties', he answered: 'Yes, but I do not miss that so much as I do my bicycle.' And during critical attacks of his illness, curses, blasphemy, real outbursts of anger continued.

"One Wednesday evening, after I had once more attempted to make him pray without success, I was thoroughly distressed at feeling him so near the end and still so badly disposed. I sought the Superior of a community of contemplative nuns, and recommended the boy to her prayers. She promised me an hour of adoration for his intentions. The next day I had a catechism class and a Guild Meeting, and had no opportunity to pay sick calls. On Friday morning I returned to my patient. As soon as I came in he said to me: 'Look here, I've had an amusing idea. Can you hear confessions when you are not in your little cupboard?' What four months of visits had not achieved, one hour of adoration had."

Even if we do not see an exterior sign of repentance, we can never know what is happening in the hidden depths of the soul during the last moments of life. On December 2, 1920, Jesus said to Marie Fidèle (Sister Marie Fidèle Weiss, 1882–1923, lived a very holy life in the monastery of Franciscan Tertiaries of Reutberg, in Bavaria. Her life has been written by her confessor, Mgr. Jean Muhlbauer). "I love sinners; I thirst for their souls. The sufferings which you have endured through my grace and in intimate union with me, I have united to the sacrifice of the Cross, from which they derive all their strength. I want you always to leave to me the choice of the sinner to whom I shall give the benefit of your sufferings and sacrifices, now or later. I am the Lord who disposes of everything for the best, ensuring that it will redound to my glory and to the salvation of souls. There are sinners facing death who urgently need my mercy. Do not give up any soul as lost, even at the last moment of life. As the Redeemer and Good Shepherd my love and concern follow the sinner until death, to save him and to secure his happiness; for I love sinners." Our mission is to inspire sinners to confidence in the last hours of the supreme struggle.

Sister Elizabeth of the Trinity told the Sisters who assisted her at the end: "This is a very solemn hour. The next world is reaching out to receive me. I thought I had been living in it for a long time, and yet it is the unknown. Oh, how we should pray for the dying! I would willingly spend my eternity near them to help them, for there is something frightening about it. It must be terrible for those who have lived only for pleasure, and who are attached to the things of this world. For myself, although free from everything, it seems to me, I am experiencing an indefinable sensation, something of the justice, of the sanctity of God. I am conscious that death is a punishment, and I find myself so little, so devoid of merit! How necessary it is to inspire those in agony with confidence!"

We must be careful not to ask more of a patient than he can give. Let us open his heart to hope in the goodness of God towards prodigal children who throw themselves into his arms. Saint Catherine of Sienna said: "If all the sins that can be committed were united in one creature, it would, compared with the divine mercy, be like a drop of vinegar in the midst of the sea."

What sinner can hear without emotion the words which Pascal put into the mouth of Jesus. "I love you more ardently than you have loved your sins." Does not the Master have in his heart more power to pardon than the whole human race has to sin?

The grace of our priesthood is not only one of comfort, support, and purification, but it brings a grace of sanctification to help the sick to give value to their sufferings, for the community and for the mission of the Church. "Sickness", wrote Mauriac, "is a difficult science. Of itself it does not make us any better: the world contracts as bodily suffering increases."

F. Pastorelli writes: "No more than normal life does suffering bring anything spiritual to those who do not know how to make use of it. We all have to repeat, according to our particular need, the Easter prayer for good use of the trial of sickness." Sickness is sometimes the occasion of a grace of transformation and of expansion for many sick people. The sick man is withdrawn from the normal circumstances of his life. His equilibrium is upset. It is the duty of the priest to help him to understand the true meaning of life, to show him the power of suffering united with that of Christ in the service of the Christian community. It is important to open the sick man's heart to love, precisely because the world contracts as suffering increases. Very soon all the sick man's thoughts concentrate on himself.

Whenever it is practicable we must not hesitate to make the patient aware of this danger and help him to overcome it, if only by showing patience towards those around him – whether

24

they are members of his family, or the sick among whom he is being cared for. Sometimes it is a good idea to ask the invalid to offer his sufferings for all those on earth who are suffering at the same time as he does, perhaps more than he does. It is not good for the patient to be left to lonely brooding or to agonizing anticipation of his fate. "The wooden cross is heavy enough", wrote one invalid, "there is no need to weigh it down with lead".

We should encourage the sick to desire to be cured. Health is a gift of God which should be asked for like any other benefit; such a wish is in accord with human destiny, and human life. Sometimes, if the cure is not obtained, it can help the sick man to rise above his situation and "become, with Jesus Christ, one of the points where universal suffering becomes conscious of itself and fulfils its redemptive task for each and all".

"To say 'Thy will be done' is not the end. It is an initial gesture: it opens the way for us. 'Thy will be done' does not free us from trial. Suffering will remain suffering: rebellions will flare up; and doubts will obscure my sight. But it ratifies an alliance, a contract of employment. I am now 'a worker with God'. Together we are going to build, and I agree to be a tool which, in daily pain, does not understand the plans of the whole work, but is confident of the wisdom of the architect."

Visiting the sick offers precious opportunities for our apostolate in their immediate neighbourhood. Our ministry among the sick often has a fortunate repercussion extending to their family and neighbourhood. In many cases, it is a providential opportunity for priestly contact which would not have been otherwise made. There is nothing like it for breaking down the apprehension, born of ignorance and prejudice, which so many people experience at sight of us; and demonstrating that the priest is something more than an official who presides at marriages and funerals.

After the first distressing visits when everyone is embarrassed and openly suspicious, the ice melts gradually, and the priest becomes a friend, and, before long, a confidant. The devotion of the priest gradually increases their confidence, and frequently helps to reawaken in them a faith which had been torpid. The priest can use the sick call as an opportunity to give spiritual direction to other members of the family, thus helping them to show practical charity towards the invalid.

By interesting the whole parish in the sick, the priest has a chance to get Christians to face their responsibilities towards those who are suffering and to prepare them for that attitude of soul which they will have to display when their turn to suffer comes.

We ourselves are the first beneficiaries of the exercise of charity towards the sick. Monsignor Dubourg, the Archbishop of Besançon, in a conference to the students of his seminary, said this: "Of all the fruits which result from helping the sick, one of the most excellent is surely the personal sanctification of the priest. It is like a reward given without delay by Christ to his minister who is helping him in his suffering members. The fatigue which the priest must force himself to endure, especially in country districts, in order to visit the sick, the repugnance he must sometimes conquer, the prayers and the sacrifices which he offers for those he seeks to lead back to God, the example of submission to the divine will which he is given by generous souls purified and sanctified by sickness, the insight he gets into human miseries, physical miseries, and moral miseries, all these things provide a stimulant for his life and help him to advance in the path of sanctity. Every moment he has the chance to be grateful and to understand the salutary effects which trials have on truly Christian souls. His thoughts are turned towards the great realities, too often forgotten: the mortality of earthly things, the necessity for detachment, the value of faith, the suddenness of death, the virtue of prayer. When his life is so often burdened with material cares and exterior occupations, these reminders are truly beneficial; they prevent him from letting his piety grow languid and his zeal from being chilled."

Finally, for the priest who helps them to evaluate their sufferings, the powerful intercession of the sick constitutes a real treasure which makes his ministry fruitful.

There is no priest who has not experienced the power of prayer supported by suffering. Sometimes we are crushed by work and fatigued, in the face of the immense task of converting the tepid, the indifferent, the hostile; we feel ourselves poor and defenceless. It is not enough for us to offer our work and our fatigue, or to offer all the time needed for prayer, since there is so much to expiate, so much to obtain. At that moment we must think of the astonishing power of those whom Claudel calls "souls expanded and deepened in fettered bodies". Let us entrust them with specific intentions and keep them informed of the results obtained: we shall be astonished at the ease with which they will obtain from the divine Master true miracles of grace. In the real meaning of the expression, they are "lords" whose power, born of humiliation and of sacrifice, rules over the devil and over sin and its consequences, and, even more important, exercises its influence on the very heart of the Almighty. "Centuries ago in Palestine, at eventide, the call 'Sick Lords' was heard in the leper houses and during the Middle Ages it echoed in their hospitals." For the crusaders, so proud of their privileges, thus used to address their invalid peasants, and would then kneel before them to wash their wounds.

"Sick Lords, your kingdom is not of this world, and revolutions have not shaken it. You who suffer, dwell amid treasures which rust cannot destroy. Your acceptance of suffering confers on you a sovereignty over the channels of grace and over mystical wealth. The world needs you, because, in your crucifixion, you are other Christs, co-redeemers."

In the evening, the sick were conscious of their power, their soul was exalted, and they were eager to devote the sufferings of their poor bodies for the benefit of their Christian brethren.

"Sick Lords, pray for peace, that God may give us heaven on earth! Pray for the peace which the world cannot give. Pray for the peace, the tranquillity of order which must first be established in the heart before it can expand. Sick Lords, pray that pardon may make up for offense, that truth may triumph over error, that faith may dispel doubts, and that light may pierce the darkness. Pray, that men, freed from the yoke of hatred, may strive for the reign of love.

"You, who know from your sorrow how to prolong joy, be instruments of peace for the world. Sick Lords, pray for yourselves, and for the sick throughout the world."

The prayer of those who suffer for those who suffer, is the only compassionate prayer. For compassion is the suffering body shuddering at the suffering another body is enduring. "Sick men, you who know from experience how much patience and strength illness requires, pray that your sick brothers may welcome their illness with courage, as an instrument of their salvation. Your prayer, more than any other, is effective, because it knows what it must ask, because it knows the relief which grace brings, and because it derives from a fraternity of the flesh as it were, the violence with which we must storm heaven."

All these sufferings, deep wounds or pin pricks, all accumulate and, on bad days, multiply. If I let them pile up before me, they will form a wall which will shut out the whole horizon, and imprison me. But I can make use of everything. Only one "yes" is needed to transform my self-denials into sacrifices, and the wall will become a terrace, a springboard, a temple.

Sacrifice – *sacrum facere* – means to make holy. My suffering has only the value that I give to it, for in itself it is an evil. Everything depends on what I do with it. I can besmirch it, or I can consecrate it. If I take it in hand, as the priest takes the host at the Mass, if I offer it up and accept it, witness of my faith in the love of him who sends this suffering. I transubstantiate it. My suffering becomes "a holy thing", and each particle takes on an almost infinite value.

My suffering becomes a divine bread which nourishes me, and in my hands, trembling in their daring, I can offer it to God for myself and for my brothers. "For our salvation and for that of the whole world, may it ascend with an odour of sweetness. Amen."

Christ speaks to his Priest

I have chosen you that you may carry on my work on earth. That should be your principal concern. Try, then, to share in all the sentiments of my heart. As my Father has sent me, so I also send you, and first to those who suffer. Have you noticed this? Thus have I revealed myself. The sign which I gave to the messengers sent by John the Baptist was the service of the infirm and the sick. In my public life I consecrated to them the greater part of my time, and I did not hesitate to show concern for them even on the Sabbath. That was the starting point of the hatred of the Pharisees for me.

If you but knew how I deplore human suffering. I wanted to know it by experience, to purify it, to transfigure it, to give it redemptive value. And above all I wanted to give my priests the example of compassionate kindness for those who suffer, and especially for those in bodily suffering. Tell yourself that health is a blessing, a talent that should be employed profitably in my service and in the service of your brethren. Sickness is a disorder, the result of the sin of humanity, an evil which, with my grace, through love, can draw much good; but an evil which, with my grace, each one should try to cure.

Be assured I do not want mankind to suffer. Very often they themselves create their own burdens. My whole purpose is to relieve them, and to make their sufferings serve their own purification, and for the redemption of their brothers. If you want to enter into the spirit of your vocation love the sick as I have loved them, with a fraternal and compassionate love. Do all that you can to relieve them, even physically. Have faith in the healing influence of the holy oils and in the power of your sacerdotal prayer said over them. But above all, be a living comfort to them by your presence. When you go to visit them be united with me. I shall show you the way to their heart, and I shall inspire you with the words which will help them. Some of them, I know, are far from me, but your visit will often be an opportunity for them to return to me. Share my tenderness for each of them and let me act through you. Very few will resist the ardour of my love when, through your priestly heart, they feel the depth and the intensity of my divine love. Try, moreover, to see me in each of them. I may be disfigured and defaced in them sometimes, but they are all my suffering members. I am going to continue in them my Agony for the redemption of the world. I am even going to experience through them the sorrows I did not know on earth. All this is destined to fill up what is lacking to my Passion so that I may apply the fruits of it for them, in them, and for all of you.

On their part there should be at least a minimum of loyalty, of conformity to the will of my Father. It is your duty to help them with superlative kindness and strength, "gently and strongly", above all at the hour of death when there is a supreme struggle between the soul and Satan. Look at this dying man: he has given in to Satan during the course of his life. Infinitely respectful as I am of his human freedom which is the basis of his greatness and of his merit, I can exercise my mercy towards him only if he acknowledges his misery and calls upon me to help him. And if he does not do so – the tree falls often in the direction towards which it was bent – then one of his brothers do it on his behalf and obtain for him the victorious grace to say an interior "yes" to me, his saviour. By your mission, by your profession, by your vocation, you are that brother.

Realize the greatness of your task and of your responsibility. It is no light matter, this responsibility for souls. You must truly bear them along and, throughout your whole life, make them susceptible to my love. If you were more a man of prayer and of penance, few souls would resist to the end.

Insist in obtaining from me the grace that none of your parishioners die without being reconciled with me. And even if no outward sign appears to console your heart, be assured that none of your appeals to me in their names were unnoticed by me. I so want love to triumph.

There are not only sinners among the sick. There are men, women, and even children, for whom sickness is an opportunity for deep purification and an unsuspected redemptive power. It is your mission to reveal to souls little by little their power over my heart. The world would not continue to exist very long if there were not everywhere generous souls who take upon themselves expiation for the sins of humanity. Teach souls to make the most of their state by forcing themselves humbly, in the midst of their sufferings, to keep calm, gentle, and patient; by forcing themselves to be united with me as much as they can. Associate them with you in your ministry. Urge them to be willing to offer themselves with me, as living victims, at Holy Mass. Then the fruitfulness of your priesthood will be increased tenfold.

Finally, fulfil more widely still your office of mediator. Look beyond the immediate radius of your activity. Think of all the sick, of all ages, and of all races, throughout the whole world.

30

Offer their sufferings to me very often, uniting them to mine. Thus you permit me to rain down upon them showers of graces for the redemption of the whole world. Why is it that so few priests understand the power of salvation that I have put into their hands?

Examination of Conscience

1. Do I love ministering to the sick?
2. Do I see in the sick the suffering members of Christ?
3. Have I enough faith to ascribe to my visits to the sick the value that Jesus puts in it? Are not these visits included in the works of mercy which will weigh heavily in the balance on the day of judgement? "I was sick and you visited me. Come, blessed of my Father." (Matt. 25:34–6)
4. Even if I am not called officially by my priestly duties to visit the sick often, have I realized that this ministry enriches my priesthood? Do I seize the opportunities which charity offers me?
5. Do I sometimes ask God for the gift of touching the hearts of the sick and of comforting them?
6. Have I sufficient faith in the power of my priesthood to relieve the sick? As Saint James said: "The prayer of faith shall save the sick man: and the Lord shall raise him up." (James 5:15)
7. Do I visit the sick in my district or in my parish conscientiously? Do I love to visit my sick colleagues? Nothing so increases brotherly love, as the Book of Ecclesiasticus confirms. "Be not slow to visit the sick: for by these things thou shalt be confirmed in love." (Ecclus. 7:38)
8. Do I keep myself informed about the many privileges granted by the Church in recent years in favour of the sick, particularly the dispensations from the eucharistic fast?
9. Am I wise enough not to prolong my visits so that they tire the patient, or even cause scandal in the household?
10. When I am called to a sick person, do I give the summons priority, and even drop everything else if the case is urgent?
11. If I am a parish priest have I made arrangements to ensure that I am notified at once about the sick in my parish?

12. Am I not inclined to put off my sick visit until the last moment, forgetting that my visits to the sick are an essential part of my duty. Canon Law says: "With extreme care and effusive charity the priest ought to give his assistance to the sick in his parish."

13. Am I convinced that a priest who loves the sick and with discretion and kindness shows them a devoted care, can exercise a very effective influence on their family at a time when they are generally psychologically more receptive and more impressionable?

14. What is my attitude when a sick man refuses to receive me, or at least will not be converted from his ways? Do I simply rest in the knowledge that I have done what I can and keep my tranquillity of soul, or am I humbled and saddened by my defeat? Am I the good shepherd, who, for all his sadness, is not discouraged, but puts into his work every spiritual means in his power: penance, prayer, appeals to little children for prayers, to obtain the grace of final repentance?

15. Do I make Extreme Unction seem only a final cleansing of the soul before it appears before his Creator, or do I explain it to others as the sacrament of the sick, destined, in the mind of the early Church, as a cure for the body as well as for the soul?

16. Am I careful when I give the Last Sacraments to the sick, to explain to them, and to their family, the meaning of the words and ceremonies?

17. When I have given the Last Sacraments, do I not too easily believe that my duty is over, forgetting that my role as priest should continue, to the extent of course that my time permits, by helping the dying person to the very end.

18. Because I have to administer to very ordinary Christians do I not run the risk of treating all my flock on the basis of the lowest common denominator and of not knowing how to prepare for death the very fervent souls whose last moments can be so very precious for completing their sanctification and for the redemption of the world?

19. Do I feel myself personally responsible for the sick in my parish who are in hospitals or clinics? Do I take care to recommend them to the chaplain, if there is one, or at least

send them a word of sympathy which will enable me to keep in touch with them? Do I ask a nearby priest to visit them?

Resolutions

1. To look upon the ministry to the sick as one of the most important duties of my apostolate.

2. To create in my parish a favourable atmosphere for visits by the clergy to the sick.

3. To look upon the sick as privileged members of my parochial community, who have a prior claim on their parish priest.

4. When I approach a sick person, to adore in him Christ suffering. To compel myself, by my faith, to see Jesus in him.

5. Whenever possible, to use the blessing for the sick provided in the Ritual. The blessing for adults or for children who are ill.

6. To develop in my parish a feeling of love for the sick. Each year to preach a sermon on the elementary duties of the Christian towards those who are sick.

7. To enlighten the faithful on their responsibilities towards the sick, so that they may not hesitate in case of need to summon the priest either out of human respect or for fear of frightening the patient.

8. To see that the anointing of the sick may not be looked upon as an indication of impending death.

9. In catechism classes, and when preaching, to speak of the anointing of the sick and not of "Extreme Unction".

10. To neglect no opportunity of making the faithful understand better the symbolism of the oil of the sick, and the meaning of the Ritual prayers.

11. To surround the holy oils with great respect. When they are received, after Maundy Thursday, to make the day a festive occasion in their honour.

12. To re-establish the rightful place of the Viaticum, which is truly the sacrament of the dying. Whenever possible to make it the occasion of the family's farewell to the one about to enter heaven, for it is a living link between the communities of heaven and earth.

13. To give devotion to the sick a place in my parish, rendering mutual spiritual and temporal help.

14. To make effective arrangements to see that I am warned as soon as anyone is seriously ill in the parish. To visit the patient even before I am asked to do so. If it is generally known that the clergy visit all the sick without distinction, this initiative will be all the more welcome.

15. To have prayers for the sick offered regularly. To interest the parish in the sick, and the sick in the parish.

16. To keep a daily register of the sick and of the infirm.

17. To impress the sick with the fact that they are not rejected, and still less abandoned.

18. To tell them gently that they have an important role in the parish community. According to their spiritual potentialities, to entrust special intentions to them, to associate them intimately with my ministry, to keep them informed of the results obtained through their mediation.

19. To make use of every opportunity to show the sick and the infirm the interest which the parish has in them. For example, to send the sick, after every big feast, the flowers which have been on the altar, to arrange for a group of First Communicants to pay them a short visit after the ceremony. To send them palms on Palm Sunday.

20. To use my ingenuity in thinking of things for chronic invalids to do. For example: to make something for a bazaar, or for the church; listening to a particular broadcast if they have a wireless; or reviewing a book for the parish magazine.

21. To have a particular care for children suffering from a long or incurable illness, and to ensure that their religious instruction is arranged.

22. To keep informed of the different societies and charities for the sick so that those who are able may profit by them.

Spiritual Reading

And now, my God, I gather around the altar set up in my home all my dear sick brothers. I empty the hospitals, the clinics, the sanatoria, the hovels, the homes, the palaces, of all their martyrs.

From all parts of the world, lines of sick men, long as rivers, converge here. I present to your merciful Majesty this tragic assembly. Look upon them – blind, lame, deaf, hunchbacks, paralytics, men with battered and twisted faces, men without arms, men without legs; men bound hand and foot to their splints; men in plaster, men pale with anaemia; these, blue with heart trouble; those gasping for breath or trembling like trees stripped of their leaves by the winter wind. Young people spitting blood or having convulsions; others with damaged organs or flesh. Lastly, all those little children, whiter than the host, who look like dying flowers and whose martyrdom I cannot explain.

Lord, "have pity on the multitude"! They are no less bruised nor less wounded, nor more beautiful than you were on the cross, and they are only men! And you, the crucified; you know that the disfigurement of their souls is even worse than that of their bodies. Have pity on these fathers and these mothers who tremble to leave their children deprived of love or without the necessities of life. Have pity on those whose illness endangers the earning of their daily bread, which was hard enough to secure when they were in good health. Have pity on those whose hopes are crushed to atoms, their work destroyed, their affections crushed. Have pity on those who do not yet realize what you wish of them. Lord, say but the word and they will be cured.

Hear all those who are praying to you now through my mouth. Soothe their anguish. Revive their courage, light up their narrow paths. Speak to them, O my God! Tell them that every soul lives only to reach the point at which he discovers your face which is engraved in the depths of our hearts.

Tell them that human tears and blood never flow in vain, for you want us all to collaborate with you.

Arrange for them the sacred experience in which we recognize your plan and your appeal in everything and your incessant work in our souls.

France Pastorelli

35

Subjects for Discussion

1. How is a priest made aware of the supreme importance of his ministry among the sick?
2. What difficulties shall we meet in our ministry among the sick, and how shall we overcome them?

Prayer

Holy Virgin Mary, most gentle Mother, ever ready to help us, we offer for your compassion all the sick in the world. Have pity on their miseries, ease their suffering, lessen their grief. Deign to make us understand that it is our duty to make known to them the beneficent presence of your divine Son.

Grant us the gift of touching their hearts and of bringing them comfort for their bodies, and salvation for their souls. May no one whom we have visited die without being at least inwardly reconciled with your beloved Son, who lives and reigns with the Father in the unity of the Holy Spirit for ever and ever. Amen.

Thought

Sickness is a humiliation of the body. It is still a form of being poor rather than of being sick. Happy they who are prepared to live in their reduced, weakened, infirm body like a monk in his cell, a hermit in his desert, a poor man in his life of poverty.

Peyrot

3

THE PRIEST AND THE WORKER

Never before in the official documents of the Church has there been such unanimity, or such insistence, that the conditions of the workers should be improved. In this respect she is divinely inspired. God seems to use a number of distressing circumstances to encourage new methods of apostolic activity and to facilitate contact and discussion which would have been impossible a few years ago.

There is a growing danger that Communism, which does not hesitate to employ any means, will use the worker for its own ends. The working class will find itself the first victim of the establishment of any Communist régime.

Pius XI said that the great scandal of the nineteenth century was the loss to the Church of the working classes. In the second half of the twentieth century our great hope should be to see a new world built up in which Christian life will be made possible for every man of good will, and where working class life can develop in a Church which welcomes the worker as a member of Christ's body.

This problem cannot leave any priest indifferent. It is he who must answer to God for all those who live in his parish, and the attention which he gives to the one faithful sheep must not cause him to forget the ninety-nine who are lost! And this applies to those whose work does not require them to take a direct interest in the problems of the workers.

If he is teaching children, a priest is responsible for the moral formation of those who may later become employers. It is during their early years that we must instil a sense of social justice and charity into the minds of young people. And this must be absolutely genuine and sincere.

The professor in a seminary has the task of moulding and influencing tomorrow's priests, of making them able to win souls for Jesus, especially those furthest away from him.

How can a hospital chaplain understand the spiritual problems and reactions of working class patients if he is a total stranger to their environment? The priest whose ministry is mostly exercised among middle class families must, without giving offense, correct any summary judgements, remove many prejudices, and challenge a good deal of ignorance about the workers. Tremendous harm can be done by an employer who is known to be a Catholic but is totally lacking in any social sense.

Side by side with those middle class families which are genuinely Christian, there are many whose religious life is weak and ineffective, made up of petty devotions, ceremonies, gestures, rites, vulgar comfort, a religion without any hold on reality, and sometimes even completely false. Phrases we overhear, actions we observe, speak volumes of distorted consciences. But the priest, haunted by the living conditions of the working classes, can, either by himself, or through the influence of Catholic societies, or groups of young lay apostles, effectively stir up those souls which are often misled rather than obdurate.

One day the wife of an industrialist complained of the high cost of living. "I have been doing my accounts; in a year, with the same number to cater for, I have had to spend on food alone twice as much as last year." When the priest explained to her then that mothers of working class families made the same complaint, and that the men's pay was far from being doubled, she admitted frankly: "That is true. I had not thought of that!"

If he keeps his eyes open, the priest in a rural district cannot but admit that today there are effective links between the life of the industrial workers and that of the rural population. Quite apart from paid holidays which bring the urban workers into the countryside, and the rural exodus which draws so many young people away from farm life, the decentralization of the factories and the setting up of industry in the country, set the parish priest in rural areas problems which do not allow him to remain unaware of the psychology and living conditions of the proletariat.

It is not only the priest who is engaged in scientific research who has an obligation to think sacerdotally of the working class. Is not this class called to be a part of the Mystical Body, whether it knows it or not? Must not all its work, so necessary to exploit the riches of creation in the service of mankind, be offered up by the hands of priests at the same time as the Precious Blood? Perhaps if scientific research were as busy with the dignity of the man who must operate the machines, as with mechanical and physical progress, we might avoid that absurdity, the degradation of the working man by dangerous or brutalizing work.

It is to his prie-dieu, to Mass, to the recitation of his office, that the priest should first bring his concern with this problem which is so saddening the heart of Jesus. The true priest is surely not one for whom to love God is to forget the world but one who draws from his love of God the strength to renounce himself and to spend himself without counting the cost in the service of his most unfortunate brothers.

Our true mission is to enlighten: "You are the salt of the earth." Our mission is to create an atmosphere of love and of justice: "I have come to cast fire upon the earth"; to work for fraternity and for unity among men in Jesus Christ "that they may be one".

Meditation

This meditation does not set out to solve the social question, but aims to help us to share Christ's attitude to this crucial problem.

Let us adore our Lord who, during the greater part of his life on earth, chose to be a manual worker in order to sanctify in advance the work of all those who would earn their bread by the sweat of their brow. Let us think of him calling to all those who laboured, especially to those who were overburdened, worn out with their work. "Come to me all you that labour and are heavily burdened."

He alone has the power to restore to them their complete human dignity. "I will refresh you." He alone can give them the true life outside which there is only bitterness and disillusion. "I have come that they may have life and have it more abundantly."

Of course, he came for everyone. No favouritism with him. After the adoration of the shepherds, he received that of the Magi. If he chose most of his disciples from among the poor, he took with him also Matthew the tax-collector. He accepted Joseph of Arimathea, he would have been glad to receive the rich young man. "Jesus, looking upon him, loved him." (Mark 10:21) If he ate by the roadside and accepted the hospitality of Peter's mother-in-law, he also sat at the table of Zacheus the Publican, and often visited Bethany.

In his parables, side by side with the rich fool, there is the good master, who gives a living wage even to the labourers who came at the eleventh hour. And if it is humanly difficult for a rich man to enter the kingdom, he will not refuse to help him. "Things which are impossible with men are possible with God." (Luke 18:27)

His preference for the poor, for those who have a hard life, is always evident. To the messengers of John the Baptist he establishes, as proof of his message, that "the poor have the gospel preached to them". The poor, those whom the world scorns, are no longer those who count for nothing, and they can receive the good news.

Let us enter into the actual sufferings of Christ when he sees workers, towards whom his heart reaches out, living in such conditions that it is morally and often materially impossible for them to hear the divine word. Let us share in the sufferings of the Good Shepherd who beholds the mass of the workers, among whom such generosity and the spirit of sacrifice is displayed, the victims of so many misunderstandings and of so many injustices, hypnotized and led away from him by false prophets or by mercenary shepherds. Let us repeat slowly with him the words: "I have pity on the multitude."

In a universal act of charity, let us offer him the present sufferings of all workers. We must not hesitate to describe them to him in detail: the rough work of the miners under the earth, of the sailors, of the stokers at blast furnaces, of the builders of dams, of the makers of chemical products, of those working on mass-production lines, of all those men and women who accomplish, in most unhealthy surroundings, a heavy and joyless labour. Let us not forget those who are disabled at work, for there is not a day without victims on this honourable field of battle.

In their name let us unite their sufferings to his Passion, their blood to his redemptive blood, in order to hasten the hour of their return to him.

Let us ask fervently of the Holy Spirit the light and the effective will to reform all those on whom the solution of the human and Christian problems depends, which the working world sets before us today. Surely, it was the Holy Spirit who inspired that sublime call of Saint James in the fifth chapter of his epistle: "Go to now, ye rich men, weep and howl in your miseries, which shall come upon you. Your riches are corrupted and your garments are motheaten. Behold the hire of the labourers, who have reaped down your fields, which by fraud has been kept back by you, who crieth: and the cry of them hath entered into the ears of the Lord of Sabaoth." (James 5:1–4)

Let us humbly implore the help of the Holy Spirit. We should have bowels of mercy, but run the risk of being like the priest in the parable of the Good Samaritan and pass by misery and injustice without paying attention to it, and without offering a remedy. "Come, Holy Spirit." May he help us to understand what ought to be our behaviour towards our brother workers.

To give a stimulus to our prayer and to build up our meditation we could group our thoughts around these three ideas. Namely, to understand, to love, and to serve.

Yes, to understand, for if priests do not understand the worker, the breach between the Church and him will grow larger still: we shall not succeed in foreseeing, in anticipating the reactions of the worker, and we shall be surprised to find that, when we wished to heal his wounds, we have only opened them wider. How many well-intentioned priests have caused deep wounds, how many have been guilty of blunders because they were too sure of themselves?

Here an act of humility is required. We are so apt to believe that we know everything. There are some priests who spend years in a working class parish and imagine that they know their people. Yet in reality they have not understood them. The priest has many excuses for this. Difference in culture and in education, unconscious class prejudice, a totally different type of life, preoccupations and interests are diametrically opposed. All the more reason for trying to see, especially to listen. It is here that personal contacts with the homes of militant workers can be extremely profitable. At least, we ought to be "teachable", as Sister Elizabeth of the Trinity would have said.

To understand certainly does not mean to approve of everything. We shall detect here or there hasty generalizations, ready-made slogans, simplifications carried to extremes, ignorance of the complexity of economic problems, perhaps even, on certain occasions or against certain individuals, an aggressiveness that is unjustified by the facts; but let us not judge too severely. In every error there is a little truth, and little by little, as we come to share the worker's mentality, we shall find the explanation – which sometimes escapes even the best Marxist authors – namely, the cry of revolt which hurts us, or of an apparently unjust judgement.

We should find the cause of the workers' suffering. Certainly suffering is found not only in the homes of the workers, but what characterizes his suffering is that due to proletarian solidarity and the collective mentality which it creates, it is not the suffering of this or that unfortunate individual, but the suffering of a whole class.

For a hundred years now, and particularly in the last fifteen, there has been some real progress in the social order, but the improvements have not followed the general improvement in the standard of living. There are some who live near their place of employment – but that is exceptional. The majority must prolong their working day by hours of travelling. There are some jobs which are interesting because the worker can

42

put into them some of his initiative, his intelligence and even his heart, or because they are carried on in healthy and even pleasant surroundings. They are the minority. There are still all too many industries where everything has been sacrificed to efficiency and to profit, where mechanized man is dehumanized and goes out from his work stupefied.

Some working men's families can make ends meet with the salary of the father, tax reliefs, and family allowances. These are, however, a small minority. Usually the mother must work, and family life is thrown out of gear, with the inevitable physical and moral consequences which it is easy to foresee.

One of the most common sufferings of the workers is the insecurity, to which "social security" brings only an insufficient palliative. Very few working families can save any money, even with rigid economy. Unforeseen emergencies always come to disorganize the plans which they have made so laboriously. And on the horizon is the menace of unemployment, which perpetually hangs over them.

In that way we shall discover one of the reasons for the inferiority complex from which the working class suffers and the origin of its sensitiveness and of that revolt, silent or open, according to the circumstances and to the individuals, a revolt which characterizes the soul of the worker of today.

Doubtless workmen understand that men's aptitudes vary. They accept inequality of duties as inevitable but, as human beings, they are not prepared to be treated as eternal inferiors. The mentality of the worker unites a conscience very alive to human dignity with a very painful feeling of the inferiority in which the proletariat finds itself in many countries still. The painfulness of this feeling is increased by their knowledge of the insolent and extravagent luxury of some wealthy people who spend in one week what many workers only just earn in a whole year.

Perhaps we shall also succeed in discovering why they have lost confidence in the Church and in us. There are various, alas converging reasons. From the beginning there has been the fact of overwork. When workers were made to work twelve and even fourteen hours a day, without even leaving them Sunday for a day of rest it was inevitable that they should forget the way to church. In historical accounts read of pathetic appeals voiced by fathers of boy apprentices that they should not be obliged to stay every Sunday morning in the shops "to sweep them".

The inevitable result was the widespread conviction that the Church is for the well-to-do, and this idea has been handed down from generation to generation. Today, on the other hand, most workers are being brought up in schools which give them no idea of religion, even though they may be sympathetic to it. In most cases there is no compensating atmosphere of a religious family background. Often the mother herself has been brought up without religion, and has other things to do than teach her children to say their prayers. They are fortunate if, from the tenderest age, they have not heard God mentioned only through blasphemies.

Let us be fair: some children, nevertheless, attend catechism classes and make their first communion – but in what circumstances! We all know from experience how little importance can be attached to these classes, which just add to the fatigue of regular school routine and which one escapes from on the least pretext. Very often their first communion is also their last. How many children, moreover, victims of the influence surrounding them, make their first communion because it is the fashion to do so, yet have not the spirit of faith and are without a desire for our Lord?

Nevertheless, some have come to us. If we had been real directors of souls as well as practical organizers we could have shown a true spiritual fatherliness towards them. They are the *élite,* our future Catholic leaders. Our work with them has not been fruitless, but it is only the minority who will persevere, for they are thwarted by a terrible and inexorable phenomenon, that of the social pressure exerted by their surroundings on young people in the early years of their apprenticeship. Over and above the ragging, the exhausting work, the immoral atmosphere which is so dangerous at an age when boys as well as girls are at the mercy of all temptations, there is all that stream of ideas, prejudices, slogans, and scales of value, which claim that the Church is an institution of another age and of another world, religion a matter of money. . . . The priest is a parasite sold to

44

capitalist society. The stream sweeps over them, submerges them, impregnates them without their realizing it: one would have to be a hero or a saint to hold out alone.

It is a fact that the workers have organized their leisure, thought, and work outside the Church.

We must add the influence of press, radio and television, which is sometimes obliquely and sometimes openly anti-religious. And we can understand why the Christian life, as things are today, is to all intents and purposes made morally impossible for most of the working class. Is that not one more reason for our apostolic hearts to love the workers and, by our conduct, to drive away all their misunderstandings and prejudices?

Let us first of all dispose of one possible misunderstanding. There is no question of love being against some one, against another class. When we truly love with the heart of Christ, we love *for* and not *against*. Nothing is more opposed to the Christian spirit, and, *a fortiori,* to the priestly spirit, than the sectarian spirit. The Christian spirit is essentially a spirit of love which does not display any partiality. The sacerdotal spirit is one of meditation, of reconciliation between God and humanity, but also between man and man.

"Saint Paul's phrase, 'Everything to all men' is more than ever the order of the day", wrote Monsignor de Bazelaire. "The priest is a universal man. He must feel as close to the poor as to the rich, to the old as to the young. He must in turn, and with equal facility, enter into the mentality of the industrial worker, the tradesman, the labourer, and make his own the sufferings and the joys of others; nor should he be indifferent to any human feeling, whether it be the pride of a young mother, the anxiety of the father of a family, the confusion of a poor luckless devil without work or a roof over his head. You are a priest in order to carry the burdens of all those who are entrusted to your care."

But it is axiomatic that every priest should love with a more tender, in fact, with a more partial love, those who suffer most, those who are victims of injustice, those who are so often mis-understood, betrayed, abandoned, those who for all sorts of reasons, are not able to defend themselves by their unaided efforts and whose advisers are so often those who are paid agitators or instigators of hatred. In spite of the undeniable progress made, the condition of the worker class is still too often – to repeat the energetic expression of Monsignor Cardijn – only "coagulated sin", bitter fruit of the primacy granted to "profit" over "man" by our economic system.

A priest who loves as Jesus loves cannot condone such things. He must pray for the realization of the prayer to the Holy Spirit: "and thou shalt renew the face of the earth". He must strive with all his heart and with all his mind to promote more justice, more dignity, more humanity.

A priest who loves as Jesus does feels a fraternal sympathy for the working man; he must show tact, respect, sensitivity and simplicity towards him, avoiding all complacency, patronizing airs, all condescension as well as any trace of vulgarity or familiarity. A priest who loves as Jesus loves looks at the working class with favour; he understands certain reactions which are sometimes expressed clumsily, and sometimes explode brutally: excuses without necessarily approving certain faults and certain enthusiasms. He emphasizes especially the admirable qualities and real virtues springing from generosity, from courage, from joint responsibility, from mutual aid, leading always to sacrifice, which are characteristic of the working class.

None of those vital problems, which have such grave consequences for the moral and spiritual life of apprentices or families, should leave him indifferent. A priest who loves as Jesus loves works gradually to achieve the unity of the whole of this class, so that he can speak to them and be understood. He grasps their true cares, their real difficulties, their deep aspirations, their hidden resources; by degrees he discovers at what point he can bring the divine into their lives. A priest who loves as Jesus loves must have absorbed something of the immense love of Jesus for the workers. That is the secret which has made great apostles among the working class.

Quite recently there was discovered among the unedited papers of Father Anizan, founder of the Sons of Charity, the following prayer, written in his spiritual notebook. "My God, my divine Master and Friend, send apostles to the people. There are plenty of flatterers who despise the poor and use them for their own ends. But where are the friends of the poor who love them, who are willing to be sacrificed for them, to be their slaves, to live and die for them? My God, who died for the poor and for the workers, as well as for the powerful, how you must long to save our dear and well-loved poor. Yes, you desire it, and the proof is in the love and desire with which you inflame my heart. Lord, send them not one, not ten, but a legion of helpers. I offer myself to you, O my God. You have sent me, here I am. Help me, multiply the powers of my body, that I may work and sacrifice myself for the poor for a long time. Send other helpers, too, other, better helpers, more powerful, more holy than I."

When a priest loves in this way, even if he has not had personal experience of manual work or of poverty, everything about the working class affects his heart if not his whole body. Then he finds that he is neither self-conscious nor awkward when circumstances, prearranged or accidental, put him into contact with the workers. He feels at home with them. Many subjects of conversation arise. Since his interest in them is not purely formal or merely polite, the atmosphere is favourable for discussion. Conversation is carried on without constraint or uneasiness: the day is near when these souls will be ready to receive the divine message.

It is as men of God that we approach our working brethren, and the most precious service we can render them is to prepare them to receive their God. The ideal would be that we should be so filled with God ourselves that they might say of us as a peasant said to his wife when he returned from a visit to Ars: "I have seen God in a man." Then by our life we should be authentic witnesses of the Gospel. But we are not alone in this cause. The whole Christian community should follow us. Let us help the practising Catholics in our parish to realize their responsibilities in this matter. If they could demonstrate true Christian charity, not a caricature of charity, mere cold and abstract virtue, but charity drawn from the heart of Christ, alone capable of being stronger than hate. As long as egotism separates men, reforms must be imposed by force; they will be short lived or they will claim other victims.

47

Some years ago the French writer, Joseph Folliet, told a Congress of Catholic workers: "If the immense liberation of human energies which mechanical progress has achieved, if the great relief men have secured by slaves of iron and steel establish the technical conditions in a city, minds and hearts are far from drawing the moral and social consequences from these facts. Two dangers follow: either the continuation of a purely technical movement and the oppression of men under the weight of the determinism they have established culminating in total stupefaction engendered by a civilization of machines and comfort; or violent reaction against the resistance and privileges of the past, the paradox of bloody revolutions which are ends in themselves, which claim to make love grow out of systematic violence, freedom out of tyranny, truth out of lies, and the universal embrace of the human race in concentration camps, torture chambers and bases for atomic weapons. Love alone, creative and constructive love, will allow us to avoid these alternatives. Ingenious, diligent, and generous love will discover new forms of economic association, new working communities towards which capitalist enterprise must advance; it is love which will give the privileged the spirit of sacrifice and moderate those who are striving to rise. What is needed is an eruption of liberty over the determination of a world which through its wish to dominate matter, has finally become material itself. Who will bear the burden if not love?"

It is part of the priest's mission to help the workers to realize their divine vocation, in the midst of their pride in their working life. But let us have no illusions: it is not sufficient to do good to a few isolated workers, to make the Church understood by a few families of workers; it is the whole working group of a village or of a region which we must penetrate and lead to Christ. That requires an action like fermentation which can only be achieved by militant Christians. It is the duty of the priest, wherever he can, to detect, to train, to sustain, to encourage, to give spiritual inspiration to those who will act as leaven.

This movement must not be limited to the workers. Many problems about the life of the worker and his christianization can be solved only if all work together. So, too, all possible ways of enlightening opinion, creating an atmosphere of understanding and of love, making the middle classes and employers assume their responsibilities, inspiring those with influence at various levels must be attempted. There we are fully in line with the mission we have in the Church.

It is, then, of the highest importance that all priests without exception, and through them all Christians, enter resolutely into the way indicated by the Holy See and the hierarchy, to help raise the working man towards Christ, as well as to enlighten and convince all our colleagues of the importance of the working-class problem at the present time. Never have there been so many reasons to hope for the solution of this problem. Without any sectarianism, but with intense love, every one should heed the appeal raised in anguish by Cardinal Suhard shortly after the war. "The fact that stands out since the beginning of this century, but particularly during the last twenty years, is the increasing importance and the prime necessity of the workers in the destiny of nations, and of the Church.

"This emergence of the working class has very deep-seated causes: particularly a legitimate reaction against the inhuman conditions of the 'proletariat'. It has very important consequences. One of these is to make it vital that our apostolic activity should be focused on the working class. Will the world which is now being built and in which the strength and feelings of the workers will have such a prominent place, be Christian or pagan?"

Christ speaks to his Priest

I have pity on the multitude. Today as ever I have pity on the multitude. The material and moral misery of the people, my people, rends my heart. That is not just in a manner of speaking, my Son. It is truth. You must study deeply the mystery of love. With me you must share the suffering love brings. May your heart bleed with this wound in my heart. Only then will you understand.

In them, my poor people, in them, workers who earn their bread with the sweat of their brow, in them I am often misunderstood, scoffed at, humiliated, cheated, forsaken, abandoned.

49

If you but knew how much I love them because they have shared my life, because more than others, they have the solidarity which unites them to other men, because I continue to be a worker in them. I love them because they are victims of bad shepherds.

You must love them very much in order to be able to understand them. You should love them so that you may recognize me and find me in each of them. You should love them in particular so that I can help them, enlighten them, sustain them, in their legitimate effort for liberation. You should love them so that, through you, I may teach them the power of a love stronger than hate.

Sometimes you will feel in your soul the shuddering of my soul, in the face of certain injustices, of certain unmerited miseries. Indignation made me cry out: "Woe to the rich." Woe to you evil rich, who abuse your riches and your culture to exploit the poor! But let your indignation, my Son, be ever an indignation springing from love and not from hate. Establish peace and light. Teach those who have responsibilities that they will only incur reproach if they do not treat their employees as brothers and if they do not respect in them my divine dignity. Teach those who own businesses that the soul of an apprentice, the honour of a woman, the health of a man are worth more than all the gold in the world. Teach them that one day they will have to give an account to me of the way in which they have acquired and managed their finances, and that at the moment of judgement the wiles, the cleverness, the finesse, and the technique will avail nothing.

Be not unjust, cast a stone at no one, but proclaim the truth with respect of persons. Be pure and disinterested yourself; love detachment and poverty. Show by your example the priority of the soul over perishable goods. Use this world as if you used it not. Let money be your good servant, never your master; never attach your heart and soul to it.

Above all my great pity goes out to souls. I have multiplied loaves of bread to nourish the body, but I have given my body to nourish souls. I desire them to desire for me, I thirst for them to thirst for me. What will it profit them to gain the whole earth, if they lose their soul? What good will come to them from their struggles for liberation, if they become slaves of Mammon and become in turn exacting and harsh masters? It is your mission to attract them to me, for I am the only substantial reply to the deep longings I have put into their hearts. To me, without whom liberty is only a word, happiness only a chimaera, prosperity only dust, riches a lie. To me, without whom every effort towards advance is doomed to defeat and to disappointment.

You see how great is your mission. Yes, give yourself completely to your worker-brethren; but take care that you are so intensely and faithfully united to me while giving yourself, that it will be I whom you will give.

Examination of Conscience

1. Do I feel myself responsible for all men living in my parish, all, including the workers?

2. Am I humble enough to believe that I am far from knowing everything, and that, whatever may be my age and experience, I always need to learn more?

3. Do I understand the suffering of the worker, and do I suffer with him in my heart?

4. Without becoming exclusive and sectarian, do I give to the problems of the workers all the importance they deserve?

5. Am I careful to keep informed about working men? Do I like to make contact with the militant workmen to learn from them the various current trends in my parish, in the world, the suffering of the worker, and the trends of opinion which unite the proletariat?

6. Do I truly look upon the workers as my brothers in Jesus Christ, the more worthy of my devotion and of my respect as they are so often victims of injustice and of disdain?

7. Do the workers feel that I am a priest who understands them and loves them?

8. By my life, am I a witness to the Gospel?

9. Do I desire to create in my parish, in the homes of all Christians, an atmosphere of understanding and of love for the workers?

10. If, personally conscious of the gravity of the social problem, I do nothing to make those around me conscious of it, do I realize that I am an accomplice in the actual disorder and that I ratify the evil by my silence and by my passivity?

11. Do the militant workers find in me the spiritual nourishment which they need? Am I concerned to help them to become the true Christian ferment which can carry the spirit of the Gospel into the centres of influence where the soul of my parishioners is fashioned?

12. Is Catholic Action the lynch-pin of my parochial missionary activity?

13. Have I created an atmosphere in my church which makes it possible for workers who come there to feel entirely at ease?

14. Have I considered that the solution of the problem of the worker in all its aspects flows over into my strictly parochial activity?

15. Is the desire "Thy Kingdom Come" written deep in my heart, that is to say, the advancement of the Kingdom of God in the city of men?

16. Do I often offer the working man to Jesus Christ, and pray for the development of Catholic Action among the workers?

Resolutions

1. To spread far and wide the love of our Lord for workers.

2. To remember at the altar and in divine office the needs of the workers' homes in my parish and in the whole world.

3. To lead a life that is completely priestly and evangelical.

4. Never to let a worker feel uneasy with me.

5. To take into account the legitimate sensitivity of the worker. To assure all those who come to me of a cordial and understanding welcome.

6. To make all possible contact with the workers.

7. To avoid all vulgarity as much as a patronizing and condescending air.

8. In conversation with workers, to show myself frankly open and sympathetic, desirous to know everything, without thinking that I am automatically obliged to approve everything.

9. If necessary as our Lord did, "spending the night in prayer" before choosing his apostles, to force myself to discover militant workers, to instruct them, to help them, to rouse them spiritually.

10. The world, for so many years steeped in capitalistic materialism, is infiltrated more and more by Marxist influences. To beware of these poisons. To know clearly, without any simplicity, what are, besides the incontestable values, the noxious characteristics of what one might call the filtering viruses of the contemporary social world.

11. To consider as a pastoral duty the study of the social doctrine of the Church. To reread from time to time the pontifical documents on this subject. To keep myself aware of the workers' problems and of the history of the working class in its effort for freedom and for legitimate promotion.

12. To neglect no occasion to make the psychology of the worker more comprehensible to those in other walks of life.

13. To reflect sometimes, and induce others to reflect on the suffering which went into the making of the objects which we use in daily life.

14. In my sermons and in my spiritual direction to insist on the justice and the charity which should be shown towards their human brothers.

15. If I am a teacher, to be careful to develop a social sense in my students, a knowledge of the realities of the working world, the respect and even the love due to their workerbrothers.

16. If I am a chaplain to young Christian workers to try to understand my brothers in the ministry, to try to understand the complexity of the problems with which they have to cope, to take good care not to be severe in my judgements about them. To show them by what means and under what conditions the working man can become open to their priestly action.

17. Whatever post I hold, never to cease to draw my colleagues' attention to the importance, vital at the present time, of the Christianization of the working class. The day when all priests of France without exception are able to bear testimony that they love all their brother workers, that they are, consequently, "aware" of the problems of their temporal and spiritual life, the scandal denounced by Pius XI will be very near an end.

Spiritual Reading

The priesthood is a social service. The priest is a mediator; he is the providential intermediary between men and God. He must never forget this. And he must feel on his shoulders the weight of responsibility for the people he must lead to God.

We call him mediator. He is also turned towards men. And in a new sense the social spirit becomes necessary to him. The people for whom he is responsible are not a people having souls only. They have bodies, too. We do not separate soul and body; that would mean death. If man suffers from ignorance, from error, from sin in his soul, he suffers also in his body from illness, misery, cold, hunger, sorrow. In face of all this, can the priest be disinterested? Surely, you will say, he must be on his guard against getting involved in temporal affairs. That is true; trade associations, joint consultation, claims, strikes, are not his business. But do not all the economic problems whose importance is growing in our modern civilization raise questions of justice and of morality? And who will solve them if he remains a stranger to them?

Perhaps because they did not see the importance of them, the clergy in the last century lost the working class, a fact which was, in the opinion of Pius XI, the greatest scandal of that era. No, the priest cannot live outside the world around him. It is not his place to take the laymen's place in their own sphere, but he must observe and pay attention; he must weigh up the misery, the difficulties, the hopes, the claims, the exigencies, so that he can judge them impartially, in a Christian manner. He must try to see clearly into the conflict of interests, not to be an arbiter, but to make known the doctrine of the Church, to recall principles, to inspire a sense of justice and of charity, to be the herald of the Gospel in a world which disregards it. Men have the right to ask him for advice and he must be capable of giving it. He must study the thought of the Church; he must let it soak into him completely. Many priests are not well informed about the encyclicals and other papal documents. They remain on the fringe of the social evolution, because they have not studied its problems sufficiently in the light of Christianity. If the priest is asked not to interfere in the unhappy dramas which set men

54

against one another, he is asked to make the voice of Christ heard, Christ who loves all his brothers and who wants to spread peace among them with respect for rights and with love for souls. That is what it means for the priest to have a social spirit.

Monsignor de Bazelaire

II

Some one has asked me a question about the "class struggle". The phrase implies a doctrinal error and a philosophical error somewhat like racialism. According to racialism, there was a privileged race, the Nordic race, which had the right to impose itself on the rest of the world and to destroy anything that opposed its domination, in particular the Jewish race. Racialism was always accompanied by anti-semitism.

According to the theory of the "class struggle", there is a privileged class, the proletariat, which has the right to monopolize power and to impose itself by force on other classes although in a different way. Although he did not use the word, Lenin presented the theory of the class war in his work on the infantile disease of "Leftism" in Communism. The Marxist theory of class ends with the suppression of all classes by their absorption into the one proletariat. In the meantime, the class war vigorously opposes every form of capitalism, that is to say all those who aim at private ownership of the means of production. Lenin was particularly set against the middle classes.

The class war, like racialism, is a totalitarian doctrine which aims to impose not only a political and economic régime, but even a common way of thinking for all men. To achieve this purpose, the class war, like racialism, must be organized in a dictatorial way, and it must repudiate all deviations. One education, one type of youth, one union, one party! Once we have seen what the class war implies, we can understand why it is condemned, and for the same reasons as racialism.

But some reflections are in order. Without doubt we must condemn the claims of the proletariat to dominate other classes, but we can do so only if we refuse to other social classes their claim to impose themselves on the working class. In other

55

words, the only people who can logically oppose the "class war" are those who have decided to help the working classes to take the place in the nation which belongs rightfully to them.

We must recognize a hardening in the opposition which exists between social classes especially between the working and middle classes. Each class seems to be more occupied with its own interests than with the common good of the whole country. It is a grave disorder. Without expressing any decision, we should work for a reconciliation of the classes while making an effort towards mutual understanding.

Without going into the excesses of Marxist class theory, we sometimes find ourselves facing certain claims by the proletariat which are not acceptable. Some of them assert that the middle classes have no right to exist if they do not put themselves at the service of the proletariat and adopt a common way of life with them. This claim is contrary to the liberty of men and of social groups. We must demand union among all. We cannot insist on a complete fusion and assimilation. The ideal in a social body is not homogeneity but unity in diversity.

There is a graver error. Some claim that true Christianity will be born again in the middle classes only if they are willing to be integrated into a proletarian religion. Some go so far as to say that the Church will be saved through the proletariat. I have heard this error maintained by at least two priests who were very devoted and very generous, but had let their enthusiasm lead them astray from the truth.

The Church is not committed to any country, to any class. She is there for all those who desire, through her and in her, to find the Lord Jesus who saves those who believe in him. The Church respects earthly institutions, and does not ask men to renounce their preferences of a temporal order. It is from within that she will change all these institutions by christianizing them. At the same time, she asks men to renounce their selfishness, individual egotism, family egotism, class egotism, or national egotism, so as to work in common agreement for the good of all. Finally, in the Church, there is neither working class nor middle class, neither French nor German, neither American nor Russian, but all are one in Jesus Christ.

Monsignor Ancel

Subjects for Discussion

1. Why is it so vitally necessary at the present time that all priests, without exception, should be interested in the problems of the worker?

2. In what sense ought and can the priest be a link of love between the different social groups?

Prayer

Most Holy Virgin Mary, so maternal towards all human distresses, cast a look of pity on the moral and material situation of the working masses. Enlighten all those who direct economic and social life on the seriousness of their responsibilities. Make concern for human life and the divine vocation of their brothers take precedence in their minds over the search for profit and wealth. In all of them may love be stronger than hatred.

Multiply in the working world vocations of militant Christians who, by the testimony of their radiance, make a true Christian life desirable to their brothers. Inspire among priests numerous apostles of the working class who can understand it and sustain it in its efforts to rise towards your Son. So through your beneficent influence as universal mediatrix, may the Kingdom of the Father slowly rise in the City of Men. Amen.

Thought

The misery of people is in their body and soul. Providing for their immediate wants makes little difference if we do not open their minds, if we do not reform and strengthen their will, if we do not fire the best with a high ideal, if we do not succeed in suppressing or at least reducing oppression and injustice, if we do not make the humble ensure the progressive achievement of their happiness.

L. J. Lebret

4

THE GREATNESS OF OUR VOCATION

Meditation

It is good for us, from time to time, to meditate on the greatness of our vocation, not to stimulate our pride or vanity, but as an incentive for thanksgiving, a constant motive for encouragement and for confidence, and a spur to our zeal and to our generosity.

In the third chapter of Saint Mark's Gospel we read how the apostles were called. "And going up into a mountain, he called unto him whom he would himself: and they came to him. And he made that twelve should be with him, and that he might send them to preach. And he gave them power to heal sicknesses, and to cast out devils. And to Simon he gave the name Peter." (Mark 3:13–16)

Strange though it may appear, it is the priest himself who finds the mystery of the priesthood most obscure. The laity can deceive themselves and stop short of the real mystery. This is not possible for the priest. The reality that is hidden within him is *very* real to him.

"It is easy for you to think about the priesthood today", said a priest to a young seminarian. "To you the priest is another person invested with prestige. But tomorrow it will be quite different. Then the priest will be you. You will scarcely see the vestments you wear. The sacred words and actions will be yours! You will find yourself with your faith stripped bare." It is in this spirit of faith, stripped bare but sustained by all the love of which we are capable, that we shall try to meditate on the three things which constitute the greatness of our vocation. These three things are the greatness of him who has called us, the greatness which he has confided to us, and the greatness of the powers conferred on us.

One of the mysteries of our priesthood is the mystery of the call, which is at one and the same time the mystery of he who has called us, the mystery of the choice he has freely made of us, the mystery of the anointing which transforms us into "another Christ".

Let us look at Isaias. "Thus saith the Lord God that created the heavens, and stretched them out: that established the earth, and the things that spring out of it: that giveth breath to the people upon it, and spirit to them that tread thereon. I the Lord have called thee in justice, and have taken thee by the hand, and preserved thee. And I have given thee for a covenant of the people, for a light of the Gentiles: that thou mightest open the eyes of the blind, and bring forth the prisoner out of the prison, and them that sit in darkness out of the prison house. I am the Lord, this is my name: I will not give my glory to another, nor my praise to graven things." (Isa. 42:5–8)

And a little later: "And now thus saith the Lord that created thee, O Jacob, and formed thee, O Israel: Fear not, for I have redeemed thee and called thee by thy name: thou art mine." (Isa. 43:1)

"You are my witnesses, saith the Lord, and my servant whom I have chosen: that you may know, and believe me, and understand that I myself am; there was no god before me, and after me there shall be none. I am, I am the Lord: and there is no Saviour besides me." (Isa. 43:10, 11)

"You are my witnesses, saith the Lord, and I am God. I have declared, and have saved, I have made it heard, and there was no strange one among you. And from the beginning I am the same, and there is none that can deliver out of my hand: I will work, and who shall turn it away?" (Isa. 42:1)

He who has chosen us is the Master *par excellence*, free in his choices and in his preferences. "You have not chosen me but I have chosen you." (Isa. 41:9) He has first singled us out and

59

loved us. "He has first loved us." We have been blessed among all other men, without our having any right to this privilege. "Whom he himself desired." In one way or another the scene on the mountain has been renewed for us. "Going up a mountain he called them."

For a few moments let us recall the story of our vocation. In what circumstances we became aware of it – gradually or suddenly – how many other young people in our group could have been chosen instead, and would perhaps have responded better than we did. Let us adore the Lord who, one day, said to us: "Behold my servant whom I have chosen, my beloved", and who always repeats to us: "Thou art my servant, I have not cast thee away."

Let us note, moreover, that in calling us he did not impose his choice on us. He accepted that we could refuse, and experience bears witness that he set the freedom of our reply before everything else. "*If* thou wilt . . . follow me."

Our assent to his call determined something more than our mere admission into an *élite,* like a teacher looking for prefects. "Blessed is he whom thou dost choose and adopt." (Ps. 64:5) The choice in question must end in an "assumption", that is our soul taking control, ensuring a real identification with Christ.

There is only one Priest, Christ Jesus, and in him is our priesthood. At the moment of the incarnation he became a priest, his divinity anointing the human nature which he assumed. The sacerdotal character is nothing else than a participation in this anointing of the Incarnate Word. This imprint, this seal, this *sphragis,* as the Greeks call it, which neither sin, nor death, nor heresy can efface, is not any ordinary sign, it is a transforming reality which consecrates the very being of the priest, and makes him a consecrator. It is this which ensures that the priesthood, if it is not intrinsically linked to the person of the priest is, nevertheless, by a free disposition of God, something of his very being. It is not an official garment, but an abiding disposition which permits God to say to us as to his Son, to each of us as an extension of his Son: "Thou art a priest forever."

The mystery of the call is, then, the mystery of the one Priest in whom we are called to become priest, like him for ever.

Priests by all our acts, priests by our state, priests before everything, priests whatever happens. Said Cardinal Suhard: "Consecrated even in his limbs, the priest is no longer and should be no longer profane. All that he touches is exorcised and blessed. In all that he does, in all that he is he should give the impression of sacredness. By his very presence he establishes the existence of an order of invisible and of superhuman values in a world which despises them or struggles against them. He makes 'palpable', so to speak, the infinity of God, while reflecting the mystery of it."

"The priest is understood only in heaven", said the Curé d'Ars. "If people understood him on earth, they would die, not from fear but from love."

The reason for the greatness of our vocation is likewise the greatness of the mission to which we are called. This mission is, in fact, identical with that of Jesus Christ himself. It combines unity and great variety. *Unity* because its essential purpose is to unite all humanity in Christ, through whom, with whom, and in whom all honour and glory are rendered to our heavenly Father, in the unity of the Holy Spirit. *Great variety* because its aspects, for our finite mind, are many and diverse, though always complementary.

To develop our meditation we can reflect on the three following points. Firstly, the mission entrusted to us is a mission of mediation. Secondly, it is a mission of redemption. And thirdly, it is a mission of sanctification.

In reality there is only one Mediator, Christ Jesus. It is precisely in him and with him that the priest should give God to man, and man to God. Christ is a mediator because he is at the same time true man and true God. In *Le Sacrement de l'Unité,* Father Charmot wrote: "He was the first to achieve this meeting of the finite and the infinite. Priests, in the likeness of Christ, reconcile in themselves, as it were, two natures, that of God and that of men." "The human and the divine", wrote Monsignor Mathieu, "are united in Jesus Christ without contradiction, even to the point of effecting a personal identity. This synthesis of the human and the divine is the mystery of the Incarnation

61

and the mystery of the priesthood in the Word made flesh. Priests, prolonging in time the Eternal Priest, are bound, after the example of their model, to maintain in themselves the union of the divine and of the human. They should grow nearer God without ceasing to be men in the process. They should grow nearer to men without ceasing to be sons of God for that purpose."

One can say of us what Canon Masure said of Christ: "Jesus is not only a priest at the Last Supper or on Calvary. He is always a priest, since his priesthood is co-extensive with the incarnation itself. He never ceases to exercise his mediatory functions. A living and substantial sacrament, he is a priest also in all his ways with God and men." "God indeed was in Christ reconciling the world to himself." (2 Cor. 5:19)

To fulfil his mission of mediation, to be this permanent link between God and man in his personal entity, the priest must be simultaneously a man of God, a man among men, a man of the Church. He must be a man of God, responsible for the interests of God. "For every high priest . . . is ordained for men in the things that appertain to God." (Heb. 5:1) "Did you not know that I must be about my Father's business?" (Luke 2:49) Responsible also for the homage due to God, for the honour due to God, for the glory of God, which consists not so much in exterior pomp as in the growth of the divine life in the hearts of men. "Man", said Saint Irenaeus, "is the living glory of God."

"The great mark of a priest", said Cardinal Saliège, "is what no other characteristic can replace, namely, the example of a life which can only be explained in terms of God." A man of God is a man consecrated to God. God is our heritage, and we are the heritage of God, God's "share", set aside for God. A man of God is a man into whom God enters, a man whom God penetrates, a man of whom God makes use. The priest makes the sign of the cross; it is God who blesses. The priest pronounces words; it is God who speaks. The priest acts; it is God who makes the action fruitful.

A man of God, because he represents God, and, whatever he does, works with God. The priest is never alone. God dwells in him in a special manner. "For Christ, therefore we are ambassadors." (2 Cor. 5:20) He is a man of God because it is his responsibility to represent him, and all the divine attributes, truth and justice, but with special emphasis on kindness and mercy.

The priest is a man of God, because before he tries to fill his mind with the thoughts of God, before nourishing his soul with the word of God, he seeks to be penetrated by the love of God, in all things thinking the thoughts of God, in all things seeing things with the eye of God. Finally, because he is an official messenger of God, the priest is his "plenipotentiary" to men.

These considerations indicate the priest's need to keep what amounts to a permanent contact with God, and, in order to talk to him, to preserve times for prayer silence and contemplation.

In his encyclical *Ad Catholici Sacerdotii Fastigium,* Pius XI wrote: "It would be a very grave and very dangerous error if priests, led on by a false zeal, neglected their own sanctification to plunge completely into external works of the priesthood, however good they may be. By so doing he would endanger his own salvation, he would run the risk of losing, if not divine grace, at least that unction of the Holy Spirit which gives to the exterior apostolate a strength and a marvellous effectiveness."

Many of the faithful feel that if the priest is to measure up to what they expect of him he must be first of all a man of God. The following letter, quoted by Canon Boulard in his book *Essor ou Declin du Clergé Français,* confirms this. "The priest is he whom God has called to make his prophet. Throughout the history of the Jewish people there have ever been men to remind them of the Eternal, so the priest, too, is always there to exhort, to awaken consciences, to track down errors, to refuse compromises, to spur on souls that are self-satisfied, and without any respite to guide us on the way of the Kingdom, towards unity, towards God. We should think of the priest as a silent soul, who breathes God. We should *want* him to live his glorious vocation."

The priest is a man among men, because the powers he has received have not been given to him for himself, but are all directed towards others. Thus a priest cannot give himself absolution nor can he give himself Holy Communion other than during Mass, nor can he give himself the sacraments. "He is a priest for others."

He is a man among men because, as we read in the Epistle to the Hebrews, taken from among men, he is destined for men (Heb. 5:1). He is a man among men because he represents men. Not that he owes his priesthood to popular election, but because he represents authentically the Person of our Lord who contains and gathers to his own body all baptized persons. He is a man among men because nothing human should be alien to him, since his mission is to purify, to spiritualize, to sanctify, to offer all human assets. Although not of the world, he must live in the midst of the world; because in his reading of his office and in his Mass his prayer should rise to God carrying with it all human suffering, and all the needs of souls.

He is a man among men because, like Christ, he must view the world as it is with a feeling of infinite respect, pity, and love. "I have pity on the multitude." (Mark 8:2)

Like Christ he, too, should be sympathetic in contact with human suffering and try in every way to relieve it, always displaying understanding and helpfulness. He should communicate to men the gifts and the teaching of God, but also make them feel that he is vitally concerned with their salvation, so that they may realize that he feels the necessity of their redemption more keenly than they do.

He is a man among men because, as a microcosm, he carries in his heart all the souls for whom he is responsible. Like Jesus he can say: "For them do I sanctify myself." (John 17:19) He elevates them to the same degree as he raises himself. The story of the people he must bear within himself is in part the projection on the map of the states of conscience of his consecrated soul. He is himself like a battle-field.

Cardinal Suhard said: "He must be the first to realize in his own person the triumph of 'the new man'. In order to 'exorcise' human effort and to make the universe get rid of its 'ambiguity' the priest must dissipate his own 'ambiguity' and establish unity in his person. It is clear that this identification in Christ, far from turning the priest away from the city, leads him straight to it. How can he bring humanity to God again if he has not first allied himself to God? Human nature will not follow any way but its own. The dilemmas of the priest will become the dilemmas of the people; his personal victories will be a preparation for those of the world."

Canon Boulard reports the testimony of a lay missionary to confirm this. "In Christ there is a human life and a divine life. In the priest we expect to find again a truly human life and a truly divine life. Unfortunately many seem to be cut off from either the one or the other.

"There are some priests who seem never to have had the life of a man. They do not know to weigh the difficulties of a layman, of a father of a family, in a truly human way. They do not realize the real, the true, the sad aspects of the normal life of a man or a woman. When Christian laymen have once met a priest who has 'understood' them, who has entered whole-heartedly into their life and their difficulties, they never lose the memory of that blessing.

"Nevertheless, if he intertwines his life with ours it must not be indistinguishable. For a long time priests treated laymen like children. Today some go to the other extreme, and try to be their equals. It would be better if they remained fathers. When the father of a family sees his son is grown up, he treats him as a man and not as a boy, but he always looks on him as his son: as a son and a man."

As a man of God, and as a man among men, it is in the Church and with the Church that the priest accomplishes his role. As Cardinal Suhard says, the priest, cut off from the Church, is unthinkable. "For we must not think of the priest as an isolated being, to whom Christ entrusts individually and directly his mission and to use his powers according to his own discretion. It is unthinkable to imagine a priest cut off from the Church in this way. Not only because he is incorporated in the Mystical Body by his baptism, and because the sacrament of holy orders which he has received is a sacrament of the Church; but above all because his mediation on this basis would be counterfeit. For it is the Church which, on earth, prolongs and continues Christ. If he is the one mediator, the Church is the one media-trix; it is in this sense that one says outside the Church there is no salvation.

65

"But the Church, as the Mystical Body of Christ, is identified with him in everything. Through her whole being, and then through her members, she shares in the sacerdotal mediation of Christ. To think of the priesthood as an additional intermediary between the soul and God, is meaningless."

Even if he were alone in a desert, he is never isolated. If he is in a diocese it is in union with his bishop and all his diocesan colleagues that he has wedded a church, that is to say a portion of humanity which he must support in order to expiate in its name and pray in its name, a faint reflection of Christ who, when he became incarnate, wed all humanity and spent himself for it unto death.

If he is a religious it is in union with the Pope, through all the links of the hierarchy of his superiors, that he devotes himself to the needs of the Church wherever obedience sends him. He does not do personal work, his is the work of the Church. He may depart, but the Church he has nourished and enriched lives on.

Said Father Michonneau: "Aware of this, the missionary feels from the start that he is a man of the Church, that he serves the Church, that he represents her, that he is responsible to her, that he assists her progress, or obstructs it, whether he wishes it or not, whether it is burdensome or not, it is a fact, and a fact that we must never forget. My attitude, my words, my smile, or my surly air, the way I hold my hand, the manner in which I judge, my manner of administering the sacraments, and my way of offering Holy Mass, all that I do inspires criticism, good or bad, of the Church of Christ."

Let us be under no misapprehension. We must try to improve our ability to carry out our apostolate. It is our duty to make full use of all the talents given to us by God. We must apply our intelligence to a better understanding of the divine mysteries in order to be able to explain them better, to be better acquainted with the current ideas prevailing in the world, to make a better analysis of the nature of the sociological trends which influence the lives of our contemporaries, to have a better grasp of the complexity of their problems.

But let us read again the words of Saint Peter, the apostle who goes straight to the point. "For unto this are you called: because Christ also suffered for us, leaving you an example that you should follow his steps." (1 Peter 2:21) We are co-redeemers. By his whole being and through his whole life Christ redeemed the world. He is a redeemer by his very existence. As Canon Masure said: "The idea of priesthood overlaps in time and metaphysics the idea of sacrifice. The priesthood endures, it is a state. Sacrifice accomplishes and achieves, it is an art. But, on the other hand, if the priesthood logically precedes the sacrifice rendering it possible, what would a priesthood be if it did not fulfil itself in the offering and immolation of a victim? It is through the sacrifice that the priesthood asserts its authority, fulfils itself, and in a certain sense passes from the potential to the actual."

It is by the cross that, obedient to the will, full of the love and of the wisdom of the Father, Christ, embracing and elevating all human sufferings, has redeemed the world. Surely we are co-redeemers, too, by our whole life. But it is above all in the hour of suffering, suffering with love, that we apply the fruits of the redemption for the benefit of those entrusted to us.

"Without shedding of blood there is no remission", said Saint Paul (Heb. 9:22). Thus did Christ show his love. "Christ also loved the Church and delivered himself up for it: that he might sanctify it, cleansing it by the laver of water in the word of life." (Eph. 5:25–6) Father Chevrier said: "The priest teaches by his words, he saves by his suffering." Suffering is not an end in itself. But as humanity stands it is a means of compensation. By fraternal substitution, the priest fulfils one of the reasons of his existence, taking on himself some of the expiation due for the sins of men, and completing in his flesh what is lacking in the Passion of Christ for his body which is the Church.

There is no priest worthy of the name who has not at some time or other come to know his Gethsemani or even Calvary. It is our "business" to make reparation. Jesus has not misled us. "If any man will come after me, let him deny himself and take up his cross and follow me" (Matt. 16:24)

"The victim of our priesthood", "to prolong the immolation of a God". These are not just rhetoric but phrases which each of us should accept as part of our lives if our priesthood is to attain all its dimensions. Many of our brother priests have so understood it, and, either drop by drop in their daily life, or by crucifying trials, have shed their blood for Christ and for their brothers. It was Paul Claudel who said: "This is what the world expects today. We need priests who give the body and blood of God, and their own at the same time."

The world around us tends to be more and more mechanized and material. The extraordinary development of science in every field means that unless men receive that "spiritual reinforcement", of which Bergson spoke, they will become robots. Modern man seeks a liberation. He is conscious that he is a slave, either to machines, to social pressure, or simply to himself. We know that only a strong and genuine spirituality can help him to recover his liberty as a child of God. It is our mission to give him, together with a relish for higher things, a hunger for God, a longing for the infinite, as well as a sense of men and a sense of the Church.

What does this mean? It means restoring sight to the blind, hearing to the deaf, the use of their limbs to the paralyzed, health to the lepers. It means announcing the good news of salvation to all the poor, not only to the materially poor, but to those who have not the riches which rust and worms cannot affect. It means kindling the flames of so many wicks that are still smoking. It means rescuing even those walking corpses who have lost him who is the way, the truth, and the life.

It is the whole mission of the priest to spiritualize humanity and to make a health-giving stream pass through all the cells of the Mystical Body. He must fulfil his mission first of all by his handling of the sacraments, by the radiance of his priestly grace, by his example, words, and life.

On Thursdays at Lauds we recite this passage from the Prophet Jeremias: "I will fill the souls of priests with fatness, and my people shall be filled with good things, saith the Lord." (Jer. 31:14) The two parts of this statement are related. It is in the measure that priests' souls are filled with the Lord that their people will obtain all the good things they need. Independently of the visible radiance of the sanctity of the priest which is a surprise and a mystery, there is all that action from within which, invisibly, spreads out in mysterious waves to purify, calm and sanctify humanity.

Who can gauge the range of a priest's prayer and its weight in the hour of last decisions. There can be a source of hidden strength when everything seems to have failed. Enquiries in various dioceses have shown that many are estranged from the Church because of social pressure, the force of which has been unsuspected until now. As a result their freedom is not complete. But it is precisely one of the aspects of the priest's mission to help them invisibly by his prayer and sacrifice.

That does not, however, relieve him of the obligation to help them by his action as teacher. The priest is by profession a spiritual teacher, guiding consciences, forming characters, inspiring prayer, directing and co-ordinating the apostolate. All that we have – doctrine, sacraments, graces, liturgy – is destined to be received, to be shared, to be vitalized in human lives, to germinate there, to flower, and to bear fruit. But since all these things often do not penetrate because souls have been rendered impervious by egotism, pride, luxury, and have been blocked by prejudice, misunderstandings, and by what are often the most improbable errors, it is the role of the priest as teacher to find cracks, points of insertion, *"points through which grace can filter"*.

It is not a question of reducing the essentials of Christianity or of modifying the substance of doctrine, but of awakening the appetite for God and the things of God, and of gradually educating those who ought to receive him to be capable of assimilating him. In other words, is not the mission of the priest to form saints, to cause Jesus Christ to be born and to grow a little more in the souls, and to share the fatherhood of God? Can he not say, "These are my children to whom I have given birth"?

Cardinal Suhard said "that which gives peerless dignity to the priest is that all the sacerdotal power of Christ is at his service. In calling us to the priesthood the Saviour did not hesitate to entrust to us powers beyond all that the human imagination can conceive. Our privileges include power over the devil and the infernal powers, power over the eucharistic host, and power over the Mystical Body."

"He gave them power to cast out devils." (Mark 3:15) Saint Luke says the same thing: "He gave them power and authority over all devils." (Luke 9:1). In fact, after their apostolic journeys the disciples, returning to Jesus, described all their adventures and related having seen Satan cast out. "And the seventy-two returned with joy, saying: Lord, the devils also are subject to us in they name." (Luke 10:17).

It is not without reason that among the minor orders we have received is the order of exorcist, with the duty and power to cast out devils. There is in us, by the very fact of our priesthood, a power to restrain the activity of the devil. Doubtless, we must not see the working of the devil everywhere and in everything. Human nature has been wounded by original sin, and man possesses the dangerous power to say "no" to God. But the more man resists God, the more he offers a field of action to the devil who has no pity, who inspires error, deceit, and division. He is the enemy who sows discord everywhere.

Without necessarily giving regional specification to the activities of the devil, as missionaries, who are by no means naïve men, sometimes do, we know that the power of the devil increases as men voluntarily give themselves up to evil.

There are many historical examples of people offering themselves to Satan, Satan has skilful helpers everywhere, under one form or another, and without falling into a kind of psychosis which would not be without danger, we can say truly that there are, here or there, poisoned realms.

Revelation and the liturgy allow of no doubt that the devil "roams the world seeking the ruin of souls". He is crafty, he knows how to assume the most diverse forms, forms most suitable to his foul purposes. Those that he assumes, in our age of reason and of discoveries, are subtle, and as Beaudelaire said: "his smartest trick is to persuade us that he does not exist."

The victory of Christ is not only over sin, but over Satan. In Jesus we also can say: "Get behind me, Satan." We are more formidable to Satan than we realize. Every evening at Compline we read the warning given by Saint Peter. "Be sober and watch: because your adversary the devil, as a roaring lion, goeth about seeking whom he may devour. Whom resist ye, strong in faith." (1 Peter 5:8, 9)

Let us have faith in the efficacy of our power against him. To be sure, we may not use the solemn exorcisms against the possessed without the bishop's authority, but it is not for nothing that the Church uses at Mass, in the breviary, in its ritual, formulae against the evil activity of the devil. This power is the more effective if the priest does not give Satan any opportunities, and is faithful to his duty of watchfulness and of sacrifice. There are some demons who depart only after fasting and prayer. "When the devil ceases to deceive children and to draw them into hell, then shall I cease to sacrifice myself for them", said Don Bosco. Wherever a priest carries out his mission holily, the kingdom of Satan recedes.

We should often meditate on our powers over the eucharist, for we exercise them every morning. But it is salutary for us to deepen its riches. There is still a mystery which will always escape us. At least, under the eyes of Christ the Sovereign Priest who makes himself our victim, let us try to get some glimpses of it.

Yet it is an extraordinary power which enables us to change bread into the body of Christ and wine into his blood. Think of it, there is in us a "power" which comes from God, which likens us to the Father and permits us to say to Christ "Thou art my Beloved Son; this day I have begotten thee." Thanks to this power, we are strong with the very strength of God, and as van der Mersch put it, "he is no less in our poor sinful hands when the words have been spoken over the bread and wine, than he was in his own hands the night he instituted the holy eucharist. Unprecedented dignity of the Christian priest who has Jesus Christ and gives him. Yet more, it is Jesus Christ who gives himself as never ceasing gift."

Thanks to this power, we offer him validly, as the perfect victim, pure and without stain, to the glory of the Father, and for the effective gain of all humanity. Thanks to this power, we give him as nourishment to all those who hunger, that they may become, in Saint Augustine's words "him whom they receive".

71

Our power over the Mystical Body of Christ has many facets. Firstly, the power to communicate Light, secondly, the power to communicate grace, and lastly, the power to guide the people of God.

We are not the light, but we bear witness to the Light, and we communicate it. We possess a special grace when we speak in the name of the Father, the Son, and the Holy Spirit. We possess this grace also to render luminous the testimony of our life which can only be explained in the context of God. Our preaching should be the fruit of contemplation. Everything is linked. "Share with others the things learned in meditation." We are the professional trustees of the word of God, but trustees who will emphasize the value of this sacred trust. Péguy said: "God has not given us dead words to guard, but he gives us living words to nourish."

It is not a question of involving souls in the complication of unimportant things. We must go straight to the essential, that is, to the Gospel. "Woe is me if I do not preach the Gospel", said St. Paul. Unhappy the priest who, by his life and by his word does not announce the good tidings, especially to the poor. "The poor shall have the Gospel preached to them."

The priest can say of himself what Jesus said. "I have come that they may have life and have it more abundantly." He is neither the equal nor the delegate of Christians. He is their father, because he begets them to divine life by faith and by baptism, of which he is the ordinary minister. He gives them birth, and he nourishes his sons until they die. As Saint John Chrysostom said: "To the priest has been entrusted the spiritual childhood of souls."

The Tridentine expression, "The power to rule the people of God", can be understood in many ways, and it can be the cause of errors and excesses. It corresponds, however, to a reality which is nothing more than a higher service, whose greatness does not consist so much in honours as in the burden, often exhausting, which it assumes. "It is fitting that the priest should be in command." It is not only a question of presiding at prayer or at liturgical gatherings; it is also a question of guiding the faithful, in the spirit of the Good Shepherd, of defending the people against the attacks of the enemy, of going out to seek the lost sheep. Authority is regarded by the true priest as an opportunity of showing the ultimate proof of love with the complete gift of his life. As Saint Paul said, "I most gladly will spend and be spent myself for your souls." (2 Cor. 12:15)

As Pope Pius XII told the Congress of Lay Apostles in 1951, Catholic Action, far from taking away the priest's responsibilities, has only emphasized their urgency. The good government of the people of God imposes on their leader the duty of rousing, educating and supporting militant laymen capable of collaborating with the hierarchy and of co-ordinating their efforts, without any sectarianism, with all those who are working in the service of the Church; and on the other hand, the duty of spiritually animating all those who are called to bear the Christian message through what are often the pagan districts of the modern world. This is what Cardinal Suhard wanted to bring out in the two sentences which sum up the greatness of our vocation: "In order that the spread of the Church may be accomplished without clumsiness, according to the mind of God, a divine artisan is needed, and that is the priest." "A city without a priest is a dead city, an unintelligible and incomplete civilization."

In conclusion let us remember that God has entrusted himself to us, and he has entrusted what he held most dear. It is a question of not disappointing the Lord, of not disappointing the souls who await him through us. There is only one way of replying to so much love and confidence. It is to give ourselves entirely to all that God asks of us, without ever losing heart. It is hard sometimes, it is true. The burden is heavy, the cross weighs us down. But let us not forget that he carries it in us. "The Lord ruleth me, and I shall want nothing." (Ps. 22:1) Let us strive then "to walk worthy of the vocation in which we are called". (Eph. 4:1)

Christ speaks to his Priest

Come to me more often. Outside me all that you can desire or seek is only vanity or nothingness. I alone should count for you. All the rest will be given to you in addition, as you come to need it for your mission. Only close to me will you discover the splendour of your priesthood.

There are some secrets that you can understand only when united with me. You will not be able to translate them into human language, but they will give you a longing for what I wish you to be, to realize fully the vocation to which I have summoned you. Concentrate on what concerns me, then I shall be able to help you more in the solving of your own problems and of those of your ministry.

What concerns me is this above all: to be able to make use of souls who are consecrated to me in order to purify, to cleanse, to sanctify all humanity from within. All else will follow: all else, that is to say the peace of the world, the turning to good account modern scientific discoveries, and above all, the union of hearts and minds. Those who are consecrated to me have great responsibilities. I have a right to count on them. Their eternal glory will be dazzling, but they must help me on earth by struggling, by working, by suffering with me. If, consciously or unconsciously, they refuse me their co-operation, their brothers will be the victims.

There are several categories of consecrated souls: all baptized souls are consecrated, but among them many have never been aware of it! If all baptized persons lived up to their title of "sons of God", how changed the world would be. Above all, I count on my priests to make baptized persons aware of their mission in this world. From them I expect a faithful adherence to my life, to my spirit, to my love, in a word, to my whole self, so that through them I may give myself without reserve.

Priests are my special friends. If they are obedient to interior prompting, uniting their will with mine that I may insert my life into their life, if they have no other ambition than to carry out my desires, then I can act in them, and by them, then I can give light, inspire ideas, develop courage, help them to achieve progress and reforms which seemed unthinkable. With me nothing is impossible, provided only that I find a sufficient number of priestly souls living loyally according as their state requires.

There is not a priest who will not one day give himself wholly to me. They must take this gift seriously: it is the pre-requisite for my passage through them for the service of all humanity.

The more intimately you live with me, the more I shall be able to guide you. Make time for silence and prayer. You will never regret doing so. You will see how, when the time comes for action, I shall inspire you, and render your work, your fatigue, and all your activities fruitful.

It is true, Lord, that you never forsake anyone who entrusts himself to you. But there are times when you seem so far away! There are hours when, rather like Peter, I feel I am letting down my nets without taking anything. Doubt almost overwhelms me. I am so often disappointed.

Do not be surprised that you have disappointments; that is part of the great mystery of redemption. By offering your heart-aches, which, I know from my own experience, are so distressing, you learn to understand my sufferings better, you make reparation you make up for them, you earn grace by your fidelity, grace for yourselves and for others. Sometimes men may disappoint you. I will never disappoint you. I give infinitely more than you expect; not always in the way you expect, but in a much better way. Besides, it is not necessary to be understood in order to do good. Do you think that I was always understood?

There are so many, even among priests, who are afraid of me, afraid of my intimacy, afraid, perhaps, of the effort I may ask of them. And yet, if they but knew of all that I dream of doing for them, with them, and through them! There are so many souls on whom I ought to be able to reply who let themselves become involved in trifles. They have not understood, these "chosen ones", the urgency of my appeal. Certainly, I leave them free, as I left the rich young man free, not to follow. But how sad it is for me.

Weakness, error, a momentary forgetfulness are not significant and do not compromise the work of love, provided that you correct them by a fresh effort as soon as you notice them. What does retard the work of my love is the refusal of pride or of cowardice. It is the fear of silence, the lack of attention to what I ask, to what I inspire; it is the habit of living in and for the material world; it is the gradual reduction of the spirit of faith, the blindness of mind, the hardness of heart.

You should know that I am waiting for you, not to reproach you, but to give you my gifts, to inspire you, to inflame you.

75

I want to grow in my priests. The day that men see in them only me, the day I am able to act freely in them to the extent that the weakness of human nature permits, the peace of the world will be assured, whole groups of humanity will know the light, an era of prosperity will open up for the earth, the proportion of saints will increase in every region across the earth.

Examination of Conscience

1. Have I a clear enough knowledge of the nobility of my priesthood?

2. Am I happy and proud to be a priest, happy without selfishness, proud without arrogance?

3. Do I often thank God for having called me, in preference to so many others whose talents were so superior to mine?

4. Does the thought that I am "above all, a priest", regulate my life and give it a special stamp?

5. Do I try always to think and to act in a priestly way, even when I am not officiating as a priest?

6. Am I truly a man of God, a man among men, a man of the Church?

7. Do I understand that I ought to reveal to men the true image of Christ, and also the true image of the Church?

8. Am I on my guard against certain professional weaknesses, which in a priest may be described as clericalism, dictatorship, bureaucracy?

9. Am I really concerned about the salvation of my brothers?

10. Do I keep my ears open for requests from my fellow men for a little more light, a little more justice, a little more real charity?

11. Have I trained myself to discover automatically when each individual is ripe to receive grace?

12. Is my priesthood concentrated on the work of redemption so that I accept with the full force of my faith that my actions are made fruitful by my sufferings united to those of Jesus dwelling in me?

13. Do I understand that a priest's supernatural virtues should be supported by the true natural virtues, practised super-

naturally: loyalty, courage, order, accuracy, tact, breadth of view, a keen sense of justice?

Resolutions

1. To ask our Lord frequently that I may be more and more the kind of priest he wants me to be.

2. To act as a priest in all circumstances, even when I am not performing my priestly functions as such.

3. To live the priestly life as fully as possible. "It is the function of the priest to offer." In the life of the priest everything is material for a fruitful offering.

4. Never to attribute to my own merits the good that the Lord permits me to do. To fear as one of the most certain causes of a priest's sterility self-complacency and anxiety for the satisfaction of self-love, whatever form it takes.

5. To have a great respect for the priestly character of my fellow-priests. Men will respect it in me as I respect it in others.

6. To become more and more a man of sacrifice and a man of prayer. I am a priest for my brothers, but I am a priest of God.

7. In all my dealings to try to live according to the standards set by Saint Paul, who said: "For me to live is Christ", and "Christ truly lives in me".

Spiritual Reading

Keep me, O Lord, from the grave sin which I fear so much; from despising thy love. That I may never sin against the Holy Spirit, who is love and unity and peace and concord; that I may never separate myself from the unity of thy Spirit, from the unity of thy peace, while committing the sin which will never be forgiven, neither in this world nor in the next. Keep me, O Lord, among my brothers, help me that I may announce the peace which comes from thee. Keep me among those who keep the unity of the spirit in the bond of peace.

My beloved brothers, let us watch over with care all that relates to the profession of our common life, keeping the unity of the Spirit in the bond of peace, by the grace of our Lord Jesus Christ and the charity of God and the communication of the Holy Spirit. From the charity of God proceeds the unity of the spirit; from the grace of our Lord Jesus Christ, the bond of peace; from the communication of the Holy Spirit, the communion which is necessary for those who live in common so that their life may truly be in common.

That unity, which the charity of God creates in us, is preserved in the bond of peace by the grace of our Lord Jesus Christ. He is our peace, he, at whose birth the angels sang: "Glory to God in the highest, and on earth peace to men of good will", he who, at the moment of his ascension, said to his disciples: "My peace I leave you, my peace I give unto you."

What is this peace given to us by Christ, the bond of which preserves the unity of the spirit? It is mutual charity, by which we love one another, and which is never broken, speak with the same voice and there are no schisms among us. Saint Peter warned us: "Above all, have this mutual charity." What is it, if not at one and the same time yours and mine so that I speak of it to him whom I love?

Such, then, is the law of this common life; the unity of the spirit in the charity of God, the bond of peace in a mutual and continual charity of all brothers, the sharing of all goods, every phase of ownership being far from the plane of holy religion. That these dispositions may be and remain in us, that we may have one heart and one soul and all things in common, "may the grace of Our Lord Jesus Christ and the charity of God and the communication of the Holy Spirit be with you all". Amen.

Balderin of Canterbury

Subjects for Discussion

1. Are priestly humility and the knowledge of our greatness compatible? On what conditions?

2. What are the principal professional aberrations to which a priest is liable? How can we preserve ourselves from them?

Prayer

O Heavenly Father, you who have chosen me from all eternity, without any merit on my part, to be your priest in Jesus, make me understand better the glories and the responsibilities of my priesthood. Have pity on my weakness and on my frailty. Grant that I may never disappoint you. Grant that my life may be such as you desire it to be, for the glory of your name and for the good of the Church. May no one of those whom you have given into my charge be absent from the eternal assembly; this I ask of you humbly through the same Jesus Christ our Lord, who lives and reigns with you in the unity of the Holy Spirit for ever and ever. Amen.

Thought

The priest is a man called by God to share in the priesthood of Jesus Christ to prolong the redemptive mission of Jesus Christ, by doing what Jesus Christ did, in the way in which he did it.

Saint Vincent de Paul

5

HE WHO ABIDES IN ME

He who abides in me and I in him, he bears much fruit."
(John 15:5) This saying of our Lord is a frequent theme of
meditations for priests, yet we need to return to it often, for it
is the natural propensity of flowing water that it loses contact
with its source.

Theoretically we are all persuaded of the necessity of the
interior life, but it is well from time to time to strengthen our
convictions. After all, men today make more and more demands
on the priest from this point of view. What they want to discover in us is evidence of Christ's indwelling.

Concluding his remarkable book, *Essor ou Declin du Clergé
Français,* Canon Boulard wrote: "The sacramental ministry of
the priest, though it remains essential, is no longer sufficient. Or
rather, if it is still the last step by which a priest gives a soul to
Christ, this ministry can no longer be the only one, or even
normally the first. It seems now that it is no longer possible to
make converts simply by having a well-organized parish, by
running a well-directed confraternity or sodality. The priest
must exercise the personal influence of a religious man, the
authority of a spiritual man. Like the light of the Gospel, he
must be able to shine into all the corners of human life. He must
be able to establish a spiritual contact between souls and Christ,
who alone has power to transform them." Let us recall the
blunt but profound observation of a student: "A priest must be
seen to be a man who lives for God, or he is a humbug."

In his book, *L'Esprit Missionaire,* the Abbé Michonneau
appeals to our personal experience. "Whether we are young or

old, let us compare the manner in which we visit the sick, give direction in the confessional, give spiritual guidance, even the way we treat visitors, after having made a retreat, with the same manner we display at other times. Let us profit by this recollection to deepen our idea of the interior life, to revive our reasons for developing it, and to verify the means we can take to make it grow in us.

Meditation

What is the interior life? Or rather, let us begin by asking what it is not! It is not the constant and explicit thought of God, nor an emotional craving for divine consolation, or a form of escape from the duties of our life.

It is not the constant and explicit thought of God. We must realize that always to be thinking of God in an explicit way is beyond normal human powers. We must have the humility to recognize our limitations. It is not a question of serving God as we might dream of serving him, but as he wishes us to serve him. Indeed, there can be times when, by a special grace from our Lord, the soul experiences moments of intense recollection and feels itself infused by God and thinks of him without effort. But, except when this particular help is available, the constant thought of God is beyond our human powers. We must be realistic about our potentialities.

What counts in the eyes of God is not the gift of our mind, but that of our heart. What counts is not so much the intellectual action of a conscious thought, as the conformity of our will with his. Certainly there are some material occupations which leave the mind free to think of God. No doubt that is why the founders of religious orders have given their religious a certain number of manual tasks to perform during the day. Manual work done calmly, not only does not prevent, but facilitates thought, and for a fervent soul, the orientation of its thought towards God. But there are also a number of occupation which require sustained attention and even definite mental concentration. Grace transcends nature, but it does not dispense with it. Trying to force nature at all costs is likely to end in madness. While we are on earth, our soul is conditioned by our body. God does not demand a purely spiritual life from us; continual tension can lead to a breakdown.

Let us remember the story told of Saint John, who did not hesitate from time to time to enjoy a few moments of relaxation. When his disciples were astonished at this, the apostle told them of the bow which, when constantly strung, loses the power to despatch its arrow. The interior life cannot then be defined as "a constant and explicit thought of God".

That does not mean that we should not try, from time to time, to think only of God, but we have duties which prevent us from doing so continually. We must therefore accept, with confidence and simplicity, our human frailty which prevents us from thinking exclusively of Christ.

The interior life is not an emotional craving for divine consolation. The word "consolation" has come to be devalued, due to a certain more or less romantic language in manuals of piety during the last century. Yet it is none the less true that our Lord, from time to time, draws a soul more intimately to him. There are few priests, however, ungenerous they may be, who have not encountered this. The result is the appearance of those phenomena, sometimes independent of the will of the priest, which consist, either in an ascendence of God who absorbs attention, or in a sort of very sweet and very pleasant feeling of his Presence.

Think of certain pages of the *Imitation of Christ* or certain verses of the hymn for the feast of the Holy Name of Jesus, *Jesus Dulcis Memoria*.

There are, however, other times when the soul is no less generously disposed, yet when God seems distant and a stranger. The soul finds it difficult even to think of God. A real effort is needed for it. And yet, if it examines itself loyally, it can say in all sincerity that it is working truly for God. The interior life does not endure only during that time when one feels oneself penetrated by God. We certainly should not distrust the touches of grace. We must accept them as a merciful help from our Master. They can help us at certain moments to orientate our life more towards him, and the remembrance of them can strengthen us in hours of trial. But we must realize that the interior life can be perfectly authentic without our feeling these graces.

Thirdly, the interior life is not a form of escape from the duties of our life. For some souls who are badly instructed in what God expects of them the interior life has become a kind of alibi. They would willingly dispense themselves from carrying out the duty of their state, and even from the great duty of fraternal charity, so as not to disturb their meditation. We certainly must not make devotion to our duties an excuse for abandoning our meditations on our Lord or failing to keep part of the day reserved for deep prayer. Since we are so inclined to seek ourselves instinctively in our activities, we must if we want to be sure of working truly for God and according to his Spirit, ensure that we keep in contact with him and direct our thoughts and our efforts towards him.

Work done for God is prayer, but only if the prayer runs through the work, at least implicitly. But if, after a time, we do not devote a minute to correcting our basic motives, and retrieving the mentality of a member of the Mystical Body, the work becomes pure routine or sterile ferment. But the interior life does not consist in thinking of God until we forget the world. On the contrary, it makes us draw from the love of God the strength to devote ourselves and sacrifice ourselves for the good of others, if this is necessary.

Saint Vincent de Paul did not hesitate to say to his Daughters of Charity: "Even in the midst of prayer, if some one comes to disturb you and asks you to go to care for a sick man, you are but leaving God to find him again."

It is always difficult to put supernatural truths into a formula, since it is axiomatic that human words never express an essentially living reality which transcends them on all counts. There is even the risk that they will cloud and distort it, and it is only by a series of approximations that we succeed in giving an inkling of the splendours of divine grace. Nevertheless, to prepare the way for our meditation, it seems that we can define the interior life as "a life of friendship with God who lives in us by grace, a life of friendship which leads us to delight in conforming our will to his in every circumstance".

It is a life. That is to say, it is a force which must be active. It is not something static, coagulated, artificial, set. The activity of the interior life does not manifest itself in a transitory way, but can influence the whole of our existence. It is a life of friendship, a life of loving, cordial, trusting relationship, in which the heart has as large a share as the mind. This relationship runs the whole gamut of expression from the cordiality of neighbourliness, to the most profound and most intimate fusion which can be imagined. It will be expressed by exchanges of words, by exchanges of gifts. It will be expressed, as the soul advances in the interior life, by a deeper and deeper union, in which emphasis on the conscience alternates with times when the union is underlined by the mutual will to live for each other.

It is a life of friendship with God! That is an overwhelming truth. God not only wishes to make man his creature and his servant, but also his friend, his son, his partner, and with special emphasis, his priest. There is an infinite distance between the Creator and the creature, all the distance which separates being from nothingness. Our Lord could say with all truth to Saint Catherine of Sienna, "I am he who is. You are she who is not." This infinite distance, the no less infinite love of God has annihilated. With that humility which confounded Bergson, God stooped down to his creature, raised him to himself, made him a sharer of his life, and, to the extent that the creature accepts it, is always ready to let him share of all his riches.

As God only appreciates a love that is voluntary and free, he has granted man the dangerous power of resisting his advances. Infinitely respectful of human dignity, he plays the game to the limit, and observes "fair play" to the point of running the risk of losing for eternity the being whom he has created with love and for love. He neglects nothing to draw all men to himself, and he goes to the limit in the game of human liberty. To show us how far this love will go he has done what all true lovers do – what Saint Paul described as "acts of folly". He has loved us unto the folly of the crib, even to the folly of the cross, even to the folly of the eucharist. And not only everyone in general, but each one of us individually. And he has made himself one of us in order to make each of us a part of him.

By the grace of baptism, he has linked us with himself, and has infused himself into us, as the live seed which asks only to be developed and grow, like sap which asks only to penetrate all the fibres of the tree, and to be transformed into buds which burst forth, into flowers which blossom, into leaves which spread out on branches and into fruits which grow ripe. As long as there is no rupture, by formal disobedience to his law of love, God dwells in us, God lives in us, God gives us life.

God dwells in us. "If anyone love me, he will keep my word. And my Father will love him: and we will come to him and will make our abode with him." (John 14:23) Let us never forget that God is one in three Persons, God is a community, God is a family: Father, Son, and Holy Spirit.

God's dream is that we should consciously and willingly become members of this family. In every soul in the state of grace God ever begets his Word and the Word praises the Father; and from the mutual love of the Father and of the Son there proceeds the Holy Spirit. Thus do we understand the words of Saint Paul: "Glorify and bear God in your body." (1 Cor. 6:20)

God lives in us. "I am the vine: you are the branches. He that abideth in me and I in him, the same bears much fruit." (John 15:5) He is not in us as a precious but lifeless object, or as a distant, unknown being. He is in us as a living being, whose presence is always real, and whose activity reflects our attention to him and our willingness to work with him and for him. His is a presence more intimate to us than we are to ourselves. He is interested in everything that takes place within us, and by mysterious communion, he experiences all that we feel.

Nothing of our most intimate desires escapes him. He sees us from within. From within he evaluates us. From within he wants to give us life.

Father Marmion wrote: "The desire of God in giving himself to the soul is to produce in it something analogous to what

85

happened in the Word made flesh. There was in him a very intense human activity; but the Word to whom humanity was indissolubly united, was the rich source from which this activity was supplied and from which it radiated. Without establishing a union as close as that of the Word with his Sacred Humanity, Christ in giving himself to the soul wishes to be, through his grace and the action of his Spirit, the principle of the whole of its interior activity.

"Et ego in eo : 'And I in him.' He is in the soul, he dwells in it, but he is not inactive: he wants to work in it, and when the soul stays committed to him and to his wishes, then the action of Christ becomes so powerful that this soul will be infallibly carried on to the highest perfection, according to the plans God has for it.

"For Christ comes into the soul with his divinity, his merit, his riches, to be its light, its way, its truth, its holiness: *qui factus est nobis sapientia a Deo et justitia et sanctificatio et redemptio ;* 'who became for us justice and holiness and redemption', in a word, to be the life of the soul, to live himself in the soul."

God gives us life. We are the "members of God", and God gives us life by his grace as the trunk of a tree gives its branches life by its sap. The true Christian has been defined by Saint Paul in these words which are a way of life in themselves: "I live, not I, but Christ liveth in me." (Gal. 2:20) The ardent desire of God is to be able to make use of us, to fill our mind with his thoughts, our hearts with his feelings, our will with his energy, so that in every circumstance we may act as he would act in our place, that we may fulfil, under his influence, the mission which each of us has received in the synthesis of his plan of love for the world.

But, and it is a moving example of the delicacy of divine love for us, our Lord gives us life only if we desire it. "Behold, I stand at the door and knock. If any man shall hear my voice and open to me the door, I will come in to him, and will sup with him: and he with me." (Apoc. 3:20) To penetrate deeper into us, to associate himself more closely with our activities and make them fruitful, he awaits our invitation, one gesture of love from us, even the blink of an eye. This collaboration is most important. Without him we can do nothing to transfigure our life. But he wishes to do nothing without us.

This life of friendship leads us to delight in conforming our will to his in every circumstance. The value of our actions in the sight of God depends not on the fact that they are extraordinary or difficult, but on the intensity of love with which we accomplish them.

This love is a love which makes us alert, not only never "to cause him sorrow" as children say, but to long to give him pleasure in all we do and to adopt the same feelings which animate the heart of Jesus. "Behold, I come to do thy Will, O God" (Heb. 10:9) "I do always the things that please him." (John 8:29) "My meat is to do the will of him that sent me." (John 4:34) "Not as I will, but as thou wilt." (Matt. 26:39) Moreover, he has warned us that "Not everyone that saith to me, Lord, Lord, shall enter into the kingdom of heaven but he that doeth the will of my Father". (Matt. 7:21) The best way of always doing his will is to succeed, through our love, in making ourselves one with him.

This interior life, this life of friendship with a God who is pure spirit demands from us a true and loyal effort, the more so as so many obstacles, interior and exterior, often oppose its development.

It will therefore help us towards more intimate and more intense relations with our Lord if we get a clear understanding of the reasons which should urge us on to this. These reasons are threefold. Firstly, the cultivation of the interior life is the very logic of our faith. Secondly it is one of the very best means of assisting the working of grace in us. And thirdly, it is the basis of happiness and fruitfulness.

The cultivation of the interior life is the very logic of our faith. "Life with the divine host in our heart is the moral state which all baptized persons should strive after", said Monsignor de Ségue. Since God dwells in us by his grace and wishes to link us to himself, it would be absurd not to pay attention to his Presence and to his action. Our Lord is certainly extremely sensitive and infinitely discreet, but that is only one more reason to make us recall, at least from time to time, the reality of his presence, and to put ourselves under his influence. It is a serious thing to forget Jesus, not to treat him as God, that is to say as the master of life, as the centre of the world, as the source from which sanctity flows unceasingly.

It is a serious thing to forget him who has loved us unto death, to forget him who has given us everything and who asks in return only that we give ourselves to him. It is a serious thing to forget him who thinks of us unceasingly and who can act in us only in so far as we give him freedom of action. It is all the more serious at a time when many men do not know him. Among those who know him many act as if he did not exist. Only God can effect the spiritual revolution of the world. He wishes to do nothing without us, and we can do nothing without him.

It is one of the best ways of assisting the working of grace in us. As we develop our interior life our hold on the divine life increases. The more our will clings to the divine will, the more he can make use of us as he wishes to inspire our thoughts and actions. The more we try to live intimately with him, the more his influence enables us to avoid mistakes, to recover from any lapses, and to purify our intentions. The more we act as a member of Christ, the less are we tempted to withdraw into ourselves. The more we cling to him with all our strength of will, the more abundantly can grace enter our soul. Contact between God and the soul only increases the flow of divine life and that is what is supremely important.

The difference between men in the eyes of God is not their race, rank, fortune, or knowledge. It is on the basis of our interior life that God considers and judges us. What makes the difference in the value of men in his eyes is the difference in the degree of divine life in them. Our glory in heaven will depend precisely on grace at the hour of our death. Here below the more we share in the life of God which is in us, the more we share in his power. That is why the interior life is the basis of our happiness and of fruitfulness! When we have a true interior life, our life is transfigured.

What consolation this clear knowledge of the presence of God brings to our souls! What strength, what an incentive is the conviction that he knows us from within, that he feels in his heart what we experience, that he asks only to inspire our thoughts and to guide our activities! Under his influence nothing that one does is vulgar or commonplace. Everything is grace, everything can be of service. When we try to live in Jesus Christ, as Saint Paul recommended to the Christians, meals, rest, leisure, as well as work and suffering, everything can be of service, everything can be for the glory of God.

When we try to live united to Christ, the most disturbed life finds unity and peace, however varied our tasks may be. As all is done for our Lord, by him, with him, and in him, everything leads to unity, and whatever complications beset us, everything is wonderfully simplified. A well-developed interior life wards off every crisis of discouragement and does not allow depressing feelings of loneliness to attack us. What strength we derive from being able to say at a difficult time: "God is within me, and he never forsakes me."

There are occasions in our lives when, as a result of some chain of circumstances independent of our will, our intentions are distorted and we become victims of unhappy misunderstandings. One of our greatest sources of comfort is to think that God who sees within us knows the exact truth and will help us, if he thinks good. The Psalms are filled with these trusting appeals to him who knows our hearts. Above all, intimacy with Christ becomes a source of fruitfulness for our life. "He who abides in me and I in him, he bears much fruit", said Jesus. "He who does not sow with me, scatters. He who works with me, gathers."

The words of the Psalmist are always true: "If the Lord build not, they labor in vain who build." He who is not united with the Lord when he builds, erects his house on sand, and is at the mercy of the first storm. Our least actions, our least words, since it is God who acts through us and who speaks through us, have an unsuspected power on the interior plane of the communion of saints, for we never know all the good that we do, since it is God who accomplishes this good through us.

Sometimes that is confirmed in a visible way. "An apostle is a chalice which is filled with Jesus and flows over", said Father Mattheo. "Men should discern within me the host my soul adores. Everything in me should speak of Jesus", wrote Elisabeth Leseur.

There is in fact a real irradiation which emanates, at least at certain moments, from a soul which lives intimately with God. The ideal of the apostle is to make the interior presence of Christ our Saviour so evident that all those who approach him experience unconsciously his irresistible attraction. Mother Marie de Sainte Cécile of Rome, in her autobiography lets our Lord say this: "My priests rule all religious society. If they were all truly saints, the very sight of them, whether in church, in the streets, or anywhere, would evoke a thought of me; they would draw souls to me; when men met them they would think, that is another Christ passing by. The devil fears one soul in whom I act freely much more than an army of tepid or indifferent souls in whom my action is paralyzed; because in the former I act with all my power, while I am forced to leave the latter to their weakness."

"The apostolate", said Father Pierre Arnaud, "means allowing Jesus to grow. In the Mystical Body, which is the whole Christ, I am a vessel through which the blood of Jesus should pass and be spread abroad to give life. The saint has the dimensions of a great artery, and I must aim at that. The mediocre priest reduces himself to the dimensions of a capillary and the place he holds in the Mystical Body is sad and disastrous! To be an apostle is to be a channel for Jesus, the only Holy One, the only Saviour."

How shall we develop our interior life? It is not something man invented. It is a filial and persevering surrender to the interior grace which works in us unceasingly and which calls us constantly to turn towards God. Its essential elements are in overcoming every obstacle which can prevent or handicap the interior life making a positive reply to its appeal. The principal obstacles which obstruct the acquisition and development of the interior life can be grouped under three headings. First, superficiality and a natural tendency to dissipation; secondly, concentration on ourselves; and thirdly, lack of faith and love.

We live in the century of speed and of noise. Modern life makes us superficial. We must make a real effort to concentrate our spirit and to recollect ourselves. If we are not careful, we find ourselves caught up in a hectic whirl which exhausts us and

90

leaves us empty. We eventually lose the faculty of deep thinking. We are at the mercy of our impressions, imagination, and whims. We eventually forget the essential, which is God himself.

To counteract this dissipation and superficiality, we must organize our activities and not let them get the upper hand. It is especially necessary to plan periods of silence; meditative reading, prolonged prayer, contemplation. We certainly cannot expect every one to adopt the same form of contemplation, nor give the same amount of time to it. It is certain, nevertheless, that if we are not willing to take energetic means to reserve enough time to allow our soul to expand and to recover itself before God, we run the risk of finding that our spiritual life is anaemic and flabby.

Today, priests and religious, no less than the simple faithful who wish to live loyally and logically in the faith, are encouraged to reserve occasional periods for meditation, spiritual reading, prolonged prayer, silent recollection, and even retreats.

In his *L'Esprit Missionaire,* Father Michonneau insists on this, bearing in mind the conditions of the modern apostolate which, he says, requires a more rigid control of our interior disposition. "At the age of fifty, we are no more firmly established in complete union than we were at twenty-five and so distrust of ourselves, self-control, and the employment of sound methods are necessary. We must take special care not to pay compliments to ourselves, and not to claim as 'contacts what are only idle conversations', not to talk about giving advice to families, when we are gratified at being invited to a meal at certain houses, or to spend a pleasant evening in a home.

"We are right to want an apostolate of increasing spirituality, and to reject tasks which are irrelevant to the priestly ministry. But then, what spiritual depth we must have. Otherwise we will accomplish nothing at all, neither the material tasks we rejected, nor the spiritual work for which we kept our hands free.

"To sum up, we think that a priest cannot keep his spiritual character if he does not keep up his life of prayer – a point we shall return to – spiritual reading, contact with Scripture, and in the afternoon a fervent visit to the Blessed Sacrament. The celebration of his Mass will have all its intensity only when it has been stimulated by careful preparation, and we fear that even his Office will become a painful routine if the priest does not frequently take up some of its texts to meditate upon them."

Another obstacle to the interior life is our egocentricity, that is to say, the very natural tendency to make ourselves the centre of the world. What would we say of a branch which was so proud of its foliage that it wished to live independently of the trunk, and so cut itself off from the sap? What would we say of a limb which, proud of its pliancy or of its strength, wished to be able to act independently of the body and shut itself off from the vital bloodstream?

This is a serious matter. It is real worship of self. For it is making self the centre and the source of life instead of God. All vain, egotistical, sensual self-seeking, whatever form it takes, hinders the action of grace. If it is conscious and voluntary it could even end in a mortal rupture with God. Interior life is possible only where there is a minimum of asceticism, particularly the cultivation of humility and of mortification. Pride makes the soul impermeable to divine grace. Vanity, susceptibility, a desire to predominate, to lead, all this impedes the action of God in our souls.

The "now not I" of Saint Paul, the renunciation of my pride, is the condition on which rests the vitality of Christ in our souls. It is the same for the renunciation of the sensual. From the moment when we let ourselves yield to gluttony, laziness, or an uncontrolled desire for our comfort we begin to be engulfed in a way which is a particular handicap to spiritual intimacy. It is not that one cannot find the Lord in an exultant way in joy, but this joy should be wholesome. The grain of sacrificial salt is often necessary to safeguard purity.

Basically, it is because our faith is not alert enough, and our love not ardent enough, that our hearts are burdened by self and by all that is not God. We have received the seed of faith, but the seed must be developed. Faith must be increased, for God is not seen directly by sight, hearing, and touch. The presence of God can be perceived only by faith. Not a theoretical or speculative faith, but a supernatural knowledge which is called the spirit of faith, better still the habit of reacting as the supernatural realities require which can be described as the "presence of mind" of faith.

It is the same with love. The love which God expects from our hearts is not a sentimental love. A life of friendship without love is a contradiction. There is an understanding of the divine friend which can proceed from only a loyal love. Villeneuve says: "Even if I do not keep him consciously in my thoughts, I feel that a muted and a deep consciousness of him never leaves me. It is that consciousness which often in my prayers and sometimes when I am most preoccupied, continues in an undertone like a never ending litany of 'Jesus, I love you', or simply 'Jesus!' thought, felt, spoken within, I hardly know how to explain it.

To love Jesus with an infectious love, is my life, my concern, my anguish, the inspiration of all my undertakings . . . Jesus has become the obsession of my life; that name, on which I lavish all my powers of jubilation, compassion, tenderness, admiration, gratitude, love, and devotion, passes through my mind and my heart every day more often than I can say, or rather, he dwells in me where I adore and help him."

It is not a question here of emotional love, but of true love. It is not a question of love which is put to the test, but of love which proves itself. Our Lord said: "Greater love than this no man hath, that he gives his life for his friend." Too often we think that we love him, whereas it is ourselves that we love, through him whom we think is the object of our love. Disinterested service will always be the touchstone of true love, the anxiety to give pleasure, even and indeed most when it costs us dear, the gift of ourselves as generously as possible whether it is gradually in our daily life or in an act of complete sacrifice, when God asks it.

Positive collaboration with grace will, in the first instance, show itself by perseverance in prayer to obtain the gift of the interior life; acquisition of the mentality and the general attitude of a member of Jesus Christ; and by a prudent and courageous multiplication of points of contact with our Lord.

A deeper interior life is a grace which the Master is waiting to grant to us, but he wishes us to persist in and press our demands for it since it is so very precious and is the starting point of a real spiritual expansion. Too often we complicate the Christian life. It is not by technical devices or clever tricks that we make ourselves ready for contemplation. The life of union with God is first of all and above all the effect of divine grace. The most elementary way, but also the most effective way to obtain it, is to beg for it with humility, but also with persistence.

"He who acts according to the truth comes to the light", said our Lord. The truth is that we are branches of the vine, members of a body of which Christ is the head, and that with him we form the total Christ, as Saint Augustine said. Each of us, as an individual, has a mission to carry out, and this mission will be accomplished only under the influence of his spirit.

Though we have our own specific and unique role, we are only instrumental causes; and we can accomplish our task effectively only if we are docile and faithful to the action of the divine artist. We are so tempted to think of ourselves as independent, and to act accordingly, taking the lead, and doing everything as we think appropriate!

One of the most effective secrets of the interior life is to ensure that we remain conscientious and responsible members, who realize our *raison d'être* the more we find our basis for action in the thought of Christ the sovereign priest and the strength for what we do in our union with Christ the universal mediator.

We have already noted that we cannot think and speak continually of God. We would run the risk of a breakdown. But let us profit by the chances we are given to resume contact with the divine guest of our souls, in faith and in love. Habit is often described as second nature. With the help of grace it can greatly assist the life of deep union which will blossom forth from time to time in a clear conscience, and even when we are not thinking of it, will bring to bear the divine influence which is so beneficial in all our activities. When we have acquired the habit of this interior life "everything becomes a symbol of spiritual realities, everything speaks of God.

Guy de Larigaudie said, "I am so accustomed to the presence of God within me, that I always have deep in my heart a prayer rising to my lips. This prayer, scarcely conscious, still goes on, in spite of the distractions of a train journey or the humming of a propeller. Even in excitement of body or of soul, even in the bustle of the city or in the tension of mind caused by an absorbing occupation. There in the depths of my soul, it is an infinitely calm and transparent water which neither the shadows nor the eddies of the surface can reach."

These points of contact will vary greatly with the temperaments, and in the same individual, with his interior dispositions, the nature of his occupation, and the time of the day. Father, Poppe, a saintly Belgian priest, whose cause has been introduced at Rome, recommended the regular practice of ejaculatory prayers. He said: "It is just like a match. You strike it once, it does not catch; the second time you press on it and get a spark; the third time, you press even more heavily and the flame bursts forth. So it is with ejaculatory prayers. The first time, perhaps your heart remains cold; close your eyes, repeat the invocation slowly, it is a little better, but there is no flame yet. Concentrate and repeat your prayer. The third time the flame of love will burst forth from your heart."

These points of contact can be also explicit acts of union, interior acts of oblation, pleas for forgiveness, acts of thanksgiving, intense, wordless acts of love, acts of adoration of the presence within us or in other souls. The essential thing is to keep watch over yourself in his presence with an open soul and a heart on fire, so as to be able to say in truth: "He is beloved to me and I to Him", in the service of the whole Christ.

Christ speaks to his Priest

Why be perturbed, why be troubled, why multiply your cares? I alone am necessary. Seek me. All else will be given to you as well. If you do not act with me, you dissipate your efforts without profit to anyone. Let the scum of useless worries be drained off, and then come to me. Enter deeply into the incessant current of my prayer in you, for you, and for the souls in your care. Then you will see more clearly and you will be more responsive to my direction. I shall then be able to inspire you more easily about what I wish you to think, to say, to do. You will

95

act under my influence, and then you will see how with less effort, less fatigue, less nervous irritation you will accomplish more.

You should feel me in you. Long for me. Yearn for me. Speak to me often. Be more united with me in spirit. Be united with me in those whom you approach. Be kind and gracious to all. Increase in love and I will make you grow in the other virtues. Remember, that it is better not to see than to see without love. It is better not to act than to act without love. Your interior mission is more important than your exterior mission. The real good that you do is to allow me to operate in the interior life of souls. I do not regard things or souls from outside, as is so often believed. I see from within and close at hand, in the intimacy of the heart. It is not necessary for people to know who is the source of their happiness once it reaches them.

Seek only one thing, my look of approval. Desire only one thing, to love with my heart. Yearn for one thing only, to be nothing so that I may be everything in you and that through you I may grow in every soul. A soul that is attached loyally to me has sufficient power over my heart to transform the world! There are too many souls that are superficial, victims of futility. There is not enough real silence. I call, but I am not heard. I seek to attract, but souls remain unmoved. Under these conditions, how is the world to be influenced?

People are attracted by things which are transient because they do not rely on me; they are not interested in me. They do not see me in themselves or in others. I cannot act as my heart dictates. I am passive so often, and there is so much I want to do! How sad that makes me. I want others to be more aware of my presence in you. Alas, the great majority of men are inaccessible to love. Almost exclusively it is the thought of their own interests, of their ambitions, of their personal satisfaction, in a word, of their egotism that fills their heart.

Exterior action is always limited. It is necessary. I want it, but its field is limited. Interior action has no limit; it extends to the ends of the earth, and plunges beyond reality. I want you to see me more and more as your objective and your reason for everything you do. Do not leave me willingly; cease thinking

96

of me as seldom as possible. Let me always be your guide. In me you will find the solution of your problems and the cure for your deficiencies. If people only knew what power souls possess to obtain from my heart the decisive graces needed to bring about the invisible and spiritual revolution of the world. It would be so simple! But men complicate everything. Since it is I who make action fruitful they only need to desire to work loyally with me, and I would inspire each of them to do what I expect from him, I would guide him secretly, but without his ever feeling any hesitation. It is my work of love which makes headway. Yes, apostolic action is too complicated. The essential is lost sight of. People exhaust themselves in fruitless discussions. They lose precious time, as all work, all activity, all effort which is not influenced by me is doomed to fruitlessness.

There are too many troubled souls. They think they are serving me by wasting their energy in useless effort. I do not overlook their good will. Originally at any rate there is a praiseworthy desire to do what is good, there is a zealous will which is sincere. How many useless steps, useless words, useless efforts, ill-regulated lives, exhausting strains, all sheer loss, a quest for incidentals, forgetting the essential thing: myself. They do not want to take time to pause before building, they do not want to make the humble effort of considering what I think of the work done and of that which they plan to do.

Do you imagine, my poor children, that it is by ceasing to long for me that you will be able to change the face of the earth? Come to me more often, with more confidence. Seek me more often in everything, in everybody, above all in yourself. You must attain to the stage at which you will not want to be without me, so that I may work through you as much as I desire. Then you will see what wonderful work we shall do together.

Examination of Conscience

1. Am I as truly united to Jesus as I should be, so that I can say with Saint Paul: "I live, no it is no longer I that live, but Christ who lives in me"?

2. Just what is my interior life worth?

3. Do I really regard Christ as my best and greatest friend, the guest of my soul?

4. Do I not suffer from being too active, so that my energies are dissipated and my life disturbed and ineffective?

5. Do I really act under the impulse of Jesus? If I try to analyze my modes of action, can I say in all truth that I always act from supernatural motives?

6. To do what I have to, do I unite myself to him from time to time?

7. I have faith, but have I really got the spirit of faith, and above all the "presence of mind" of faith? Are my reactions to events, difficulties, reverses, humiliations, suffering, always supernatural?

8. Do I automatically see God in souls? Am I above all anxious for his growth in every soul and for the expansion of every soul under the inspirations of grace?

9. Is the principal source of my energy really my love of God and of my neighbour? Is it not only too often a subtle self-seeking?

10. Are the glance of Jesus towards me and the presence of Jesus in me, realities which influence the practical details of my daily life?

11. How faithful am I to the practice of ejaculatory prayer?

12. Can I say, as did Saint Paul, "For me to live is Christ"? Is my reason for living, for working, for obeying, for smiling, for acting, Jesus Christ?

13. Do my discouragements arise too often from the fact that my life is not sufficiently impregnated with faith in his love?

14. Am I not inclined to forget that the interior life is a gift of God, and that I should ask for it humbly?

Resolutions

1. To pray to Jesus often for the gift of a deep interior life. It is a grace which the Master longs to grant to us, but we must ask for it perseveringly.

2. In the morning when we awake, to resume contact with God living in us, and to base our whole day on his wishes.

3. While celebrating Mass, to renew the offering of all activities which will make up our day so that they may be influenced by him and effectively based on him.

4. When we are busy, without any lengthy interruption, to make him feel from time to time that the pact of the early morning still holds, and that it is for him that we are working and that we are bearing any suffering.

5. To take advantage of any journeys, by any free moments, however short, and above all of any manual work, to converse with him in our hearts.

6. To acquire the habit – and it is extremely difficult – of seeing him and of adoring him in all that we do.

7. Often to share his love for those around us. To send out to everyone, waves of kindness, of goodness.

8. To try every day, for a few minutes, to unite ourselves with him to accomplish what we have to do. Not to overstrain our mind, not to get jaded. To stop as soon as we feel exhausted. It is not necessary always to be thinking of him. The essential thing is to want to act for him. But from time to time to resume this practice. Gradually, with his grace, he will attract us and he will unite us with himself without any effort on our part.

9. From time to time to follow the advice of Saint Vincent de Paul and gaze within us at his Majesty, and talk to him.

10. To train those souls who are capable of it – and there are many more than we think – to practise a life of intimacy with our Lord.

Spiritual Reading

"Abide in me. Abide in me by constantly remembering me and by turning your soul constantly towards me. Live in me. Seek nourishment in me. Try to know me, not only from without, but from within. Read into the depth of my Heart. Do not weary of this occupation. Let it be your only concern, the centre of your life. Stay there, as at the source of all light, of all energy, of all joy. Attach yourself to me strongly by your love. You will be firm and strong in my firmness and in my strength. Nothing will be able to trouble you, to disturb you, to separate us, except sin. But if sin threatens you, come closer to me by a more generous and more ardent love. Far from doing you harm, the trial will only have made your union stronger."

"How do you dwell in me, O Jesus?"

"I am in you as a friend in the home of a friend, as a guest in the home of his host. I have made myself the master of your heart. I have expelled from it every affection which rivals mine. Your heart is mine; it is for me that it beats unceasingly. It is I who move it. I am the strength which carries it along, the power which sets it in motion, the light which guides it, and I show it the path along which it must advance. I have changed it spiritually in my heart. What I love, it loves. What I reject, it rejects. What I want, it wants. It is every day a little more like my own heart. I am in you more intimately than you are in yourself. In one sense it is true that I am more you than you are yourself through the love which has transformed you into me. My apostle said: 'It is now no longer I that live.' That is precisely the position. Or again: 'He who clings to the Lord is one spirit with him.' One mind, one heart, and if you so wish it, for ever."

"Your gaze, O my God, is not only pleasant, it is salutary. It does not find us lovable, it makes us so. To look with love and create and enrich the being whom you have created is all one for you. May you deign to turn your gaze towards my soul and keep it there. Nothing is so pleasing to me as to know that I am always under your gaze. It seems to me that I should keep myself in an attitude of most profound respect and of most humble modesty. But what enlightenment shall I not receive with your eyes on me. It is your gaze that lightens my path, and shows me the true value of things, and whether they are obstacles or assets. It is your gaze that allows me to enlighten others in my turn. Without it there would be only darkness. I want to feel your eyes upon me always. Your gaze, O my God, is not something exterior to my soul; it is within, intimate. My soul seems to be infused by it as if from its depths. Your gaze is in fact yourself, living in my soul, and enlightening it about yourself, about itself, and about everything. My soul is conscious of this interior illumination. It is like a very pure crystal exposed directly to the sun, penetrated by its brilliant rays and knowing it. But that is a very feeble comparison. The soul is a spirit. God is a spirit.

100

Nothing can give an adequate idea of what takes place when God enters the soul and fills it with himself. He who is truth! Blessed is the soul without fault and without stain which the divine rays can illuminate fully. It is so wonderful to see God within us in this way. It is already a little touch of heaven."

Robert de Langeac

Subjects for Discussion

1. Why is it that for the priest who has an active ministry the need to set aside time for meditation is more pressing today than in the past?

2. What is the role of the emotions in our intimacy with our Lord? The danger of excess in two respects.

Prayer

Holy Virgin Mary, mother and model of interior souls, keep mine faithfully united in will and heart with your divine Son. Obtain for me the grace to think of him often, without fatigue and tension of mind, and to base all my activities on him.

Grant, O Mary, that I may be united to him in such a way, that no one can approach me without feeling himself nearer to Christ. May everyone sense his divine presence through my poor humanity. Let me find in him all the graces which I need to understand all that he expects of me, in the service of his Father's glory and of the salvation of my brothers. Amen.

Thought

The only way to be happy is to live in a world full of the presence and the reality of God.

Thomas Merton

6

ON READING THE ENCYCLICAL "MENTI NOSTRAE"

One of the most moving texts issued by Pope Pius XII is without doubt the encyclical *Menti Nostrae* on the subject of priestly holiness, addressed to the Catholic clergy throughout the world. It is a document which every priest should keep by him for frequent reference and as material for his meditations. A document like this calls for more than a superficial reading. It should be studied, pondered, and prayed over in the spirit which inspired it. To assist us let us select certain passages, grouped under three main headings: Why should we strive for sanctity? How should the sanctity of priests be expressed today? and From which source should we nourish our spiritual life?

Meditation

WHY SHOULD WE STRIVE FOR SANCTITY?

Without holiness the ministry cannot bear fruit. Priests are bound, because of the nature of their calling, to work untiringly for their own satisfaction.

"The priest is a 'second Christ'. Sealed with an indelible character, he becomes, as it were, a living image of the Saviour." (*Menti nostrae 7*)

"He is ordained for men in the things that appertain to God." (Heb. 5:1) "To him, therefore, all those must have recourse who would live the life of the Divine Redeemer and receive strength, comfort and nourishment for their souls; and those,

102

too, who would seek opportune remedies in their efforts to recover from moral collapse."(7) "Be holy because your ministry is holy."

"The ministry of the priest will be the more fruitful, the more closely he is himself united with Christ and guided by his Spirit." "The priest must not be content with submitting to the duties by which the faithful are bound, but must pursue daily more vigourously the perfection of life which the high dignity of a priest demands, according to the canon: "The clergy should lead a holier life interiorly and exteriorly than the laity, and be an example to them by the standard of their virtue and right conduct." (14 [Code of Canon Law, Can. 124])

Sanctity in the ministry is necessary for the sake of the sanctification of the world. To be the "consecrator" it is right that the priest should first of all be "consecrated" himself. It is he who should be the first to realize in his own person the triumph of "the new man". Before, and in order to "exorcize" human effort and to remove the world's doubts, the priest must dispel his own doubts, and to achieve unity in his own person. It is clear that this mystical identification with Christ, far from turning the priest from the needy world, leads him straight back to it. How will he lead humanity to God if he is himself not already united to him? "The human race will not take any other route than his", said Cardinal Suhard, "the dilemmas of the priest will be the dilemmas of the world: his personal victories will prepare those of the universe."

Every priest should strive to be and to show that he is a pattern of the priestly life, which for the young who approach him and in whom he discovers signs of the divine call which can take as an ideal to imitate. The vigour and the fervour with which young priests give themselves to their first priestly duties can sometimes overshadow and certainly reduce the example and influence of older priests, if they do not shine by the brilliance of their virtues, or prefer passive life on the excuse that they do not want to change some routine they have adopted.

The souls of our lay apostles provide us with a particular reason for striving after holiness. Here is what a girl studying at the University of Paris wrote: "For us, a priest is a man living in God. I remember the first time when I was preparing – at the age of twenty-one – to visit one. For the first time I was going to be alone with a priest, I was going to be able to study him, to hear him, and to speak with him. In my mind was the idea that I was going 'to see' some one who lived in God and with him. For me, a priest was a man living in God. I told myself that that had to be seen or it was a lie."

"You priests do not appreciate that it is on this, on the almost external testimony that you give of God that we judge you. The faith of the priest must flow out from him. The priest must radiate God. He must convince us that he definitely lives in God. It is then that God who was 'impossible' becomes 'possible' for the atheist. We cannot help being struck, upset, confused by a priest who is truly a witness of God. We do not forgive him for failing completely to be one."

In *L'Esprit Missionaire,* Father Michonneau writes: "The more we reflect on the chances of success or failure facing the missionary effort being deployed in France, the more we are convinced that it depends on the priestly merit of the men who undertake it. Let us question the lay apostles, or rather, simply listen to them. What do they expect from a priest? Namely the virtues expected of priests. Of what do they complain? That we are not sufficiently holy.

"They have a very exalted idea of us, or to be more exact, a very superior ideal, and this ideal is essentially the priestly ideal. They do not expect us to be artists, scholars, administrators, business men or specialists. They expect from us nothing outside our calling. Even the intellectuals do not expect to find us brilliant in erudition, or clever in juggling theories. They ask us merely to give them something solid: they do not want to be undernourished.

"The workman will not necessarily trust a priest who has adopted so-called working-class ways. He may treat him as a 'good type', but if he does not feel something more in him, the day he needs a serious adviser, he will go to some other priest in whom he has sensed a man of God."

"But the priestly ministry cannot be fully effective to meet the needs of our time, unless priests surpass their people by the brightness of their eminent holiness ...."(4)

104

"The increased needs of Christian society today more and more require of priests the pattern of interior perfection."(6)

"We are priests of Christ, and it is therefore our task to bring to individual souls the fullest efficacy of the redemption which he accomplished. A consideration of the conditions of our time urges upon us the need to bring back to Christ and his teaching those whom error and passion have led astray, to bring to the world the light of Christian doctrine, the rule of Christian law, the standards of a Christian conscience. In a word, we must inspire all to fight with courage for truth and justice. We shall achieve this only when we have reached such a height of sanctity, that what we pour out on others shall be life and virtue we have ourselves drawn from Christ". (129)

HOW SHOULD THE SANCTITY OF PRIESTS BE EXPRESSED TODAY?

"Let your apostolate radiate sympathy. Error must, of course, be refuted and vice resisted. But the heart of a priest should always be moved by pity; so that while he does his best to overthrow evil, he yet evinces ardent love for the erring brethren whom he is trying to convert. What wonders have saintly men been able to achieve by their kindness of heart among those classes whose circumstances and environment occasioned little else but deception and vice! True, the priest would be failing in his duty who sought to please men by being indulgent towards their evil propensities and their wrong ideas and principles, to the detriment of the purity of Christian faith and morality. But, provided the precepts of the Gospel are not whittled down, the priest, when dealing with sincerely repentant sinners, should remember the words of the Divine Master to the Prince of the Apostles who had asked how often he should forgive his brother: 'I say not to thee, till seven times, but till seventy times seven times.'" (Matt. 18:22) (62)

"After the pattern of his Divine Master the priest should do his best to supply the needs of the poor and of the workers; and indeed of all who are in straitened circumstances, among whom are to be reckoned, as is well known, many from the middle classes and from the ranks of the priesthood. But he should not neglect the well-to-do who are suffering from poverty of soul; he must summon them to the amendment of their lives, recalling the example of Zacchaeus who said: 'The half of my goods I give to the poor: and if I have wronged any man of anything, I restore him fourfold.' (Luke 19:8) In dealing with the social question, the priest should never forget the obligations of his office; frankly, therefore, and unhesitatingly he should propound the principles which concern the right of ownership, wealth, justice and charity and their application to the various classes of society, and he should show by his own example how these principles are to be put into practice." (120)

"We exhort you, therefore, to persevere in your fatherly efforts to ensure that the workers in the Lord's vineyard do not want for their daily bread." (123)

"Tell your people, then, that they are bound to supply the needs of their priests. Our Divine Redeemer's words, 'The labourer is worthy of his hire', (Luke 10:7) never lose their force. How can the people expect from their priest an energetic ministry if the necessities of life are wanting to him? Moreover, the faithful who neglect this duty are unwittingly assisting the policy of the enemies of the Church who in many countries endeavour to force the clergy through indigence into rebellion against ecclesiastical authority." (127)

"We should like to thank those priests who, regardless of personal inconvenience, are continually assisting their needy brethren, the aged and infirm especially. They give a wonderful example of that mutual charity which Christ designated as the hallmark of his disciples: "By this shall all men know that you are my disciples, if you have love one for another." (John 13:35) (125)

"We desire to give a word of special encouragement to those priests who, as counsellors, directors or confessors, unassumingly but most devotedly apply their talent to the sanctification of their fellow-priests. The incalculable service they render to the Church is often passed over in silence during their lifetime; but it will be manifested to the full one day in the glory of the heavenly kingdom."

106

"Not many years ago, We had the great consolation of raising to the altars the priest of Turin, Joseph Cafasso. He, as you know, in times of great difficulty, was a wise and holy director to many priests. He helped them to grow in holiness and to exercise a very effective ministry. We are confident that through his powerful intercession our Divine Redeemer will grant us many priests as holy as he, to guide themselves and their colleagues to perfection so exalted that the faithful, seeing their splendid example, will be moved willingly to follow it." (67, 68)

"We therefore exhort all priests, both secular and regular, in a brotherly spirit to combine their forces in pursuit of the common goal, which is the good of the Church and the sanctification of themselves and their neighbour." (71)

"Every priestly action of the sacred minister must be directed to this purpose; for it was he called by God, appointed to a divine office and endowed with divine grace. He must collaborate diligently with Jesus Christ, the one, eternal Priest. He must follow and imitate him whose ruling intention during his earthly life was to demonstrate his burning love for the Father and to bestow on men the infinite treasures of his Heart."

"The main motive force actuating a priest should be the determination to attain the closest union with the Divine Redeemer." (12, 13)

"The priestly life takes its origin from Christ, and to him, therefore, it should at all times be wholly directed." (15)

"Perfect sanctity further requires constant communion with God." (37)

"A priest should not rely on his own strength nor take immoderate delight in his gifts. He should not seek the esteem and eulogies of men, nor eagerly long for posts of greater importance. But let him imitate Christ who 'came not to be ministered unto, but to minister' (Matt. 20:28); and let him deny himself, according to the rule laid down by the Gospel, (cf. Matt. 16:24) and cling not too closely to earthly things, in order that he may follow the Divine Master more easily and more freely. Whatever he has or is comes from the goodness and power of God. If, then, he would glory, let him remember the words of the Apostles of the Gentiles: 'For myself I will glory nothing, but in my infirmities.'" (2 Cor. 12 : 5) (17)

107

"The priest's ministry is concerned with the affairs of the supernatural life. He forwards its growth and makes it share in the Mystical Body of Jesus Christ. He must, therefore, bid farewell to 'the things of the world' in order to care only for 'the things that belong to the Lord'. (1 Cor. 7:32, 33) To ensure his emancipation from worldly cares and his complete freedom for the service of God, the Church has established the law of celibacy, whereby it might be made more and more manifest to all that he is God's minister and the father of souls. By this law the priest does not lose the office of a father, rather he enhances it immeasurably, in that he brings forth children, not for this earthly and fleeting life, but for the life of heaven which will last for ever."

"The more brightly the priestly chastity of the sacred minister shines, the more completely does he become, along with Christ, 'a pure victim, a holy victim, an unblemished victim'." (Roman Missal: the Canon.)

"To guard the integrity of his chastity with every care, as a treasure of priceless value, it is useful and indeed necessary for him scrupulously to obey the injunction of the Prince of the Apostles, which we repeat daily in the Office: 'Be sober and watch.'" (1 Peter 5:8)

"Be very watchful, then, beloved sons, for so many dangers beset your chastity, dangers arising from the public immorality, from the allurements of vice which are so smoothly insidious today, and finally from the excessive freedom of intimacy which both sexes indulge in, which at times dares to creep into the exercise of the sacred ministry itself. 'Watch and pray', (Mark 14:38) always remembering that your hands touch most holy things, remembering, too, that you are consecrated to God and ought to serve him alone. The very vesture you wear admonishes you that you live, not for the world, but for God." (20–23)

"We consider it opportune to give you a special warning that, in directing the associations and sodalities of women, you should behave as priests. Avoid all familiarity. Whenever your service is needed, give it as sacred ministers. And in guiding these associations restrict your activity within the limits which your priestly ministry demands." (24)

108

"We exhort you, beloved sons, not to love overmuch the fleeting and perishable things of this world. Set before your eyes and revere the example of the saintly men of the past and of today. They have combined due detachment from external goods and the fullest confidence in the Providence of God with the most ardent zeal. Trusting in God only, who never denies the help we need, they have achieved most wonderful results. Sacred ministers, it is true, are not bound by a special vow of poverty; but they should be drawn by a love of poverty, manifesting itself in a simple and restrained manner of living and in the inexpensiveness of their dwelling, and proved by their generosity to the poor. Let them particularly avoid such business transactions as would draw them from their sacred duties and lessen the regard of the faithful. Since a priest must spend all his energy in procuring the salvation of souls, he should apply to himself the saying of the Apostle Paul: 'I seek not the things that are yours, but you'." (2 Cor. 12:14) (25)

"The proper object of your zeal is not the fleeting and transient; it is the things of eternity. Hence the priest who desires to fulfil his obligation to be holy should have, as his chief aim in life, to work only for the glory of God and the salvation of souls. The Apostle of the Gentiles was satisfied with little and sought only the bare necessities; 'having food', he said, 'and wherewith to be covered, with these we are content.' (1 Tim. 6:8) By this sober detachment from the things of the world and their trust in Providence they have produced abundant fruit to the spiritual and indeed, the social advantage of the Church." (63)

FROM WHICH SOURCE SHOULD WE NOURISH OUR SPIRITUAL LIFE?

"In this sacrifice they assume the person of Christ; they consecrate bread and wine which become the Body and Blood of Christ; and thereby they are enabled to draw from the very fount of supernatural life inexhaustible treasures of salvation and every help they need both for themselves and for the fulfilment of their duties."

"In consequence of so intimate an association with these divine mysteries, it is impossible that the sacred minister should not hunger and thirst for justice (cf. Matt. 5:6) and feel himself vehemently urged to harmonize his spiritual life with his sublime calling and, since he must after a manner immolate himself with Christ, to discipline his spirit by zeal for self-dedication. Hence he must not only offer the eucharistic sacrifice but also intimately live it." (31, 32)

"This hard and assiduous effort cannot be produced by a mere velleity: it is not limited to desires and wishes; rather, it must be an earnest and unwearied activity, endeavouring to achieve a fruitful renewal of the soul. It must be an exercise of piety, referring all things to God's glory. It must be an exercise of penance, to temper and control the immoderate movements of the soul. It must be an assiduous charity, inflaming us with love for God and our neighbour and rousing us to promote all the works of mercy. In a word, it must be an active and energetic exercise of the will, whereby we struggle and strive to attain whatever is perfect." (33)

"To her ministers then, the Church entrusts the special duty of praying in the name of the people and of consecrating to God the whole course of time and of events." (37)

"As he fulfils this duty the priest continues down the ages the action of Christ, who 'in the days of his flesh, with a strong cry and tears, offering up prayers and supplications.'" (Hebr. 5:7) (38)

"The priest's prayer is in a special way 'the voice of Christ' who 'prays for us as our priest and in us as our Head'. (St. Augustine, *Enarr. in Ps.*, 85, n. 1.) Likewise it is always 'the voice of the Church', which represents the prayers and desires of all the faithful. They are one in faith with the priest as he prays, and through him they praise Jesus Christ, give thanks to the eternal Father, and, daily and hourly, obtain from him all things needful. It is, so to say, a repetition each day of what Moses did on the mountain; with arms raised he spoke with God and begged mercy for the people labouring under affliction in the valley below." (38)

"A priest must make every effort to reproduce in himself these examples of the Gospel and the virtues of the Divine

Redeemer. Food will not nourish, sustain and increase the vitality of the body unless it is digested, assimilated, and converted into our substance. Similarly, unless the priest comes to live the life of the Divine Redeemer by meditation and by contemplation of the mysteries of Christ, the supreme model of all perfection and the inexhaustible source of sanctity, he cannot attain self-mastery and purity of soul; nor can he adequately strive for virtue; nor, finally, will he be able to exercise his sacred functions faithfully, zealously and with profit to souls." (45)

"Let the priest realize that his laborious ministry will be the more fruitful, the more closely he is himself united with Christ and led by his Spirit. His work will not then end in merely natural activity, wearisome to body and soul, and tending to lead him astray to his own and the Church's considerable detriment. On the contrary, his efforts will be fortified by divine grace." (57)

"With an apostolate of this character the priest will inevitably draw souls to himself by a supernatural attraction. He will be, as it were, a living image of Jesus Christ; and all those he teaches will feel an inner conviction that it is God's words he speaks and that it is by God's power that he operates."(57)

"The priest who would sanctify himself and others must possess solid learning, not only in theology, but also in the various subjects which our age has evolved by study and research. With a mind thus enriched, he will be like the good father of the family, who brings 'from his treasure new things and old' (cf. Matt. 13:52); his ministry will be universally esteemed, and it will prove fruitful." (65)

"For priests study is a duty, as the Code of Canon Law lays down: 'Clerics must not neglect their studies, especially their sacred studies, after ordination.'" (Canon 129) (110)

"To encourage the studies from which priests are often debarred through lack of means, it is very desirable that the bishops should reconstitute cathedral, capitular and parochial libraries according to the ancient and admirable traditions of the Church." (111)

"These libraries should not be treated as storehouses of no interest; they should be a centre of life and activity, and be provided with a room suitable for the consultation of books. Above all they must be up-to-date, containing modern books on all subjects, especially religious and social, so that professors and parish priests, and particularly the younger clergy, may be able to obtain whatever knowledge they need in their work of spreading the truths of the Gospel and of refuting error." (112)

Christ speaks to his Priest

My Son, consider as coming from me and addressed particularly to you, this new appeal of my Vicar on earth, an appeal to a life more and more holy, more and more dedicated, more and more loving. I desire so earnestly that the fire of love may preserve the world from the fire of hatred. It is not too late yet, but my priests must become burning furnaces of charity. It is not around conference tables nor on the fields of battle that the destinies of people are worked out, but in the hearts of my consecrated priests. It is from within that I see the world. It is from within that my kingdom must be extended. "The Kingdom of God is within you." Exterior results can be deceiving. It is the interior of souls that counts in my eyes. I do not judge as men do, I judge with the eyes of love, which look beyond appearances. The more that you love with my heart, the more you will see with my eyes.

If you but knew how I burn with the desire to give myself to you, and through you to others. But you must get to the point where you cannot do without me so that I may take possession of you as much as my heart desires. Come to me, I am always waiting for you. It is with me first of all you should discuss the business of my Father. The business of my Father? That means making the great human family become a part of the divine family, through attraction, through conviction, through choice. My Father has made his choice: all men without exception. But men's choice is not made. Besides those who say "yes", there are those who say "no", and there are those who are silent and who live what is virtually an animal existence. Beside those who cry "Abba, Father!", and who work effectively to extend his Kingdom, there are those who say: "We do not

112

want him to reign over us", and there are all those who think only of squandering their inheritance.

The world is in a sad state, but it is far from hopeless. If all those whom I have chosen among thousands to train to help me in the work of co-redemption would but fulfil their mission, conversions would multiply, and men would be astonished at the era of peace and of material and moral prosperity which would begin soon. Give me unceasingly to the world through your whole life, give me unceasingly to the world by your every thought. You are a mediator. Do not slow down the current of life which should pass through you, nor the stream of appeals which you must make surge up to me.

If men but desired me more, I would come to them and make them happy. They do not desire me because they do not know me, or they know me imperfectly. They know me so badly because those whose mission it is to reveal me to them so often present me as a caricature. To present me as I am they would have to live more united with me. For that they would have to come again and again to draw from the source I provide.

What a loss of time, what a waste of energy, what useless fatigue, because they forget the essential! If a river ceased to be in contact with its source, it would soon dry up. A priest who does not keep in contact with me soon dries up spiritually. Are you astonished after that that the desert is so extensive? The most fertile valleys can become arid plains. Do not seek elsewhere for the basic cause of current dechristianization. Secondary causes are only secondary. In the beginning there is the practical refusal to remain united with me. The abundant waters of my grace are lost, without profiting any one. Masses of mud and of rocks block up those channels which should carry living water. Souls are the victims of it, entire nations suffer from it, all humanity suffers from it.

I am Salvation. I am Sanctity. I am the one thing necessary. And yet it is I who am neglected. If I long to be of use, it is for you. Without me you wander aimlessly, you waste your efforts to no purpose, you squander, you spoil, you mar everything that I put into your hands. If I tell you all this, it is out of my love. You are so unhappy seeking the solution of problems where it is not to be found.

Come, then, to me. How charity would grow in you and in all those influenced by you, if you would let yourself be absorbed by me, instead of letting yourself be absorbed by dust or trifles. Live close to me, and you will have the gift of touching hearts. Too many priests, starting out with good intentions, complicate their apostolic life so much that they dissipate their efforts and lose the thought of me and the flame of my Love. They no longer reflect me sufficiently. Then they become inoperative and ineffective. Do they imagine that it is in ceasing to aspire towards me that they will be able to renew the face of the earth? The renewal of the face of the earth depends on the way they let my Spirit breathe through their actions, their words, their gestures.

It is my Spirit alone which makes things fruitful. I send it to them without ceasing, but they do not spare the time to receive it. As they do not listen to my Spirit, so I am all too often paralyzed in them. I cannot act in them as I wish. What suffering that causes my heart! What a loss for the world! If you but knew how much I love you! Come to me more often! Be willing to give me a little of your time. The little effort that you make to keep some time for me will be richly rewarded! You will see that for you and for souls it will be time saved. My light will prevent you from committing many errors, many faults. My fire will help you to purify and to enkindle hearts. My power will enable you, with less effort, to attain lasting results.

Believe me: the hour that you consecrate to me is more important for the increase of my love than days of feverish activity lived forgetful of me. I tell you again: it is especially through you that I want to enkindle the world. It is for that I have chosen you, and it is to that I have consecrated you. I am in each of you, recording the motions of your will: your loyalties, or your rejections of my love reacting on all humanity. What I need today are priests fired with love for me, fired with zeal for the glory of the Father. To these ardent priests I shall give all the souls they ask of me, and they can obtain all the miracles for souls for which they ask me. They will see, then, on this earth, the meaning of the hundredfold I have promised to them. Do you want to be one of them?

Examination of Conscience

1. Have I a sincere desire to be a holy priest?

2. Do I accept the truth that "today the increased needs of Christian society require more and more interior perfection in their priests"?

3. Am I above all "animated with the desire to be intimately united with the divine Redeemer in all the circumstances of my life"?

4. Is my charity ardent, zealous, active?

5. Have I understood that "by the obligation of celibacy, far from losing the privilege of paternity, the priest enjoys it in an infinitely greater degree for the posterity which he does not raise up in this earthly and fleeting life, he begets a heavenly and eternal life"?

6. Have I understood that a priest is a channel of graces only if he is humble?

7. Is my fidelity to Christ expressed by trust and obedience to the lawful authority established by him?

8. Am I faithful to the recommendations of the Holy Father about the direction of associations for women, "keeping a prudent reserve, and acting only as a minister of God?"

9. Do I give evidence in my conduct of that detachment from earthly things recommended by the Holy Father "by the simplicity of my manner of life, the absence of luxury in my surroundings, and my generosity to the poor"?

10. Is the Mass the centre of my priestly life? Is it a constant reality which permits me to insert unceasingly into the never-ending oblation of my Saviour Jesus my prayers, works, joys, and sorrows?

11. Am I faithful, not only materially but spiritually, to the recitation of my office? Do I make it a subject for meditation, a means of sanctification?

12. Is my prayer centred on Christ Jesus, not only as the supreme model of perfection but as a source of unfailing sanctity?

13. Do I make the feast of the Assumption an occasion for renewing my fervour towards Our Lady? Am I faithful to the daily recitation of the rosary, or at least to a part of it?

14. Do I love to visit the Blessed Sacrament daily in order to adore God in the name of those who do not adore him, to ask pardon in the name of those who forget, to present to the merciful heart of the Saviour the distress of the souls under my care?

15. Am I faithful to my examination of conscience and to frequent confession?

16. In my sermons, in the spiritual doctrine that I teach, do I try to make the faithful understand the true doctrine of the Communion of Saints?

17. Are Catholic Action and missionary activity propagated and encouraged in my parish?

18. Do I inculcate in lay people a sense of social justice?

19. Am I sure that I am not caught up in the "whirlwind of exterior activity"? Have I reacted again to the very real danger of the heresy of activity?

20. Am I disinterested as well as zealous in my apostolate? "Let it be always apparent to everyone that the priest, in all his activities, seeks no other good than that of souls and that he has no other end in view than Christ, to whom he consecrates his strength and his whole being."

21. Is my apostolic zeal animated by "a divine love which is conquered by no obstacle and which embraces poor and rich, believers and unbelievers"?

22. Do I make sure that I am not swept away by the uncontrolled desire for success? Am I cast down if, after conscientious work, I do not reap the fruits I had hoped for?

23. Is my zeal characterized by kindness and gentleness?

24. Without falling into the defect of loving novelty for itself, am I careful to adapt the methods of my apostolate to the real need of the faithful?

25. If I have young priests around me – in my parish or deanery – do I make an effort to guide and encourage them?

26. Have I a deep concern for priestly and religious vocations? Do I often pray for this intention? Do I prepare the souls of those "who are called to God to receive the inspiration and the invisible action of the Holy Spirit"? Do I try to be an "example of priestly life" which can be an ideal to imitate?

116

27. Do I understand that it is not enough to oppose Communism or to denounce the baneful consequences of capitalism? "The damage caused by both these economic systems must convince the world, and priests in particular, of their obligation to adhere and remain faithful to the social doctrine which the Church teaches, to make it known to others and to make them put it into practice as they have the opportunity. This doctrine alone can provide a remedy for the evils which are now so widespread. It unites and harmonizes all the demands of justice and the duties of charity. It requires the establishment of a social order which, far from oppressing individuals and isolating them by excessive preoccupation with their own interests, reunites all men in the reciprocal relations of harmony and by the ties of a brotherly friendship."

28. Do I wish, with the Holy Father, that "the bonds of fraternal charity become closer among the priests of all nations so that it may be more patent that the priests, ministers of the same God, Father of all, are animated in their mutual relations by the same spirit of charity, no matter in what country they live"?

Resolutions

1. To read again with the greatest care the encyclical *Menti Nostrae*.

2. To make it for some time the subject of my meditation.

3. To make a note of the passages which refer especially to my state of soul, or to my particular mission.

4. To pray for all my colleagues throughout the whole world, that the appeal of the Holy Father may be heard and that there may be all over the earth and in all dioceses, a new flood of priestly fervour.

Subjects for Discussion

1. During the last century, what are the pontifical documents which have taken priestly sanctity as their principal subject?

2. What new factors have been brought out in *Menti Nostrae*?

117

Prayer

Most Holy Virgin Mary, Mother of the eternal Priest, and because of that, loving Mother of the clergy, cast a glance of mercy on all your sons throughout the whole world. Develop in them a deep desire for priestly sanctity. Raise up those who have fallen. Support those who are weak. Comfort those who feel abandoned. Console those who are victims of men's wickedness, especially those who are persecuted, imprisoned, exiled. Give to all the desire and the gift of gaining all hearts for you. Through your intercession, may all your priestly sons become, for each soul in their charge, another Jesus, that is to say, another Saviour. Amen.

Thought

Priest, what else can it possibly be to which you have been called, but sanctity!

Léon Bloy

7

SAINT JOSEPH AND THE PRIESTHOOD

Paul Claudel referred to "the great and rather mysterious figure of Saint Joseph, whose very name makes superior people smile". Another poet, Francis Jammes, extolling him and glorifying his humility, called him "the derided one, whose very name is an embarrassment on the lips of tepid Christians, a blasphemy on those of the impious". Indeed, without going that far, we might be tempted to treat Saint Joseph as one who does not count, to grant him only secondary attention, at the most giving him a vage salute on the nineteenth of March and on the Third Sunday after Easter, rather regretting that his feast often falls during Lent. Also, it seems that there is not a very strong tie between Saint Joseph and our priesthood. Why, then, multiply our devotions? What benefits can accrue to us, and even to our flock, from concentrating our thought and prayer on this saint, about whom we know so little!

If we study the Gospel of the Infancy, in the light of the words which the Angel of God addresses to Joseph, defining his mission, in the light of the facts which determine his behaviour and emphasize his true greatness, we see, emerging from the shadows to which he was so attached, a very different countenance from the one which was apparent from a superficial glance. His fatherhood is not unlike ours. The virtues which he practised are those practised by every priest worthy of the name. Far from distracting our attention, contemplation of Saint Joseph reveals a priestly soul united with our Lord and his Mother, in a life vibrating with activity in which we run the risk of losing sight of the one thing necessary to salvation.

Moreover, it is our Lord's wish to rescue from obscurity him whom he called Father.

The greatest saints, from Saint Teresa of Ávila onwards, go instinctively to him, declaring that they are well repaid. Many important plans and religious communities are placed under his patronage. In our troubled times, the Sovereign Pontiffs multiply their appeals to the faithful to have confidence in his power to solve crucial problems of family life, of the workers, and of international peace. It seems, then, that it may be in accordance with God's plan that we should try to integrate Saint Joseph more into our spiritual and apostolic life.

Meditation

When asking us to give up the privilege of fatherhood according to the flesh, the Lord offered us another fatherhood, of an infinitely superior order: a virginal fatherhood in relation to him in his eucharistic life, and a no less virginal fatherhood in relation to the souls in whom, mystically, he wishes to be born and to grow. It is not without emotion that a priest becomes aware of that authority which the bishop has conferred on him on the day of his ordination. "Receive the power to offer sacrifice to God", by virtue of which, every morning he brings his God eucharistically into the world.

The fatherhood of Saint Joseph is also a virginal fatherhood. The epithets which are ordinarily applied to him, such as legal father, foster father, adopted father, are all far short of the reality. His fatherhood is not borrowed. It is not a sort of guardianship with limited responsibilities. "God", wrote Saint John Chrysostom, "had decided to give to Joseph all that might belong to a father without forfeiting virginity." The words of the Angel are formal: "Fear not to take unto thee Mary thy wife, for that which is conceived in her is of the Holy Ghost. And she shall bring forth a son, and thou shalt call his name Jesus. For he shall save his people from their sins." (Matt. 1:20, 21)

By saluting Joseph as the Son of David the divine message links his destiny legally with that of Christ. By confirming and

120

sanctioning the alliance of Mary and Joseph, it establishes and makes official the rights Joseph had over the child born of this marriage through the operation of the Holy Spirit. Finally, by telling him to give to the new-born child the name of Jesus, it recognizes in him the official capacity of head of the household, with all the responsibilities which flow from that. And Joseph, fully reassured, knowing that it is henceforth the will of his heavenly Father, agrees to be the father of Jesus with the same simple and very loving dignity with which he agreed to be the spouse of the Blessed Virgin. In fact, he takes charge of the Holy Family, not with fear and timidity, but, as Father Buzy says, "with the conviction of a priest who administers the sacraments".

In himself he feels inadequate for that sublime function. But his fatherhood makes him share the divine fatherhood which is imprinted on him like an indelible character. He makes his decisions and bears his responsibilities in full dependence on the heavenly Father. It is to him and not to Mary that on several occasions the angel makes known the divine decisions, before the flight into Egypt, or of the return to Palestine. The divine child submitted to him, his wife respects his authority. Many times, the New Testament refers to him as Father or identifies him with Mary under the common title of "parents of Jesus". When he and Mary find the child again in the Temple, she refers to her husband: "Behold your father and I have sought you sorrowing." She recognizes his superior rights, and she speaks of him without any fear of causing the least misunderstanding, an evident proof that she normally gave him this title and was factually correct. She, better than anyone else, knew the essential role played by Joseph, and how, apart from the physical relationship, he is and shows himself father in the full sense of the word.

Father Stephane Piat writes: "Since God decided that his Son should be born of a Virgin, within legal wedlock, the virginity of Joseph, the assent that he gives to that of his wife, the jealous care he exercises over this treasure, take first place among the arrangements made from all eternity for the incarnation of the Word. In this conception, the most sublime of all, it is not the physical participation of the man, it is the voluntary

121

abstention from this which permits generation. Guardian of the conjugal virginity which cannot subsist without him, Joseph will be at the same time the guardian of the child born of this virginity. That is why Saint Augustine can say: 'the more steadfastly a father as he is the more chastely so'."

Saint Leo, in his first sermon on the Nativity, said of Mary, that before conceiving the Saviour physically she had conceived him spiritually. "She conceived her offspring in her soul before she conceived him physically." "In the announcement made to Joseph", said Father Bessières, "we find the clarity, the imposing simplicity of the announcement made to Mary. Saint Joseph's assent is as clear, as heroically trustful as that of his spouse; both souls are in unison."

Again, is it not a similar virginal fatherhood which we share when, at the consecration, we bring Jesus down upon the altar and place him on the corporal, and when we are, like him, made guardians of the divine presence and guardians of his life of constant oblation, by the contribution of our offering of ourselves and of the community which we represent? The very same sentiments of fatherhood animate us when our heart is concerned about the fate that so many modern Herods threaten, and when we witness the ruin of so many innocent souls. The same anguish grips us when we seek to find him in the meanderings of souls as once Joseph and Mary tried to find him in the labyrinth of streets in Jerusalem. We experience the same fatherly emotion when we bend over the weary or suffering members of Christ, and when, throughout our apostolic works, whatever form they take, it is he whom we are trying to make grow within us in the sight of God and of men.

Another French writer on Saint Joseph, M. Olier, develops this thought. "Joseph was given to earth to express visibly the admirable perfections of God the Father, to be the image of God the Father in the eyes of the Son of God", and he adds: "What must be the sanctity of this great saint whom God the Father formed with his own hands to represent himself to his only Son!" That is without doubt why the virtues proper to a priest in the exercise of his spiritual fatherhood find in Joseph so perfect a model.

What perhaps impresses us most is his silence. The Gospels have so little to say about him. They devote to him twenty-six verses only. They mention him fourteen times. He enters the scene almost stealthily; he hides himself in the glamour of Jesus and Mary, he affaces himself as if disconcerted by the role he has to play and finally disappears, under conditions quite unknown, before the glory of Christ appears on the horizon. After his death there is almost a conspiracy concerning his name.

The priest must also know how to be silent because there is a real danger of his talking too much, of his feeling that he must talk for the sake of talking, of his gradually acquiring the habit of talking aimlessly. The longest sermons are not the most effective; abundance of words often hides poverty of thought.

The Curé d'Ars kept his penitents a very short time, at most five minutes for the worst sinners. But in a few sentences full of the divine, he turned a soul right around and steered it towards the Lord. For a priest, to speak without reference to the Word, is to speak with nothing to say. There is only one word that is fruitful, Christ's. Through our lips it is he, the substantial Word of the Father, which must express and broadcast itself.

Whether it is in prayer or preaching, we easily lapse into useless talk if we do not take the means (and that means a great effort of will for most of us) of cutting short our habitual occupations occasionally and plunging ourselves into the profound silence where the soul finds itself alone with its God. The priest who does not know how to secure these intervals of silence gradually becomes a superficial man in the proper sense of the term. He can keep up a façade for a time, but before long the souls who, because of his excellent reputation, hoped to find in him a source of spiritual nourishment, find only an empty, dirty or dried-up cistern.

The priest should also know how to be silent because he ought to give an example of the control of the tongue, of which Saint James said: "Behold also ships, whereas they are great and are driven by strong winds, yet are they turned about with a small helm whithersoever the force of the governor willeth." (James 3:4). Besides those which he listens to in the confessional, the priest is the recipient of many confidences. It is not without reason that he was formerly honoured with the title of "a discreet and learned person". He can do tremendous harm by speaking uncharitably and retailing rumours which, coming from him, acquire an added authority! The discretion which enhances charity, if not justice, is an indispensable condition for gaining the particular confidence of other people.

Saint Joseph knew how to keep God's secret. Is it not true that it is difficult to keep a secret when telling it would bring us esteem? Suppose Saint Joseph had said to his neighbours: "The awaited Messiah is at my home!" Would not that wonderful news have secured him the respect of everyone? But the love of silence in the soul of Joseph was one with his love of the hidden life. One of the most precious lessons we can learn from him is that the real effectiveness of a human life is not measured by its fame during its earthly career.

"Without a moment's warning", wrote Father R. Bernard, "Joseph is enveloped and submerged in the divine mystery. God acts here not openly, as formerly, but with a secrecy and tact which adds greatly to the perfection and merit of faith. And yet, this is the greatest manifestation of the divine ever to take place, since it is the Word which is made flesh, which comes to dwell among us. Saint Joseph is treated by God as the greatest spiritual character of the new era. No publicity, nothing greatly out of the ordinary, and exterior facts reduced to a minimum. On the contrary, very intimate things, much reflection, trials of soul, unspeakable anguish and waiting; revelations and warnings in a dream, giving the essential and nothing more. From all that emerges the first Christian faith, and the last of the patriarchs gives the Word Incarnate the very welcome he desires.

"We are tempted to cry out to our Lord: 'Happy is the man who bent over your crib, and who held you in his arms' but Jesus replies: 'Happier is he that believed and knew how to understand and keep the divine secret!'"

To identify Joseph the New Testament uses a very simple term: *vir justus*. To translate this as "a just man" would be inadequate and manifestly insufficient. Today we should say that he was a dutiful, a conscientious man. The priest, too, should be a conscientious man. Over much of his life, for all practical purposes, no one exercises any control. So, if he has not an upright, loyal and sensitive conscience, all sorts of aberrations are possible. Conscience stems from loyalty to God and to the commitments we have undertaken for love of him, whatever this costs and whatever happens. This is exactly the soul of Saint Joseph: a steadfast faith in spite of obscurities; an intelligent obedience in spite of difficulties, an inviolable loyalty to complete chastity.

His faith was put to a severe test. It was not only after he had lost and found Jesus that he did not understand. "Precisely because he was a just man", said Father Bessières, "his whole life was nourished by the hard bread of faith." Whether it was at the moment when he took Mary as his wife; whether it was at the moment he left Bethlehem under the conditions we know so well; whether it was at the hasty flight by night into Egypt; whether it was at the return from Egypt with all that it involved, it was always with the same attitude of submission towards him who was the Master. It was done with a love eager to serve him who called, done with confidence, in abandonment of all his plans. For even if the ways of God are impenetrable and his paths singularly disconcerting, he repeated with the Psalmist: "The Lord directs me and I shall want nothing."

Moreover, he had an active, intelligent, prudent obedience, which sought loyally within the limits of God's plan what seemed to him the best way of expressing his fidelity, or serving the best interests of those who were entrusted to him. That was clear at the moment when his soul was battling with the most painful problem that a man has had to solve. It appeared not less clearly when he had to choose a permanent home for the Holy Family when they returned from Egypt. Authority was for him only a type of "service". For him it was based upon the divine command, not upon a superiority of strength or talents always open to challenge by men or by events. And so he never felt the least bewilderment when he saw himself obeyed by him whom he knew to be the Son of the Most High, and by the Immaculate Virgin whom he knew to be blessed among all women.

125

Equally chastity is for him only a form of highest service, a superior expression of a love which wishes to be complete. It was necessary to enable the Infant God to be born of a Virgin Mother with the assurance of an effective paternal protection. In reply to the divine call, he had no questions to ask, or rather, he accepted all without contesting it, without delay, without doubt or reflection. Saint Bernard calls Saint Joseph "the most faithful worker for the divine plan". Like Saint Joseph, we must be faithful workers. To us as to him should be applied this verse which we repeat several times on the Feast of St. Joseph: "A faithful man, guardian of his Lord."

The New Testament, speaking of Joseph, refers to his profession and calls him *faber*. Whatever trades which can be grouped under this title, it is absolutely clear that Saint Joseph was a worker who had to earn his bread and that of his family by the sweat of his brow. The priest, too, must be a worker. Nothing would be more absurd and contradictory than a lazy priest. Once a priest has seen the great distress in the world, he could not think of living in an ivory tower. "Woe is me if I do not preach the Gospel." (1 Cor. 9:16)

The priest must never say: "There is nothing to do." For the father of a family there is always something to do. The harvest is always abundant and the labourers are few, very few. There are, and there will always be, sheep who need our care. There are, and there will always be, lost sheep who will need to have us go out to find them, or who will at least need us to help them. In fact, the real temptation of a priest worthy of the name, is not so much hateful idleness, as a poor organization of his time and a faulty use of his gifts, talents and of the many opportunities which God has given him.

"Time is money." For a priest it is souls, it is eternity: time is eternity. The priest should know how to use it economically, how to ration its use to the importance of the object. We should plan ahead, twice a day if possible, the sequence, order, and approximate details of everything foreseeable, so as not to be at sea when the unexpected happens. "A time for everything and everything in its place." Observing commonsense axioms like these must have given to Saint Joseph's workshop that atmosphere of order calm, and peaceful efficiency

126

which facilitates progress in contemplation within the most active life.

A good priest once said: "What tires me is not so much what I do as what I do not succeed in doing." And that happens when we fail to organize our work, because we refuse to identify and to appreciate possible aids, however primitive and elementary they may be. Again, it is our failure to pause for long enough to think and to pray about what we are going to do. Then, instead of dominating it, we let it dominate us, and soon our most legitimate activity becomes sterile agitation, which exhausts us morally and physically. Formerly, because the priests were more numerous, because life had more rhythm, nearer nature, because problems were not as complex as they are today, many priests who were very busy on Saturday, Sunday, and fasted on Thursday, had the rest of the week to study, think, and pray. Today, especially in certain city parishes, the hustle is such that the priest who does not observe the divine law of resting on the Sabbath under one form or another, withers and becomes empty.

To meditate on Saint Joseph the Worker is a lesson and a relief. He respected the Sabbath, not only in the letter but in the spirit. To him, the consecrated day was really like a time strong in resources and full of opportunity for acquiring the interior spirit which would be expressed on other days by work happily and calmly done.

We remember what Péguy said: "Work there was an unbelievable honour, the most beautiful of all honours! All through my childhood I remember chairs being mended with the same spirit, the same heart, and the same hand with which this same people had carved their cathedrals. It was essential that the rung of a chair should be well made. That was understood. It was not essential that it should be well made because of the wages paid. It was not essential that it should be well made for the employer nor for the experts, nor for the customers of the employer. It had to be well done, in itself, for itself . . . all their work was a prayer, and their workshop an oratory."

There will always be more work than we can do. It is better to do a little less and do it very well than to do a lot and do it badly, for then we are liable to do a great deal of harm.

We know all this very well, but sometimes we are tempted to forget. It is not we who do the real good that counts, it is our Lord who wishes to make our work effective so that he can profit by it, because it has been done for him, with much love. And there again, was it not this that characterized the work of Joseph, done as it was essentially through love of Jesus and our Lady, very often under their very eyes?

In the sixth chapter of her autobiography, Saint Teresa of Avila wrote: "It seems that God grants to other saints the grace to help in certain needs. But I know from experience that Saint Joseph helps us in everything, as if our Lord wanted to make us understand that, as he had submitted on earth to the man who took the place of his Father and bore the name of Father, so in heaven he will refuse him nothing." Is this not the theme of the hymn *Coelitum Joseph*?

> He that is King, the God of Kings, the lord of the earth, at whose bidding hell trembles and before whom heaven falls prostrate, ready to do his will, yes even he makes himself subject to thee.

There is no age, no state of life for which Saint Joseph cannot be counted on to show special concern. We might say of him what the poet wrote of a mother's heart and her children: "Each one has part of my heart, and all of them have the whole of it." We have a responsibility for the children in our parishes. The massacre of the innocents continues physically and morally. How many pure souls are contaminated; how many good wills are distorted; how much spontaneity is crushed; how many possibilities for good stifled. Whatever we say, childhood is humanity in flower, and the future of the world of tomorrow depends on the children of today.

Let us entrust those who are in our care to Saint Joseph, who, with Mary, bent with so much tenderness over the crib of the Infant God, who sacrificed his rest, his sleep, his tranquillity in his service, who protected him from the assassins of Herod, who, in a word, spent himself for Jesus without counting the cost. Let us ask him to help parents to fulfil their unique mission, and to multiply everywhere throughout the world not masters but servants of the divine presence growing in the souls of children.

We may be in charge of adolescents. They are at the dangerous age of the first serious temptations and the first important choices; at an age, however, when, in spite of their constitutional instability, they are capable of admirable generosity which, if it is prudently encouraged and channelled, can influence them to give themselves to noble causes. Let us entrust them to Saint Joseph for whom the youth of Christ when it first appeared at Jerusalem was the occasion of such a trial, and who was the master of the divine Master during his apprenticeship.

> Safe under His Father's roof Jesus grows up in seclusion, to be trained in Joseph's lowly trade. He gives himself of his own free choice to be Joseph's companion in his work as a carpenter. (Hymn, *Sacra Jam,* from Matins of Sunday within the Octave of the Epiphany.)

Let us ask him to guard our young people against all the snares of the devil, to help them to come out victorious from the critical age and to direct them towards the state of life which conform to the plan of God's love for them.

We have charge of young homes. We know that the health of a parish or a nation depends on the moral health of the vital cells which true families represent. Let us entrust them to Saint Joseph. He knows their problems better than anyone else. Father Piat says: "We must not attribute to Joseph and Mary some sort of toneless tenderness, a stiff and artificial affection, dominated and numbed by a fear of the flesh. If love is essentially the gift of self, two spouses never loved as did they. Devotion, sacrifice, respect characterized them, they lived for each other, and entirely in the service of God. In the most beautiful sense of the term, they loved on the summits."

Let us ask Saint Joseph to multiply throughout the whole world and in every sphere, beautiful and solid Christian homes, homes that are open and radiant, that are in every way possible replicas of the Holy Family at Nazareth.

As priests, we have to look after adult workers. Our hearts bleed at the thought of the many men who are victims of a life which is often inhuman, made harder sometimes by working conditions which degrade their souls, whilst they produce superior products with their hands, and exposed to a social pressure which is exercised in a sense opposed to faith and to Christian living. We suffer because we find it so difficult to reach them. We want to reveal to them that true liberty is that of the sons of God, that true fraternity is that of the brothers of Jesus Christ, that true peace proceeds from justice and true love. Certainly there are a few outstanding Christian workers here and there. But the mass of workers is still far removed from us. Let us entrust them to Saint Joseph, that rugged workman with the calloused hands, who knows all the riches hidden in the heart of those who labour. Let us ask him to raise up many militant Christian workers who will be in the midst of things without flinching and who will testify without falsifying.

Let us ask Saint Joseph to bless and to inspire action in those chaplains whose mission it is to help them spiritually and to guide them according to the spirit of the Gospel and the directives of the Church. Especially let us ask him to make all priests understand, whatever may be their position or their function, that they have no right to be disinterested in one of the greatest scandals of modern times: the separation of the people and the Church.

We have charge of the sick and of the dying, because they are the suffering members of Christ; because their sufferings, if they have been accepted and united to those of our Saviour, can win for them and for humanity a more abundant application of the fruits of the redemption. We look after them also because their illness and death leave their relatives in suffering and sorrow. Are we not especially pained at the thought of the many men who die without any preparation, without any spiritual help, as poor beasts who have finished their fleeting course?

Let us entrust them to Saint Joseph. He had the great privilege of dying in the arms of Jesus and Mary:

> . . . O thrice blessed Saint, at whose last hour Jesus and Mary stood watching with tender love. (Hymn of the First Vespers of the Feast of Saint Joseph.)

130

We cannot fail to be moved when we re-read the prayer which Saint Francis de Sales puts on the lips of Saint Joseph, and which is so in keeping with his essential qualities of trust and of simple surrender: "having accomplished the work which had been required of him, he said to the eternal Father: 'O Father, I have finished the work you gave me to do'; and then to the Son; 'O my Child, as your heavenly Father gave your body into my hands the day you came into this world, so, on this day of my departure from this world, I entrust my soul into your hands.'"

Perhaps this will remind us that some day our Lord will call us. We shall be very happy then if we have often entrusted our last moments to Saint Joseph, and if we feel his reassuring presence at our last hour.

We have also many other responsibilities, and so we can continue for a long time in this meditation. Everything interests Saint Joseph, Patron of the Universal Church: vocations, interior souls, consecrated souls, workers, those in civil and ecclesiastical authority, travellers, exiles. His solicitude extends to all and to everything, including our material needs.

At this point we can profitably re-read the beautiful words of Saint Teresa of Avila, which have helped so much to spread devotion to Saint Joseph: "I took as my patron and intercessor the glorious Saint Joseph. I recommended myself to him and I have since realized that this great Saint has given me greater and prompter help than I would have dared to hope for. I do not remember ever to asking anything of him that I did not obtain, nor can I cease to be astonished when I think of the graces God has granted me through his intercession, and of the dangers from which he has delivered me, dangers both of soul and of body. Other persons to whom I commended the great saint have had the same experience as I. And so my experience of the goodness of Saint Joseph has made me wish to be able to persuade the whole world to have a great devotion to him."

The older we grow, the more we feel our limitations. Our power grows restricted. Our confidence in the power of Saint Joseph however, can be wonderfully extended. Is that not what the prayer for his feast implies: "what we cannot obtain of ourselves may be granted to us through his intercession"?

Christ speaks to his Priest

While you are contemplating the man to whom I gave the name of Father when I was on earth, and who was so truly a father to me, you rejoice my heart. For how many times have I, too, looked at him, observed him, contemplated him, and admired him! If you only knew the strength of his character, the rectitude of his judgement, the perfection of his balance, and above all, the exquisite delicacy of his heart! I was proud to be called and to be considered his son. He was so devoted to me. He took upon himself so many burdens, so many fatigues, so many trials. Thus he entered into the dolorous path of the redemption. In him I saw man in his first dimension and his final perfection. So great, so excellent a man as he is an honour to humanity! In him I saw all men, the poor, the workers, as well as the sons of kings. I saw all those who would be exiled, who would be banished from their country, who would be uprooted.

In him, especially, I saw my priests. Is not each one of you, like Saint Joseph, my virgin father? Am I not in your hands, under the eucharistic elements, as I was in the arms of Joseph when he used to hold me as a child? Have I not submitted to you, even as I was obedient to him? Like him, does not each of you protect me, defend me, nourish me, help me to grow in souls? Like him, does not each of you suffer for me or because of me? Like him, is not each of you called to live in intimacy with me and my Mother?

Go more often to Joseph. There is in him a source of hidden graces reserved for you. You do not know what you lose if you neglect him. You do not know how much you would gain by seeking his advice and by calling on him to help you. He is a good companion who understands the severe "trade" which is yours, and he will teach you to make of it "a perfect work". He is a master craftsman who will teach you how to apply your effort at the right spot, to measure your effort to the need of the task, and avoid any waste of energy, so as to give to your life its greatest efficiency. Above all, he will teach you that total submission to the wishes of the heavenly Father, which is the secret of true apostolic efficiency. What matters is not so much spending ourselves without counting the cost, as accomplishing with all the love of which we are capable what God expects of each of us.

Confide to Joseph your worries and your pains, your distress, and your anxiety; he knows from experience what anxiety and insecurity are. But he knows the key to every problem, the solution of all difficulties. For him, surrender was an active form of the total gift of himself to my Father's plan of love. He will even solve material difficulties to your advantage, provided you appeal to his immense influence. Finally, when you are at the hour of your death, no one will be able to help you so well as he who died in my arms.

Examination of Conscience

1. Am I aware of the importance of Saint Joseph in the incarnation, the redemption, and consequently in the sanctification of all humanity?

2. Have I given the mission of Saint Joseph a place in the synthesis of my sacerdotal and apostolic life?

3. Do I appreciate that, far from destroying my devotion to Christ and to Our Lady, a true and manly and trustful devotion to Saint Joseph brings me closer to a true knowledge of them?

4. Does not my neglect of Saint Joseph arise from a certain misunderstanding of his mission, from a too superficial view of his role, from an instinctive reaction against apocryphal distortion of the facts or even simply from the difficulty my simple and limited logic has in integrating this devotion into my spirituality?

5. Do I appreciate that I have no right to deprive my priesthood of the special flow of graces which would come to me if I had a trusting devotion to Saint Joseph?

6. Have I not sought to reassure myself that it is better to pray to God than to the saints, forgetting their providential mission and the very desire of God who wishes us to approach him through and with his saints?

Resolutions

1. In my spiritual life and in my preaching to give to Saint Joseph the place that is his by right. Often to ask him to inspire me and to help me in the exercise of my spiritual paternity for those souls for whom I am responsible.

2. To wage war against the distressing caricature found in so many statues, so-called religious pictures, and manuals of piety which offend good taste and good sense, in everything about Saint Joseph.

3. In my preaching to depict Saint Joseph in his full stature as a man, as a father, and as a saint.

4. To unite myself sometimes with Saint Joseph to greet Our Lady. From time to time to recall with him the salutation of the Angel and that of Elizabeth. The "Hail Mary" said in union with Saint Joseph takes on a richer flavour.

5. To unite myself with him to say the "Our Father". Jesus must have taught it to him, and on his lips the words "Our Father" cannot fail to be profound.

6. To be united with his fundamental virtues which are so essential for the enrichment of my priesthood.

7. To believe in the power of Saint Joseph which God wishes to be made more and more manifest, but which depends for its development on our appeal. To confide in particular to Saint Joseph the great cause of the christianization of the worker's world, especially of the adult workers about whom we should all be concerned.

8. To recite more often the prayer to Saint Joseph which is found at the end of my breviary, in the thanksgiving after Mass.

9. To recommend to him all the dying, and to ask him now for his special protection when the hour comes for me to cross the great threshold.

Spiritual Reading

When Joseph was approaching the end of his life, his holiness reached its zenith. The virtues which from the beginning he had practised so conspicuously, then blossomed out in their fullness.

It was because of his manly integrity of soul and body that he received as spouse the woman who as a widow will be later entrusted to the innocence of Saint John. Contact with Mary, whom the Fathers hailed as "the root of virginity", only deepened his love of chastity. The influence of the Saviour, so veiled, so discreet, added to him that supernatural magnetism which had once sanctified John the Baptist in the womb of Elizabeth, and which later cured so many afflictions. Mortification, which Joseph practised to an heroic degree, did the rest. In short, he attained to that level of candour and detachment in which all that is created is assessed at its true value, and ceases being a snare to become a voice ringing out in the great symphony of mortals. In him purity finds again its essential meaning of transcendent simplicity.

He whom Jesus called his Father retained the charming ingenuousness of the heart of a child until his last day of life. Pride had no hold on him. He was a realist with clear and deep insight. He lived wholly for truth. He had relinquished any desire for prestige as far as family, fortune, or social position were concerned. A resident of a small town, a craftsman of no renown, an unostentatious existence were all that he desired to be. When Mary sang in the Magnificat of those who hunger, and of the humble she must have thought of Joseph. When she saw herself suddenly involved in the most sublime mysteries she drew closer to Joseph in the peaceful certainty of his littleness. On the stage where the incarnation unrolled its splendours he was like an actor without any lines, who is anxious to keep in the background. He is silent about the revelation of Gabriel. He buries in his solitary meditation the marvels of Bethlehem. After the prophecy of Simeon he disappears: we hear nothing of him until he finds the Child in the Temple. Do we realize how overwhelming it was to keep such a secret for so long? In this age of publicity and propaganda are we not amazed that neither scripture nor tradition has preserved a single word of the man who, after Mary, is the most perfect model of sanctity?

All true greatness is from within. His only thought is of the Lord; his only desire God's desire. He has no other light, no other rule of action. He breathes only for God. His every impulse is towards him. If Christ could say that he who does the will of

135

his Father in Heaven is his brother, his sister, and his Mother; if, taking up the interjection of a woman of the people, he praises Mary less for her glorious physical maternity than for her willingness to heed the message of the Most High, is it not right, to compare like Saint Augustine the complete surrender of himself by Joseph to a kind of spiritual generation, to a conception through faith which makes him truly a father and gives him the right to the title and privileges of that status? The parents of the Saviour were his parents in the loftiest sense of the term. Joseph his father in spirit only; Mary his mother in spirit and flesh.

Father Stephane Piat

Subjects for Discussion

1. In our own sphere is there an increase or reduction in devotion to Saint Joseph? What are the reasons for this?
2. In what sense and under what conditions can Saint Joseph make our love for our Lord and Our Lady increase?

Prayer

Lord Jesus, who lived so close to Joseph in your hidden life, teach me to understand him better, to love him more, to imitate him more closely. Through his example, through his intercession and through your grace, may I become more deeply united to you in the midst of the cares of daily life, and without any seeking for human reward, may I serve you in everything with a maximum of love and of humility, according to the desires of the heavenly Father, who lives and reigns with you in the unity of the Holy Spirit, for ever and ever. Amen.

Thought

Saint Joseph is the purest man in his virginity, the deepest in his humility, the most ardent in his charity, the most elevated in his contemplation.

Saint Bernardine of Sienna

8

OUR RESPONSIBILITIES TOWARDS
WOMEN RELIGIOUS

Meditation

To correct the opinion which too many of the faithful and too many Christian families hold about the religious vocation of young girls", said a recent report issued by the French hierarchy about the status of women religious today, "it is essential that the priest himself should be convinced of the excellence of religious perfection". In fact, how can a priest who does not esteem the religious life understand those who are called to it and help them effectively to conform to the demands of their state?

It is true that as long as we are on this earth, there will always be a gap between the ideal and the practical reality, but just as the discrepancies or errors of churchmen should not affect our faith in the Church, so weaknesses found here or there among religious and nuns should not lessen our respect for the religious life. There are sometimes strange errors or at least narrow-minded views expressed on this subject which can distort the idea which we ought to possess.

Let us try to see clearly and precisely what the religious life is not, what it is, and its place in the life of the Church.

The religious life is not a refuge for sinners. Certainly some sinners may be filled with the desire to make reparation. The grace of conversion has made them realize not merely the gravity of their offense but how they have offended the majesty of God. Having experienced a feeling of disgust for vain

137

pleasures, they thirst for the absolute which can lead them to seek admission to the religious life. But if the vocations of Magdalens are legitimate, they are not the only ones, and it would be a ridiculous simplification to look upon convents as nothing more than a refuge for repentant girls.

Neither is it a spiritual shelter for a weak nature. To be sure, a community affords a support. The rule, the traditions, the example of the sisters, the counsels of superiors are meant to guide, to encourage, to stimulate. But what a serious mistake to direct weak souls to the religious life on the grounds that it will shelter them from the world, and they will accordingly find it easier to save or sanctify themselves! In the convent, as in the world, there are temptations and there are trials. In the convent, as in the world, and perhaps more than in the world, energy, courage, and strength of will are required.

It is not an asylum for those who have lost hope or those who are suffering from frustrated love, or from disappointed hopes. God's ways are indeed not our ways, and sometimes he makes use of a setback to make his light flash forth, and to make his appeal felt. But, in general, we must distrust vocations inspired by disappointments, since a sudden improvement in their affairs will cause them to give up the religious life and return to the world.

It is not even an ecclesiastical organization for social service. It is true that the solidity afforded by their canonical rule, the strength of their organization, the stability which community life guarantees, the many varied objects which each order pursues, all enable the congregations of nuns to render outstanding practical services to the parishes in which they work, and in a general way, to society as a whole.

But if we were to look upon the religious life from an economic standpoint, and see it only as providing a valuable labour force which is reliable and relieves the clergy of a number of its responsibilities to the sick, to young children, to parish life, we would be reducing it to one of its incidental aspects and so obscure its essential reality. Need we go farther?

The religious life is one of apostleship. It helps us to love our neighbour and developes in us a pure missionary zeal. All the previous advantages we cited for social actions apply with

138

even greater force to apostolic action. Religious receive a training which makes them technically better equipped to work in the Master's vineyard. Yet we must not forget that good active laymen, married or single, can provide wonderful examples of charity, and radiate efficiency. Religious orders have no monopoly of such qualities.

What characterizes the religious life, and constitutes its distinctive element, is the final, complete and formal offering, in a community governed by rules given or approved by the Church, of all that one *is* by the vow of chastity, of all that one *has* by the vow of poverty, of all that one *does* by the vow of obedience. All this in recognition of the fact that God is everything and the creature completely dependent. The value of the exercises, the rules, the customs has been firmly established, and they must not be lightly changed, much less abandoned. On the other hand, they do not constitute the essence or the end of the religious life.

The essence of the religious life lies entirely in that sovereign, constant, irrevocable influence of the virtue of religion on the life and on the actions of those who have answered the divine call. "Since that critical day in my youth", wrote a young nun, "when I began to get a slight perception of what God was, how he alone is, that everything created only exists in him, that there is no shade of reality outside him, I understood that he alone counts, that we are made for him alone, that outside him there is no reason for living. And if I followed what I believed to be noble and beautiful in the world, I always found myself deceived and led back to him again. Finally, pursued by that thought of God, I entered the convent. I came to dedicate myself to him, to know him better, to love him more and unceasingly, and to let myself be taken over by him, obedience in my exterior existence matching fidelity to the Holy Spirit in my interior life. What I wish is to love the good God so much that there may be nothing left in me but God, that he may take possession of me and that all that remains of me may be an assent constantly renewed to my total adhesion to all that he has done and is in me."

The creature, and more especially the baptized creature, belongs *de jure* to God. But what comprises the value of the

139

religious life is that full ratification of baptism by virtue of which a soul, fully aware of what it does, declares before the Christian community, that he wishes to be *de facto* the exclusive property of God. It is that which makes Saint Thomas say that "religious profession is, after martyrdom, the most beautiful testimony of love". It is that which makes Suarez say that, "like martyrdom, it is a new baptism which blots out every trace of past sins".

To this free surrender of one's complete personality solemnly confirmed by God and ratified by the Church, correspond the graces of the religious state which reserve the human being completely for the service of God alone. To be a professed religious is to render formally to God, in the name of humanity and for the duration of one's life, the worship which is his due, the greatest worship, through the practice of the evangelical counsels. It is for every religious and every nun not only a mission, a command, a function, but a consecration, a segregation, a specific state; it is not only their reason for action, but their reason for being in the Church.

The religious life appears first of all as a corporate testimony of prime importance. Commanded directly by the truth that God is all and that everything leads to him, is not the religious life the strongest, the most complete, the most manifest assertion of the supreme importance of God? This assertion is most salutary for society, as Cardinal Suhard says. "Human dignity is the first victim when religious sense declines!" This assertion is all the more necessary as it has become the fashion to doubt supernatural realities.

Our's is a technical world, without room for spirituality or abstract reflection. Everything is reduced to graphs, to slide rules, to data, to numbers, to case histories; everything is a matter of technique; even things of the highest spiritual values like the individual, the family, the Church itself. Physical, chemical, biological, nuclear, psychological, sociological, historical sciences suppress all mysteries and our world is less and less acclimatized to accept the supernatural message of incarnate love.

For Christians themselves the testimony of the religious life is of capital importance, as it prevents their sense of the divine

140

transcendence from being dulled in the pagan world into which they are plunged. How many practising Christians have perverted in themselves the sense, the understanding of the true God, considering him as at the service of man rather than considering themselves as being at the service of God! For some, God is the fond grandfather who pardons and excuses everything; to them hell and sin are myths. For others, God is an idea, useful for the social order; the divine laws are abstract and impersonal barriers, which are binding only in so far as they do not conflict with society; the individual is free to judge and to interpret them. For others, God is a distant and creative entity, who gives life a meaning, who owes us everything and to whom we owe nothing, whom we approach when we are in need, whom we invoke in misfortune, but whom we are content to by-pass when everything is going according to plan.

As for active Catholics themselves, many fall equally into the danger of activism. Religion for them is restricted to the building up of human society, to stopping social injustices, to developing personalities. We forget that the Kingdom of God is not of this world, that the primary duty of man is that of adoration. Some people would reduce the primacy of mystical theology to an ethical code of well-being and of good humour. They cheerfully look upon the Beatitudes as a play upon words; they consider the indefeasible law of asceticism as a disastrous mutilation of personality: if you do not do penance, you shall all perish. The fundamental meaning of the liturgy, which is the service of God, gives place to that of mere teaching and instructing.

An act of pure love towards God, the religious offering is a reparative act of the first order, by virtue of the hidden network which, through the communion of saints, unites souls so mysteriously. Through poverty it makes reparation for the inordinate love of money; through chastity, for lust in all its forms; through obedience, for all the rebellion and pride of men. Thus, this life of offering is inscribed in the life of the Church, and helps to give the Spouse of Christ its note of

141

mystical ability for the accomplishment of the divine wish for love and redemption.

God does not wish to act alone. To honour his creature he makes him his associate. It is true that all who are baptized are destined to work with him in the work of salvation, and in their different states of life, each of them from near or afar, by his pain as well as by his joy, helps in the work of redemption. But their commitment is limited since each of them keeps, at least in part, the freedom to dispose of himself. That is why our Lord, whose love, although it respects a partial response, always seeks a complete one and invites a certain number of privileged souls to renounce absolutely and unreservedly a divided life in order to consecrate themselves to the salvation of the world, by a complete and final gift of themselves.

The fact that some souls are not faithful to their ideal and gradually withdraw what they once offered completely is regrettable. *Corruptio optimi pessima.* "The best, when corrupted, become the worst." On earth the very best things can secrete poisons, collective pride can unfortunately balance heroic efforts for individual humility – touchiness can coincide with a generous and ardent desire for perfection – routine and the narrowing of our horizon can be found with the minutest fidelity to observances, the spirit of which we have gradually lost. On the other hand, as Monsignor d'Hulst has said: "There is great danger that within us a professional attitude will progressively supplant the spirit of Jesus and the gift of ourselves to him." For those who are teaching, there is always the risk, after a certain time, of becoming teachers rather than priests; for those working in hospitals, there is the risk of becoming more of a nurse than a religious; for a Carmelite, of becoming more bound up in herself than in being a contemplative missionary according to the spirit of Saint Teresa; for a superior, of becoming an organizer rather than a real spiritual director.

It is not the weakness, nor the laxity, nor even the desertion of a few sisters which reduces the value of religious congregations as a whole and the splendour of their mission. If nuns live up to the spirit of their profession, if they long for God with all their being, they open up the world to God by surrendering themselves to his action – as Father François de Sainte Marie

142

put it: "The Lord, in his exquisite courtesy, awaits this consent, just as he awaited the *fiat* of Mary, before descending into the heart of the universe."

Finally, and this is a point on which we can never insist sufficiently, nuns, dedicated as they are to pay homage to the divine transcendence, usually find in God an increased understanding of their neighbour. If they share the feelings of Christ Jesus, will they like him reconcile concern for his Father's business with devotion to his human brothers? The second commandment is like the first and effective love for our neighbour is the clearest proof of our love for God. It is a fact that, without being primarily and fundamentally directed towards the service of men, the religious life, through the centuries, has overflowed in active charity to reach the members of Christ.

"Compassion for our neighbour", said Saint John of the Cross, "increases as our soul is more closely united to God by love, for the more our soul loves Jesus, the more it desires that Jesus should be loved by everyone and itself loves everything in Jesus and Jesus in everything." Truly, "living man is the glory of God", as Saint Ireneus said. Service of our neighbour is only an expression of that "praise of glory" which primarily every family of religious is supposed to be.

Father Bouveresse said: "To relieve misery, to cure, to instruct, to pacify, to make justice and love reign, is to render glory to God, and allow him to share the benefits of his Kingdom. So the Sister of Charity does not nurse to convert: she nurses, that is all; she pays homage to God and gives testimony to God, whose glory it is to make his sun shine on all, the good and the bad. She belongs to God and gives help in her works of mercy as well as in her prayers."

As priests we have thus a duty to foster vocations to the religious life, to work for the sanctification of nuns, and to encourage them to pursue the aims laid down by their rule.

God can call anyone he wishes, and sometimes he calls children whose home environment offers no encouragement. These are divine paradoxes which testify to the absolute liberty

143

of his choice. Normally, however, parents have the basic responsibility for vocations. Not in the sense that they should push their children into the religious life, but that they should make their home conducive to the flowering of vocations. Also they should do nothing which might prevent any of their children from answering a serious call from God. Many parents need to be better informed, both about the grandeur of the religious state, and about the respect they should have for the personal vocation of each of their children as the basis for their true happiness. Is this not a subject we should discuss both in our sermons and in retreats for engaged and young married couples?

In one of his pastoral letters Monsignor Béguin, Archbishop of Auch, wrote of vocations: "Sometimes there are on this earth strange wrongs, inexplicable blindnesses. For some people, who describe themselves as Christians, but who are clearly only nominal ones, a religious vocation is the worst calamity which can strike a child; if it occurs they set about stifling it by every means, however improper and even criminal. Have we not sometimes seen mothers of families, in desperate straits because their daughter had expressed the desire to go into a convent, expose her quite deliberately to the most dangerous occasions of sin? Have we not seen fathers of families threaten their child with the worst reprisals if she persists in her wish to be a nun, and try to stop her in her ambition by threatening, in revenge, to turn aside from God the innocent soul of a little brother or sister?"

Some parents who would willingly see one of their sons become a priest are reluctant to consider a religious vocation for their daughter. There is certainly plenty of scope for our attention.

In a general way we can say that God, who loves this poor world so much, multiplies his appeals. But as with the seed in the Gospel, the grace of a vocation often falls on stony ground and is choked by thorns. Many talented children, whom God wished for himself, have not been able to recognize his invitation because of the superficial character of their faith; or, indeed, have let the precious seeds penetrate their heart, only to stunt their growth by their fear of effort or sacrifice with a

144

consequent loss for the spiritualization of humanity. It is important, then, to develop in children, from the time that they begin the catechism, the understanding of the greatness of God, and it is at this stage that the cultivation of a living and practical faith is as important as the cultivation of courage and charity.

Many examples from the childhood of holy nuns (like Saint Thérèse of Lisieux) could illustrate that elementary truth so often forgotten: many more children than we think are ready to acquire a life of real union with God, provided someone shows them the way. Most of them are equally capable of a great generosity in the matter of small sacrifices provided that someone with the necessary prudence knows how to encourage them. Our priestly activity, whether in the catechism class or the confessional, will be crucial. We must not forget that faith is contagious, so is the spirit of sacrifice. "God does not work without men", Canon Leclercq has written, "and as soon as a man of God appears, vocations spring up in his path, vocations that are genuine even if they are inspired by him."

Finally, for those who have reached the age of adolescence, so favourable to self-dedication and to the choice of a noble cause, organize retreats, where recollection and meditation encourage personal contact with God, and predispose the soul to direct its life according to the will of God.

The aforementioned report of the French hierarchy insists on the following point. "The clergy must take particular care to mitigate the consequences of an excessive and unbalanced propaganda in favour of Christian marriage; they must not hesitate to teach that virginity consecrated to God is superior to the married state." We must certainly not minimize the greatness of marriage. For too long marriage has been a sort of poor relation – some people have almost considered it as a concession to human weakness. It is one of the graces of our day that we have plumbed its beauty and sanctifying richness. But, as always, reaction tends to pass the point of equilibrium and soon gets to the stage of exalting the conjugal state at the expense of the religious life.

"A good religious vocation does not proceed from any contempt of marriage. Indeed, more, a religious vocation is not perfect unless we have chosen it with a full understanding, with a clear appreciation of the happiness and to nobility of marriage. We see in marriage a lofty vocation, an instrument of perfection, the work of man *par excellence,* the natural condition of the blossoming of the human race, the normal basis for Christian expansion, but nevertheless choose the religious vocation because we realize that it is in the divine alone that human renunciation finds complete satisfaction." The vow of consecrated celibacy is the act by which we renounce this human perfection for that perfection which surpasses nature and is justified only on the purely supernatural plane by the offering to God of the whole of our life.

"Some well-meaning writers", says Monsignor Gegout, "talk very carelessly about the 'vocation of marriage'. We must protest against this inaccuracy. There is no 'vocation of marriage'. It is something much more than this: there is a 'universal destiny for marriage'. Every human being is destined first of all to live the life he has received, then to transmit it. If he is normal, he will inevitably feel the urge to fulfil this law. A vocation does not annihilate those deep natural desires nor does it extinguish all attraction towards marriage. A vocation leads us to a more perfect life, it is an invitation to renounce marriage, 'in full knowledge and of our free choice because of a greater love and to a higher service'."

We can see how serious the exceptional attitude described by Pierre Le Frontalier can be. It is the story of two young girls who told their parish priest of their impending entry into a convent. The priest burst out: "Today, we do not need nuns, but Christian homes. By such homes our country will be regenerated, re-christianized; to enter religion would be a mistake, a grave mistake; marriage is a duty, the most important duty."

The French hierarchy's report made the following recommendation. "The clergy, regular as well as secular, must show esteem, devotion, gratitude to congregations and communities of nuns; they will consider it a point of honour to correct the criticisms which are often made in unjustifiable ignorance of the facts about religious life." We never know the harm we can do in criticizing or in speaking ironically about nuns, above all before a young and enthusiastic soul. But it is not enough to avoid what is negative. If we ask for prayers for vocations to the

146

priesthood we should also ask for prayers for vocations among women.

Let us consider the different kinds of women we must prepare. First of all there are those generous young girls who are both fervent and balanced, but, through timidity, have never dared to consider the complete gift of themselves to God. Just a little encouragement, or simply an opportunity to discuss the question would be enough for them to recognize that their interior aspirations correspond with the call of grace. Just as we must avoid "compulsory enrolment", so we must avoid "the principle of silence" when our priesthood gives us the vocational grace of proposing to souls of good will the possibility of the divine call.

There are other young girls who, of themselves, have considered the problem honestly. It is quite normal for a director to examine the seriousness of such a vocation, and in particular to make sure of the intention underlying it. It is his province to find out if the postulant really has the qualities of judgement and stability, spirituality and charity, humility and strong courage without which she is likely to be unable to persevere in community life.

It is true that we do not enter religion because we are perfect, but because we want to give God all our love and all our good will in order to become perfect. But it is essential that we should have over and above the right intention, the minimum of natural and supernatural qualities, without which we are heading for certain failure.

Today in particular, we can meet young girls who blithely think that they have the vocation to be Superior Generals, if not reformers of the Church! "It is renunciation", says Monsignor Gegout, "humility, the spirit of submission, confidence in the Church, which are the surest marks of a vocation." It is equally the province of the director to help a soul decide when she should seek admission as a postulant. In some cases, for example, where there is an evident lack of maturity, a delay will be desirable. In others, to defer acting on a vocation without very strong reason, can be an abuse of grace, by letting the providential hour pass by. "A vocation postponed, is a vocation lost", says the old adage. That is where the priest must be

147

particularly tactful, begging fervently for the light of the Holy Spirit, and ensuring he is not swayed by his personal preferences, or considerations extrinsic to the real welfare of the postulant.

"It is important for the clergy to make it their duty to respect scrupulously a real religious vocation, and not seek to hold a candidate back for the benefit of the parish or of some form of Catholic Action." It is the duty of the spiritual director to help candidates to choose the order which is most suited to their aptitudes and aspirations. Normally our Lord makes it clear by providential circumstances in which community these souls will best develop. Sometimes, however, it falls to the spiritual father to consider the various orders (contemplative, nursing, missionary, teaching) capable of suiting a particular individual. While we should take every care to get accurate information about their purpose and the training given, we are not called on to learn about every order before we choose. If, in order to make a choice, we had to instruct ourselves about everything that exists, none of us would ever enter religion. There comes a time when we have to make an act of faith in divine providence.

The report of the French hierarchy gives the following directives. "The clergy cannot ignore the fact that it is from the priest that the religious expect an enlightenment on the obligations as well as the privileges of the state of evangelical perfection. The direction of nuns is to be looked upon as a special ministry, a particularly delicate one, which must be carried out with due preparation and attention, if we are to avoid the risk of grave prejudice to the souls concerned."

In practice it can happen that once professed, nuns are less nourished spiritually than active laymen. We ourselves know from experience that a priest cannot be content to live on the knowledge he acquired in the seminary. After a few years he feels very keenly the necessity to renew himself, both intellectually and spiritually, and he knows very well that if he does not keep up his spiritual vitality by one means or another, study, personal meditation, conferences, seminars, and retreats, he will end more or less hardened and sterile.

In the same way, religious cannot be content with the knowledge they acquired in the novitiate, nor even in their annual retreat. Having more responsibilities, by virtue of their dedicated state, they have the right to a stronger nourishment than the simple faithful, or even active laymen. Very often we criticize or complain of them. But do we do sufficient for them?

The distinguished priest who writes under the name of Pierre de Frontalier puts the question with deep concern. "We are all a little troubled by the spiritual neglect to which country priests are condemned; counter-measures have been taken by regular days of recollection. These have been, and continue to be of inestimable good. Some dioceses even have a chaplain for the clergy, whose extreme usefulness is well known. But is there the same concern for religious and nuns who live in small communities, very far from their mother house, without any other spiritual resources than can be obtained locally and may be almost non-existent. Is anything done to assure them of a minimum of vital spirituality? Preachers of annual retreats, who receive the confidences of these religious, could say a great deal on this subject if they were not under a pledge of secrecy. If these religious and nuns dared to speak frankly, for what would they ask? They would probably ask for the following. Not to be overworked to such an extent that they are deprived of time for the regular and full fulfilment of their spiritual exercises; to be given enough leisure to seek and to find God in prayer. To be assured of the opportunity of going to confession as often as their rule requires, or as often as they need; to obtain from their confessor something more than bare absolution; to obtain from him the light, the comfort, the encouragement, the direction so indispensable in their isolation.

"To have the freedom to speak, at least occasionally, for the peace of their conscience, to a priest of their choice; for this freedom to be real and not theoretical; for this freedom which is their guaranteed right to be practically and easily enjoyed; for the exercise of this freedom not to be obstructed by conflicts of influence or personal jealousies; for the fact that they take advantage of a priest's visit not to be met by reproaches, sullenness, or a stormy atmosphere.

149

"For the parish priest to take proper steps to give, or invite an experienced priest to give conferences, or better still, complete days of recollection. If this is not a practicable proposition for a small community, why not bring together occasionally, all the small Communities in an area, even if they belong to different religious orders?"

All this is the more important as the combination of the religious with the apostolic life is a very delicate problem in the modern world. Nuns who teach, or work in hospitals, must be technically qualified and understand the world and the social pressures which influence it; on the other hand, they must not cease to make progress with the complete gift of themselves to God, if they really wish to bring God close to them. This is possible only if their life is infused with a powerful blend of asceticism and mysticism.

These, then, are the devoted services the priest must assure the religious communities which rely on him for help. He must, however, never forget the cardinal virtue of prudence. It is not a question of affecting a lofty manner, but of being faithful to the traditional rules of priestly reserve. When we have had a little experience of life we appreciate the reasons for this.

Without an express mandate from the bishop, we must take care not to interfere in the interior government of communities. The superiors are responsible for that, and nine times out of ten, when a priest is carried away by good intentions and wishes to meddle in what does not concern him, and above all to take the part of an individual nun he only confuses the situation, prevents the inevitable minor difficulties from righting themselves, upsets the normal flow of community life, and is liable to strengthen factions and coteries, and himself to become the victim of these divisions. It is the positive strengthening of the spirit of faith and of real charity which assures the full development of the spirit of religion, and it is that which, above all, nuns expect from us.

In the course of time the Lord has raised up religious orders for all needs. All of them have one essential aim: to proclaim the divine transcendence, to bring everything back to God, to share (as far as it is possible for a human creature) the very holiness of God. But the sanctity of God is a burning charity.

And that is why, in one way or another, the secondary end of every religious congregation is directed towards the spiritual or corporal service of their neighbours: closed retreats, hospitals, care of the sick, teaching, care of the aged, work with prisoners, catechism classes, parochial or educational duties and so on. The important thing for the priest called to serve nuns is to help them, to encourage them to follow the aims laid down by their rule, for in it they will find the greatest source of grace for their work in the service of the Church.

We have to respect the varied action of the Holy Spirit, and nothing would be more contrary to it than to wish to bring the life of all congregations into line with a particular way of spirituality or a particular form of activity which we ourselves prefer.

We must indeed desire, and, in so far as we are authorized to do so, suggest any adaptations required by current conditions and any flexibility which is called for by modern temperaments. To be static, to show hostility to any legitimate change is to be unfaithful to the spirit of the founder through material fidelity to the letter of his or her rule.

But that does not mean that we must bow before every caprice or fancy. Remember what the Pope said about the expression "keeping up to date". "Yes", he said, "be up to date, provided you don't make this an excuse for tearing up the precious book of tradition, destroying the earlier pages, as one tear off the leaves of a calendar."

On the apostolic plane, the collaboration of the religious communities and the secular clergy is always a delicate problem. Both should show tact, understanding, mutual confidence. It is on this note that the report of the meeting of the French hierarchy ends. "It is important that the clergy should know how to give the nuns a share in the life of the parish without asking them to carry out apostolic responsibilities which are more properly the work of laymen."

Then again, there are many excesses to avoid. We must not oversimplify the problem by paying no attention to what the nuns do, letting them act as they please, "to keep the peace", without exercising the least control, and even without demanding any reports. On the other hand we must not crush them with our attention, confiding them with so many different responsibilities that we overload them, and deprive the parochial and apostolic life of the precious assistance of the laity.

Here it is that the priest will find the point of equilibrium by creating an atmosphere of confidence in the service of Christ himself, by increasing in everyone a better understanding of the Church and the spirit of loyal and disinterested collaboration with all.

Here, too, the priest will act wisely, knowing how to make judicious use of every form of skill, and encouraging both their technical proficiency and the growth of their religious spirit. For directly allied to God and inexplicable without him, the religious vocation borrows from the divine a radicalism which does not permit mediocrity. It is God alone and his Kingdom that must be sought in everything and through everything. It is for him alone that we must equip ourselves to give more effective service. It is he alone who makes the unity, the beauty, and the fruitfulness of all lives which have been surrendered to him.

Christ speaks to his Priest

Hold the religious life in great esteem. Have a great respect for souls consecrated to me. They work for the glory of my Father, for the good of my Church, for the exalted service of my love throughout the world. If they are faithful to their vocation, they wield great influence over my heart. They have as their first duty the task of continuing Mother's work in the world. Like her they can, by their life of prayer and sacrifice, in union with my prayer and unceasing oblation, dispense the infinite treasures of my redemption.

You ought to help them live in the spirit of their vocation, and show them the demands as well as the splendour of their mission. You should teach them to see only me in everything and in every one. You should take care to stir up their faith, raise up their hope, and breathe divine charity into them. Precious graces for yourself and for your brothers in the priesthood will be the first fruits of their loyalty to the appeals of my Heart.

It is in their hands that much of the salvation of mankind rests. It is in the intimacy of their souls that much of the destiny of the world is worked out. As evil was given access to humanity by a woman, so salvation came to the world by a woman. It is also to a great extent on her that I make the abundance of my graces for the Church depend. As my Mother's acceptance permitted me to become man, so the manner in which consecrated souls live their lives enables me to multiply priestly and missionary vocations.

It was my Mother's acceptance of Calvary which allowed me to entrust Saint John to her, and through him all priests throughout the ages. It is the ardent cry "Thy will be done" of souls uniting themselves generously with my Passion which allows me to multiply graces of faith and holiness for the good of priests, and through them for all souls in their care. It was my Mother's prayers, assisted by those of holy women, which, in the upper chamber, helped hesitant and fearful apostles to receive the plenitude of that Spirit which transformed them into intrepid missionaries. It is the prayers of nuns which brings my Church the fervent priests whom my Heart needs to renew the face of the earth. That is why they must understand the importance of their mission and be enlightened as to its fulfilment. In the Church the role of women must be discreet, and often it is hidden, but it remains an essential part. For my kingdom is within. It is precisely through the interior spirit that my kingdom comes. "The Kingdom of God is within you."

Examination of Conscience

1. Have I all the respect for nuns that an enlightened priest should?

2. Am I not inclined to generalize, basing my conclusions on the deficiencies or mistakes of individuals, while I am the first to complain when I hear hostile generalizations made on the basis of the failings of an individual priest?

3. Have I not observed that if nuns are not fervent, the responsibility often rests with the priests who failed to give them the necessary spiritual direction?

4. Have I not been inclined, under the form of pleasantries or of seemingly innocent raillery, to make uncalled-for criticisms

about nuns, forgetting that the respect which they owe to the clergy forbids them to reply in the same manner? Is it not true, moreover, that priests who indulge in these attacks lose their respect very rapidly and run the risk of discouraging them?

5. Do I observe respectful reserve in language and behaviour?

6. Am I willing to give nuns the help, encouragement, and spiritual instruction which they need, taking care to adapt my instructions to their spirituality and their particular vocation?

7. Do I try to develop in them love for their founder and a confident obedience towards their superiors, at the same time increasing their understanding of the universal Church and encouraging a spirit of obedience towards the hierarchy?

8. Do I pray and do I ask prayers for the increase of religious vocations and for the sanctification of religious communities?

9. Do I seek the prayers and the sacrifices of nuns, especially contemplatives, to obtain more abundant blessings from God on my work?

Resolutions

1. To pray that the religious life may be better understood and implemented. This will bring our contemporaries an awareness of the primacy of God's rights which they need so badly.

2. To pray and to get prayers said for the increase of religious vocations, especially in my diocese and parish.

3. To neglect no opportunity of showing the importance of the mission entrusted to nuns, both on the supernatural and the natural level.

4. To avoid casting the least discredit on nuns. If, here or there, some desirable adaptations or changes are needed, it is not extreme criticism that will bring them about. If we wish to upset usages and customs indiscriminately and without the gradual creation of a favourable atmosphere, we merely repeat the action of those who wanted to pluck the tares before the

harvest was ripe. If we try to go too quickly, we are liable to suppress without replacing, and to rebel without helping anyone. The Church is wise·in being slow, which does not mean that worthwhile proposals must not receive encouragement.

5. If I have nuns in my parish, to do my best to ensure, with the necessary reserve and discretion, a confident collaboration in the service of the Lord. To avoid misunderstanding, to remember that prevention is better than cure. To define, if appropriate in writing, for the superior, everything that ought to be understood: respective rights and duties; the scope and the limits of the mission entrusted to them.

6. In case of difficulties, never to give vent to my displeasure before the faithful. There will always be good souls who think they are doing good by reporting my statements, sometimes with amplifications and distortions. Not to complain to superiors at a higher level without doing our best to iron out the difficulty with the local superior. If there is no solution, always to warn her that we are going to invoke the intervention of higher authority.

7. To put myself willingly at the service of nuns, to help them to acquire all the skills which can be useful to them. To make them a definite part of parochial life, to admit them to councils or committees on which they can play so valuable a part. To define the form of their collaboration with Catholic Action.

8. To encourage nuns to take part in days of recollection, training courses, congresses, and study days. As the quality of their service will benefit by it, not to hesitate to let the parish assume responsibility for at least part of the cost of their studies or incidental expenses.

9. To take care, in collaboration with their superiors and in the spirit of their constitutions, that they avoid overwork, which would be as harmful for their spiritual life and their life in the community, as for their physical health. To teach them in particular the art of helping themselves!

10. To facilitate the union of minds and of hearts, with the organizations and the other religious communities in the parish.

155

Spiritual Reading

1. To correct the attitude shown by too many of the faithful concerning the religious vocation of young girls, it is important that the priest should himself be convinced of the essential excellence of the religious life. On this point, suitable training should be given in the seminary.

2. The clergy must take particular care to reduce the effect of an excessive and unbalanced propaganda about the legitimate spirituality of Christian marriage; the priest must not hesitate to teach the superiority of virginity consecrated to God over the state of marriage.

3. It is important that the clergy make it a duty to respect an authentic religious vocation scrupulously and not seek to delay its fulfilment for the benefit of the parish or some form of Catholic Action.

4. When deciding about the vocation of a young girl, parish clergy, chaplains and confessors must always remember the excellence of a life consecrated entirely to God by the practice of the evangelical counsels, as well as the advantages and the security offered by entrance into a religious or secular institute canonically approved by the Church.

The regular as well as the secular clergy must show esteem, devotion, and gratitude to congregations and communities of nuns; they must regard it as a point of honour to refute critics who have spoken to them in what is often an unjustifiable ignorance of the truth about convent life.

It must not be forgotten that it is from the priest that nuns expect an enlightened knowledge of the obligations as well as the privileges of their state of evangelical perfection. In particular, the clergy have a duty to consider the collective and personal responsibility for nuns which devolves upon them and their obligation to fulfil exactly the duties which Canon law imposes on them as superiors, confessors, chaplains, preachers. Ministering to nuns is to be valued as a special ministry and a particularly delicate one which must be carried out with due preparation and attention if we are to avoid the risk of grave prejudice to the souls concerned.

156

In this respect, it seems fitting to recommend the appointment in each diocese of a priest or of several priests, both for the spiritual care of religious communities of women, and for the training of the parochial clergy in their duties as ordinary or extraordinary confessors, and in preaching to nuns; an important place in pastoral publications for the use of the clergy, to enlighten and assist them in their ministry to nuns; a more active participation by the regular clergy, who are familiar with the practice of religious life, and who are often linked to congregations of nuns by ties of spiritual affinity. Finally, it is important that the clergy should know how to bring nuns into the activities of the parish, without asking them to carry out apostolic responsibilities which are more properly the work of laymen.

Report of the French hierarchy, March, 1949

Subjects for Discussion

1. What are the advantages, for the good of souls, of a trusting collaboration between the clergy and nuns?

2. Under what conditions can we participate in this?

Prayer

Lord Jesus, who wished holy women to gather round your Mother, to pray and to devote themselves to the service of the young Church, and who, at a later stage, accepted the consecration of virgins in the religious life, deign to bless and to sanctify all souls of good will whom you have called to this life of complete self-sacrifice. Grant me and all my colleagues the grace never to put an obstacle in the way of the realization of a true vocation.

Deign to grant us the grace of discovering them and of helping them effectively to direct their lives in accordance with your will. And grant, O Lord, that all the nuns throughout the world may so live that they may encourage the faithful to a more holy life, and give unbelievers a patent testimony of your immense love, you who live and reign with the Father in the unity of the Holy Spirit for ever and ever. Amen.

Thought

We do not enter religion because we are perfect, but because we wish to become perfect.

Saint Thomas Aquinas

9

THE PRIEST AND OLD PEOPLE

The priest is at everyone's service without exception. He must not exclude anyone from his ministry. "All things to all men", the motto of Saint Paul, must be his motto, too. But life is demanding. "Priests must go to those most in need and to urgent cases." It is said they prepare the future. Are not the youth of today the men of tomorrow? They must go to those who influence public opinion. Have not adults the right of priority? Then there are the sick, the dying who so often cannot wait.

In short, our attention is so divided that if it is not drawn by a specific appeal, we are liable to leave in oblivion a whole group of people which is becoming more and more numerous and has great need of our attention and help.

Meditation

At the beginning of this meditation let us adore the divine Master who bids us place ourselves at the service of everyone, to imitate him in his availability to all. "Him that cometh to me I will not cast out." (John 6:37) He even extends a special invitation to those who are overburdened by age, worries and sickness. "Come to me, all you who labour and are burdened." (Matt. 11:28) Let us ask him the secret of meeting all these obligations. That is a secret of love of which he possesses the solution. "Charity bears all things, endures all things." (1 Cor. 13:7)

Let us examine the reasons why we should interest ourselves in the aged, and the duties which we have towards them. We should be concerned about old people because they are becoming more and more numerous; they are often alone and abandoned, if not materially, at least morally; and they have a mission in the Mystical Body which we should help them to fulfil.

The problem of the aged is an acute one today. For a century, thanks to the progress of hygiene, surgery and medicine, the span of life has been considerably extended. Many illnesses which a few years ago would have been considered fatal, are today cured. Science can achieve happy results when directed to the service of humanity. Under Napoleon III the average expectation of life in France was thirty-eight years. In this half of the twentieth century it is over sixty. The sexagenarians constitute nearly one fifth of the adult population, and it is forecast that in a few years they will be a quarter. We should rejoice in this longevity which allows affection for our loved ones to be shown for a longer time, allows them more time to merit grace, and thus to work effectively for the good of the Mystical Body.

The increasing number of old people, however, brings pastoral problems which we have no right to neglect. They are often alone and abandoned, if not materially, at least morally. When in a society the aged are few they assume the appearance of patriarchs, and they are the object of care and veneration. Formerly, men loved to hear them relate family traditions and to profit by their experience, which the slower evolution of ideas and techniques made more valuable. Monetary and economic stability normally allowed those who had reached an advanced age to live on the savings they had accumulated, and not be too great a burden on the younger members of their family. Today, all that is changed. As the number of aged people has grown out of proportion to the number of adult workers, the support of the old imposes on their children a much more considerable burden, so that the young people are more and more inclined to free themselves of the burden and to transfer it to the community. The savings of a lifetime no longer assure security for old age. Private charity has also experienced a substantial reduction in its contributions. The social services themselves can

160

give only a small amount. Hostels and old people's homes are overcrowded.

On the other hand, in spite of genuine but inadequate legislative efforts, there are still too many dying of hunger in unheated attics, or weary of suffering, sinking into despair. Even if, due to fortunate circumstances, the old do not lack anything material, they are more apt to suffer morally than in the past. The young, in the fullness of their health, do not always allow for the many weaknesses which the years bring on, and which often account for a morose disposition, frequent complaints, or demands that are almost tyrannical.

With the swift pace of the modern world, old people, who find it more difficult because of their age to adjust themselves to circumstances, are often quick to lose their moral authority and are no longer capable of giving proper advice. They soon display to their younger visitors a combination of lassitude and self-pity. This slowing down aggravates their feeling of loneliness. Soon, they feel that they are not understood. Unhappily, they do not find always sufficient compensation in the company of men or women of their own age, for complaints against the modern world are not sufficient to link hearts that are more inclined to brood on their past achievements than to develop rewarding friendships.

A community of old people often has a sad atmosphere because, concerned as they are with themselves and their past, life in common is made even more painful by egotism. Even the psychology of today demands of the old specific qualities of spirituality, and a generous effort of charity for others based on forgetfulness of self and a willingness to adapt themselves which is particularly meritorious. It is becoming for us to help them in this crucial period which, according to the guidance given to their thinking, can be the most beautiful or the most wretched of their life.

The period during which the physical forces decline can in fact be, with God's grace, the period in which power of the soul increases. Something would be lacking in human greatness if the aged no longer knew how to make visible in some way the triumph of the soul over the body. It is in this, rather than in the experience acquired throughout life, that the majesty of old

161

age resides. It is because of this that it commands admiration and respect.

Old age is for those who reach it a stage in God's plan which should contribute not only to their spiritual good, but to the general good of humanity. Youth, even with the hopes which it represents, maturity, even with the strength it commands, does not constitute the whole of the Mystical body. Old age is also an integral part of it; it is united to Christ, it prolongs him, it expresses him, in its own particular way.

The treasure of divine thought is infinite. If old age lets itself be penetrated and infused by Christ, the incarnation is accomplished in it, and the Mystical Body can attain its full stature. If old age refuses to assist God's design, the Mystical Body of Christ will suffer a reduction. The life which emanates from it will not reach all humanity, it will experience something akin to the hardening of the arteries, and we all know that the whole body suffers when life stops circulating in one of its limbs.

The very approach of death gives old age, when lived in a Christian way, its full grandeur. Old age is in fact a prison only if endured with bad grace. When it is understood and accepted, it is a liberation. What does it matter if the old man is chained to his armchair, his bed, or his fireside, if he remains free for spiritual inspiration and so contributes to the elevation of the world towards God, since "every soul that raises itself elevates the world".

"For the Christian", said Father Sertillange, "old age is not a recoiling from the thirst to live, on the contrary, it is an increase and a confirmation of hope. It is proximity to what was only forecast and foreshadowed by our active life. It is a land which appears on the horizon after a distant voyage. It is the veil of illusion which falls away, disclosing the supreme realities to our gaze. Old age is the approach of God."

"When we grow old", said Bazin, "everything departs but God comes. It is our role to facilitate this approach and this meeting for the benefit of the old and for the greater good of the souls united to them."

Our duties to old people are to understand them, to love them, and to help them. To understand them is to understand their

162

psychology, their sufferings, their temptations. Characteristic of the old is the increasing knowledge of a weakening of their powers. Sight becomes less penetrating, hearing less acute, hands less skilful, legs less sure; the heart, the lungs, and the other internal organs require more attention, and get tired more quickly; the memory loses its accuracy, the intelligence its penetration and its quickness. This deterioration in itself may not be too inconvenient for them, but infirmities lie in wait for them and few escape them.

There is another sad feature about old age: the relative loss of liberty, the need to accept dependence. "Day after day the old must have recourse to the help of others; less and less can they go where they want to, do what they wish, when they want to; in varying degrees, all of which are painful, they depend on the devotion of those around them. This is an importunate subjection to which there may be very different reactions. Some old people cling fiercely to the last vestiges of their independence. They prefer to do without the help they need rather than admit themselves defeated. Others resign themselves readily but take their revenge by their demands on those around them. To make sure they miss nothing, they enlist every one's services. Their unreasonable requests often exceed the limits of the help they really need."

There is a serious risk that the aged will become superlatively egotistical, and only be willing to discuss themselves, their suffering and their past. Reacting against the fact that everything is slipping away, some become avaricious. The character of Molière's Harpagon is classical as well as ridiculous. Saint Thomas says: "Old people, whose powers are diminishing, seek with even greater enthusiasm the help which exterior goods can give them in the same way that every beggar is in search of anything that will compensate for his indigence."

The failing of natural powers can lead to vices. Some try to sustain their strength by drinking. In others the fear that they are failing engenders a sensuality which is all the more pitiable as it leads to real disasters. Their basic anxiety makes them fall into a childish touchiness which does not secure them the satisfaction to which they think they have a right, and is the cause of the complaints and whining which cause their family such distress. Finally, as a compensation for the inferiority complex caused by their physical deterioration, they take refuge in the memory of their glorious past, at least of the time when they felt at the apex of their power. There is nothing which gives an old man more pleasure than to tell you about his memories. But as his memory of what is happening grows weaker, he relates the same stories to the same people after a few days without realizing he is doing so.

It is precisely because they suffer, because they feel their solitude more than others, because they are approaching the time their powers will weaken, because they are more sensitive to the lack of consideration, that they have a particular right to our affection. Are we not dedicated by our vocation, first of all to the poor, to those who lack wealth or love? So often they lack both.

To love them means to forget our cares in order to think of theirs, to listen again and again to the same stories, to try to arrange little thoughtful surprises for them, those delicate attentions, which cost so little and which give them so much pleasure, even when they show in return for them very little gratitude. Let us recall the reaction of the old, infirm, rather cross-grained Sister of whom Saint Thérèse had taken charge. The young Carmelite received little encouragement, little gratitude from her old patient; nevertheless one day the old Sister declared to another religious: "Sister Thérèse used to give me such a beautiful smile before leaving me that my soul was filled with sunshine!"

Basically, old people need a ray of sunshine, morally as well as physically, a thing which is lacking today in this unquiet and jostling world. To love them is to bring them love, we might almost say the tenderness of Christ, and to bring them also, as far as they are prepared to receive them and capable of assimilating them the words of Christ, the life of Christ, the grace of Christ, with a desire for the things of heaven, which alone can give their last years a meaning. To love them is to try to help them.

To help them materially at first, for many of them, many more than we generally think, are as we say today "economic casualties", and as Saint James recommends, we have no right to fob off a man who is hungry with good advice. Following our Master's example we must concern ourselves lovingly and unselfishly with their situation. We must act with discretion, of course, but also effectively.

As Saint Vincent de Paul told Antoine Portal, it can be a good and salutary thing to have "our" poor man. But the time we can give him is, of course, limited. To deal with all the cases of distress, we must enlist the help of charitable and tactful men and women, religious or lay, to bring help to the old, taking care to respect their legitimate pride. It will be one of the fields of our priestly ministry to inspire people to exercise their generosity, but also to make the public more aware of the problem of the duty we owe the aged and their hidden distress.

Often, indeed, old people are not aware of the possible resources open to them; they are frightened by the nature, the variety, the complications of the printed forms that have to be filled up in quadruplicate, declarations which to them seem impertinent and inquisitive, and by visits to offices which tire and humiliate them. This is a field in which young and active men can find an excellent way of putting their abilities and their devotion to good effect.

Undoubtedly, it is also the duty of the parish priest to encourage and support all the groups and associations like the Conferences of Saint Vincent de Paul, one of whose objects is to help the aged.

It is still more appropriate to our vocation to encourage these associations to adapt their techniques and their methods to modern conditions, to teach them the eminent dignity of old people, the elementary laws of their psychology, to remind them always that behind the wrinkled face and the apparent decay they must use the eyes of faith and love to seek and find our Lord Jesus himself.

We must also help them morally and spiritually. All old people if they are honest admit that when the swiftness of an unexpected accident, or the gradual process of "slowing down" makes a man realize that he is entering into the last stage of his life, he experiences a sadness which makes some depressed and others rebellious.

It is therefore important to help the aged first to accept loyally the state in which they are, and then, believing that "every-

165

thing is a source of grace", to discover and exploit to the full the riches which are concealed in it.

Gustave Thibon said: "The man who cannot accept the temperament of his age has all its unhappiness." Cicero said in *De Senectute :* "Life has a set course, each age has been given its own characteristics which must be assumed at the time." To know how to grow old is an art in itself. As the good old countryman says: "When age no longer supports us, we must know how to support our age!"

The true meaning of life does not consist in obstinate attempts to do the tasks of which we are no longer capable. To know how to give them up is a great grace – not to give up completely, but to take up activities that we can still do. It is by trying desperately to carry on too long that so many ruin in the last years of their life all the good they have been able to achieve in their years of maturity. To help old people morally is, then, to help them to understand the grace of their state. Our Lord makes available to each of us the divine help which our time of life, and its particular difficulties require; and it is old age, above all, because of the renunciation it entails, that can be a time of enormous spiritual profit.

Giving the aged moral assistance means helping them to understand their state, to avoid the bad temper which does them no good and estranges their friends, to try and develop a benevolent attitude which, while it does not pander to the foolish vagaries of the young wins their confidence and allows them to profit from the lessons of experience. A lot of love is necessary for that.

"The old men who have withdrawn from the tumult", wrote Anne-Marie Couvreur, "are in an excellent position to recuperate, to bring themselves under the influence of Christ once more, to recover through contact with him the divine warmth of charity. Just as they generally suffer physically from the cold, they also need warmth in their moral life. We are often forced to say that when they withdraw into themselves they seem to shrivel up, to let themselves be dominated by a preoccupation with themselves which becomes more and more engrossing. It is then that our Saviour holds out his arms to them. He alone can help them to react against the cold which threatens to numb them. If the old would only yield to this regenerating action of Christ in their souls, like the first Christians, they would compel the attention of those around them, they would inspire surprise, sympathy, and admiration. And that would be the finest testimony that they could render to the work of the Redeemer living in them."

To give the aged moral assistance means helping them to understand, to carry, and profit by the cross. "To understand the meaning of suffering", said Masson, "is the great task, and should be the great triumph of the aged." To give the aged moral assistance means, finally, helping them to understand death, and to look at it confidently and serenely.

"We only have to observe old people to reach this conclusion: some seem absorbed by an incurable sadness; they are those who are obsessed by the fear of death, who struggle in vain under the weight of this obsession. Others do not struggle with this thought, since they accept it. As a result it does not obsess them, not trouble them; they are not held back by it; they pass it by and look beyond at the perspective of the eternal horizons." The words which Pascal puts on the lips of Christ in his *Mystère de Jésus,* are always true: "Doctors will not cure you, for in the end you will die. It is I who cure, and render the soul immortal."

But is it not our task to make the hope of eternity grow in the souls of old people? The fact is that beyond death there is a life that does not grow old, or involve separation, the vision and the possession of God, the consciousness of our union with Christ, our entry into the ecstasy of love which unites the three divine Persons, a glory in which our hearts, which are now without beauty, infirm and sad, will find one day the radiance of eternal youth.

If there are some lives whose decline is an ascension, many others perish in the darkness because the light has not reached them. It is sad to think of these brothers of ours who are so near the tomb, but so far from God. Many are waiting unconsciously in the cold and in the darkness for our supernatural friendship, reinforced by our prayer and by our daily Mass, to bring them the light for which, like Goethe, every human being, in the last hours of his life calls from the depths of his heart. The approach of death, as Bernanos puts it, "shatters the façade by which we impose on ourselves as much as on other people". It is the approach of death which made the psalmist exclaim: "Cast me not off in the time of my old age; when my strength has failed, do not abandon me."

We must inspire the old with confidence. God has too much respect for our freedom to impose on us, but in those last years he knocks loudly at the door of our hearts. As on that first Easter evening, Christ accompanied the two disciples on the road to Emmaus, so in the evening of life, when day fades, he makes himself our companion. As he enlightened their hesitation, distress and discouragement, so he comforts those souls who are about to enter heaven.

We should proclaim with Victor Giraud: "Old age is not the atrocious and dark period of life, the hopeless antechamber of death, which the epicurean likes to picture. In many respects and in spite of the inevitable miseries which accompany it, it is the richest, the most fruitful period of our whole spiritual life, the only one which is worth the pain it involves."

Christ speaks to his Priest

I am in each of you making use of your humanity to send forth the divine realities by human acts. I am in you to give and pardon, to consecrate and bless, to enlighten and influence, to think and pray, to offer and smile, to share suffering and human anguish. I am in you to gather all the souls whom I have linked with yours, and which I sanctify through you.

You should not be indifferent to any human being. Whatever his age or his misery, his weakness and poverty should only make you more sensitive about him, and inspire you with an infinite respect, and an immense love for him. However busy you are, be attentive to the aged. They need you more than you think. They need your sympathy and your ministry. Among them are those whom a long life of indifference and of sin has kept from me. The years of old age which are granted to them can give them time to recover, to repent, to make reparation, provided that the humble and loving soul of a priest assists their return to God.

There are those who have led a hardworking and honest life. With all their cares and worries they have not given me the place I should have had, but they can be the labourers who arrive at the eleventh hour. With a few years of spiritual effort they can make up for lost time and work effectively in my spiritual kingdom, provided that one of my stewards, that is to say, one of my priests, invites them and guides them in this task which is so novel to them.

Finally, there are those who after a generous and holy life, end their earthly pilgrimage by suffering. They have great power over my heart; they have the right to be supported, encouraged, and stimulated, so that rising from height to height they give their militant life the fullness of achievement and of fruitfulness while they wait for the joy of their final meeting with me in the light of glory. The role of my priests is fundamental: is it not in them and through them that my spirit of holiness acts and shapes men to my own likeness?

To the priests who have taken special care of the aged I shall grant the grace to keep their moral strength intact and to revive their inner flame when they too grow old. I shall also ensure that they do not feel abandoned, and are in their turn, supported and encouraged by their friends, for whatever they did to my poor they did to me. I am hidden in each of the old people whom they assisted. The help they brought me will be returned to them a hundredfold on this earth.

There is one point I want to impress on you, above all on younger priests. It is the pressing duty of love and of veneration for aged priests. If I hide myself mysteriously in everyone, if I consider as done to me whatever you do to the least of your brethren, this is even more true when it concerns one of those venerable priests who have consecrated their whole life to my service. Blessed are those who have behind them forty or fifty years or more of loyalty and devotion to my Church. Deep is my love for them and great will be their reward in heaven! As eternity nears, the devil sometimes tries to worry them by reminding them persistently of their weaknesses or of their errors. Let them be reassured, and have confidence in my mercy: the past is over and done. I have pardoned them, repaired the damage and made it good. It is their present state of soul which concerns

169

me. All that I ask of them is to come to me more often and for a longer time, to profit by the last years which remain to them, to grow in humility and in charity.

Let them be content with the restrictions on their powers and the reduction in their exterior activity. By accepting their state they have a means of accomplishing more spiritually than they did by their material efforts when they were at the height of their powers, when the subtle temptation of pride was often liable to impede the action of my grace. Let them also increase in charity. Forgetful of self, they must try to be benevolent, indulgent and compassionate. The kindness of the old priest imprints on his forehead a halo of glory. Never does my grace operate more effectively than in a priest who has stripped himself of self and is growing in love. Nothing that is done or suffered through love is useless. In truth, I say to you, it is the only thing that is really useful. If they are willing to cling to me, their last years can be the most fruitful of their ministry.

Examination of Conscience

1. In my ministry do I pay sufficient attention to the aged?
2. Am I not inclined to think that to try to exercise the apostolate through them is a waste of time, because they are too old to change?
3. Am I not inclined to despise, or at least to look down upon the aged with the excuse that they have manias and that their piety is liable to give a false impression of religion?
4. Do I see that my parishioners are sympathetic to them, so that they are helped, respected, even spoiled?
5. Do I think of organizing occasional celebrations for them?
6. Do I see they are helped by way of services, meetings, and prayers adapted to their mentality?
7. Do I take care to surround old priests with the affection and the veneration which are their due?
8. Am I not inclined to consider as anachronisms the marks of respect which are due to the aged?
9. Am I not inclined to emphasize their inability to keep up with the times, their repetition of their experiences, and all the

other frailties of old age, forgetting the lesson of the sons of Noah?

10. Quite apart from the obligations of faith and of charity, do I ever think that if I live to an advanced age, I shall want to be helped, supported, encouraged?

Resolutions

1. To train myself to see Christ in all old people and to ask for an increase of faith for that purpose.

2. Never to be sarcastic about the old. They have the same right as others to my love, and more right than others to my respect.

3. To believe and proclaim that the old can have as much and even more influence on the Mystical Body than those at the height of their powers, as God does not judge the worth of a man by his strength but by his love.

4. To help the old whom I visit to have confidence in the Lord who loves them so much, and who is so near them. Is it not true for them more than for others that "the Lord is nigh"?

5. To watch the material conditions of the old people of my parish or of my district, to help them or to get help for them discreetly, mindful of their legitimate sensitiveness.

6. An old man is never so happy as when he can render a service. To suggest to my active laymen the organization of mutual aid rather than charity in the ordinary sense.

7. To try to understand the aged and to make them understood: their psychology, their sufferings, their tendency to recall the past, to reminisce, but also their need of affection and tactful attention.

8. Often old people do not know how to get their rights, they get lost in a maze of detail surrounding the help to which they are entitled: national assistance, homes, tax relief, etc. To persuade devoted and competent young men to see to the formalities for them.

9. To encourage and to publicize the organizations which exist to serve them on the moral and material plane.

10. To consider it an essential duty in priestly charity to visit an aged priest.

Spiritual Reading

First of all, old age implies detachment. It forces us to dispense with all the material and moral superfluities which encumber the most serious lives and even more those which are not. No more pointless visits, no more frivolous curiosity, no more aimless reading, no more common or vulgar preoccupations, no more superficial friendships. Henceforth, we must restrict ourselves to essentials, concentrate on ourselves and return to the pure spiritual life.

Old age is a time of memories. Detached from the world, the soul looks back over past problems, of things perpetually postponed in the past by the so-called necessities of daily life. If many old people revert to matters of conscience and, to be candid, return to thoughts and the practice of religion, it is not as so many imagine, through fear of death and of the mysteries of eternity; it is simply because once they are disengaged from all that has hitherto filled their life to no purpose, they return to the essential mysteries of the basic problem, which underlies everything, namely "the one thing necessary".

Old age is revelation. When in the evening of life we try to take in the sequence and train of the innumerably events, great and small, which make it up, we cannot help seeing that often unknown to us they have been following an external plan. Without knowing it we have obeyed the conductor of an invisible choir.

Finally, old age is rejuvenation. It would be quite wrong to imagine that the old cannot love any more. "When we grow old", said Lacordaire, "we only enjoy souls." But we enjoy them with an intensity and a depth that youth did not know. We should remember the profound words of Saint Paul. "Though our outward man is corrupted, yet the inward man is renewed day by day." (2 Cor. 4:16) Freed from the constraint of flesh and blood and purified, his past affections – whether in his memory or still present – are for the old man younger and more vivid than ever. He has even become capable of new affections – nor will these betray him. The good old man is loved for his discreet kindness, for his smiling indulgence, for his disinterestedness, for his experience, for his keen intuition, for the charm of his greeting, for his strong emotion, for his charity, for his chastity, for his piety. And as under these different aspects there is only one love, all these affections, old as well as new, combine, increase, and are made fruitful by the Communion of the Saints, providing a path to the eternal tenderness of which we catch a glimpse here below, but can only attain in the next life.

Victor Giraud

II

Our first duty towards the old is to respect them. Man needs always respect more than bread. Besides when we truly respect some one, we do not let him want for bread. But when we give him bread without respect, we demean him.

Let us try first of all to meditate on respect. Instinctively we respect only those who are superior to us or are stronger than we are. In patriarchal societies the old man was the unchallenged head. Everyone feared him: he was respected. He was never thought of as "a poor old man". And he was fully conscious of his dignity. But the world has changed completely. Today it is production which counts. A man is judged according to his capacity for producing. As his ability to produce lessens, his human value decreases. So as we advance in age we become "poor old men".

Everything was not perfect in the patriarchal societies, but it is not good, however, that a man should be judged only according to his economic value. Ability to produce is something. Man is someone. We must not confuse things and people. Personal dignity is not recognized. That is why, instinctively, we do not respect the old. We feel stronger than they, and we have nothing to fear from their supremacy. They have "gone down", so we despise them.

There must be a reaction. First of all, let us remember that an old man is one who has done his work. It is good to honour work. But, then, we must honour aged workers. An old man is one who has suffered. I am not referring to the sufferings of his old age, but of the suffering that has interspersed his whole life. It is through suffering that he has grown up, established a home, raised a family. Think of all the trials he has had. When we reflect on all those sufferings we feel instinctively that respect for the aged increases.

Moreover, this respect should be impregnated with gratitude. We must be grateful to the old. We are profiting by those who have gone before us. We should be grateful. We do not think of this enough. We are told that the destruction caused by wars is one of the principal causes of misery. But what has been destroyed? Precisely what our forefathers had built.

Our anguish in the face of destruction and ruins is an involuntary homage to the work and to all the efforts of those who have preceded us. A generation which is not grateful to the old, is a generation without a heart. It wants to profit by the work of others and does not even know how to say "thank you".

Assistance to the aged should not be considered as humiliating "charity". It is a debt of gratitude. To provide a suitable standard of living for our old people is a duty for us. And the accomplishment of this duty should take precedence over many other considerations.

I fear that the materialism of this present generation makes this essential readjustment impossible. I do not think that a true renewal can be achieved outside the faith. I would like to depict an old man in the light of God. One whom God is preparing for heaven. He suffers, and this suffering is primarily an expiation for his sins. It is a purification of his soul, to make him more ready to meet God.

He suffers, and this suffering detaches him from the earth. Life here no longer brings him joy. No longer is he ruled by his passions. He knows from experience that life often deceives. Detached, he can direct his thoughts more readily towards God and heaven. He feels abandoned, and he realizes he can no longer lean on his fellow men. And so, he turns more readily towards him who never forsakes those who seek him. And when death approaches, the old man becomes more and more like the Son of God who wished to suffer and die.

When we see an old man, let us think of the mystery of the meeting with God. Yet this view that faith inspires is not instinctive, either for the old or for their friends. We can, however, help the aged to see things this way, which alone will bring peace to them, and will make them understand the true meaning of their trials.

I do not suggest you should preach to them indefinitely of what I have just said. Undoubtedly they would want to reply: "I hope, indeed, to see you there", or again, "It is very evident you do not know what heaven really is!" But they should live in an atmosphere of respect and of tactful attention which will help to buoy them up as much as possible. That is why I should like to give those who are looking after old people some suggestions on how to help them carry out their mission better.

Learn how to listen. They will, of course, tell you about their times and they will criticize what is done today. Do not express surprise or try to argue or dispute. Listen. An old man will be more sympathetic with the young when he feels that he is listened to. Besides, by listening, you enrich yourself. An old man has had the experience of a whole lifetime, limited as all experience is, practical rather than theoretical. If we listen to the old, really listen, sympathetically, carefully and respectfully, we will make more progress than by reading books. You must understand that the old will not listen to you, and if they do listen, they will promptly forget. That is not their fault.

You can nevertheless ask him questions. Provided these questions relate to the past, he will be able to reply. Perhaps he will confuse dates, but the facts will be there. Those facts will no doubt be idealized as the facts of today will be painted black, but a little poetry does not harm history. And so he will have a pleasant conversation. And remember, a pleasant conversation for an old person is one in which he has done all the talking and you have done all the listening!

Love the old tenderly. You must overcome any natural repugnance to establish an affection which will become more and more real. You will prove your affection at first by listening to their complaints. Even a poor whining old creature recovers his dignity when he realizes that some one understands his suffering. Tell yourself that he probably suffers more than you realize. He cannot complain effectively; he never knows how to explain his suffering.

You will prove your affection for them by accepting their reproaches without trying to defend yourself. However much you do for old people, you will never satisfy them because they are always ill. Consequently, do not try to defend yourself. It is true we shall never be able to do enough for them. It is impossible to satisfy them. Above all, do not scold them, but ask them to forgive you because you have not done enough for them. It is easier to pardon than to acknowledge oneself wrong.

Finally, and most important, show them that you count on their affection. An old man has the heart of a grandfather. He needs to love and be loved as grandfathers know how to love. Let the old love you and tell them you are grateful for their affection. Then there will be no more "poor old men". There will be old people surrounded by affection and respect, who are preparing to meet our Lord.

Monsignor Ancel

Subjects for Discussion

1. How can we make old people understand and value the grace of their state?

2. How can we develop in the young a respect for the aged?

Prayer

Lord Jesus, make me understand better my priestly responsibilities towards that period of life which has its servitude as well as its greatness. I offer to your merciful kindness all the old people in my parish and my district.

Have mercy on those who are far from you, on those who have forgotten you. Make those who feel lonely sense your presence. Be the certainty of those who doubt, the light of those who seek, the strength of those who struggle, the warmth of hearts that have grown cold. Come to the help of those who are in need, material and moral. Above all give them the graces they need to sanctify the last years of their earthly life, in preparation for the great day of their eternity. Amen.

Thought

The spiritual man has no age, but he accepts the ages of carnal man. He dwells not in time, for his fatherland is in eternity. He no longer revolts against time, for he knows that time is the road which leads to eternity. He loves what is permanent.

Gustave Thibon

10

THE PRIEST IS A MAN

Before being a priest one must be first a man, and not only a man, but a gentleman, and an honourable man." This was said by the rector of a famous seminary. It is a serious mistake to harbour sentimental ideas about the priesthood. Is it the result of nineteenth-century romanticism, of the false sentimentality of the past? Perhaps it is because, for so many years, women have been going to church in greater numbers than men. Also the training given in junior seminaries might be responsible.

There has been, without doubt, in the past, a type of churchman who was far from measuring up to what is required by the Gospel, far from what the Church militant needs, namely, a man of conscience and character. The priest is not simply a sign post which indicates the way; he is a guide who sets an example, who leads and assists.

On the day of our ordination we were told that the priest should be in command. This does not mean that he should seek out the first places or show off, for it is not by making a display that either we enter paradise or lead others there. It means having a rugged mentality, which knows how to combine boldness and prudence, and which makes the exercise of authority a service for the common good.

Nothing is more misleading and more contrary to the true spirit of the Church than the attitude of so-called leaders who have no backbone. They can be lucid and brilliant, but what characterizes them is their fear of responsibility: fear of being compromised or committed, fear of making a decision and above all of sticking to it. Disciples of Pontius Pilate rather than of

Jesus, they are always ready to "wash their hands" to avoid "getting into deep water".

The Church asks for priests who are men of God, but men also in the full sense of the word, not overgrown choir boys, not eternal adolescents nor cranks with bees in their bonnets, wrapped up in themselves. It is misunderstandings about this which explain both our failure to influence most of our contemporaries, and the all too little use of the grace of the Holy Spirit who longs to renew the face of the earth! Let us recall the words of Péguy: "To make progress in grace it is not sufficient to abandon nature. To mount to God it is not sufficient to abandon the world. Because pious people haven't the strength to face nature they think they have made spiritual progress. Because they have no temporal courage, they think that they have entered into the eternal. Because they have not courage to play their part in the world, they think they are doing God's work. Because they have not the courage to commit themselves to a human cause, they think they are serving God's cause. Because they do not love anyone, they think they love God."

It is vital that we should avoid or correct these distortions, which are often unconscious but can do grave harm to our spiritual development as well as to our apostolic efficiency. "Be a man, act courageously." Expressions such as these occur frequently in the works of the inspired writers. "Do manfully and be of good heart: fear not, nor yet be ye dismayed at their sight." (Deut. 31:6) "Show yourself strong and courageous." (Jos. 1:18)

The Psalms often have courage as their theme. "Expect the Lord, do manfully, and let thy heart take courage." (Ps. 26:14) "Do ye manfully, and let your heart be strengthened, all ye that hope in the Lord." (Ps. 30:25) In the first Book of the Machabees there is a hymn in honour of courage and heroism. (Macc. 2:64) Our Lord does not mince his words on the subject of manliness. "The Kingdom of heaven suffereth violence and the violent bear it away." (Matt. 11:12)

"You are the salt of the earth", said our Lord to his disciples. "And salt is not honey", comments Father Torcy, a character in Bernanos' *The Diary of a Country Priest*. When the salt loses its flavour, our Lord tells us that we throw it away.

179

Saint Paul and Saint Peter both say the same thing. "Watch ye; stand fast in the faith; do manfully and be strengthened." (1 Cor. 16:13) "Be sober and watch: because your adversary the devil, as a roaring lion, goeth about seeking whom he may devour. Whom resist ye, strong in faith." (1 Peter 5:8)

The manly and fighting character of the first Christians is constantly referred to in the annals of the early Church. Besides, our Lord never promised his disciples an easy life. He never promised his apostles a tranquil ministry. He continually refers to struggles, opposition, persecution; but at the same time he calls on their valour, their courage, their tenacity, their confidence. And, at the very moment when he was about to enter into his agony at Gethsemane his last word was a cry of triumph: "Take courage, I have overcome the world." (John 16:33)

All the martyrs, and indeed all the saints, both men and women, displayed a fine spirit. It is a deplorable mistake, as well as lamentable taste, to depict Saint Thérèse of Lisieux as fragile and languishing. She was in reality an energetic girl, much more like Joan of Arc and Teresa of Avila than the insipid niminy-piminy so often depicted.

A childlike spirit signifies neither childishness, nor puerility, nor faintheartedness. It is a way of giving ourselves with confidence to the infinite gifts of the Holy Spirit, and of placing our hand in the hand of God to change the face of the earth.

Meditation

For a few moments let us adore our Lord in silence who asks us first of all to be men and leaders. Let us share in his great-heartedness and the strength which emanates from him. In his presence, let us reflect on the example of manliness which he himself gave us. Let us examine what it is not; what it is; how to develop it in ourselves.

Manliness is not harshness, nor aggressiveness, nor feverish-ness. As ever, the most simple virtues are often exposed to the risk of excess, especially following a period in which they have

180

been little practised. Manliness must not be confused with harshness, abruptness or cruelty. Some people think it is a good thing to adopt, in reaction to the past, a certain abruptness in manners, a harshness of attitude, and sometimes even a real hardness of heart. That is not only a mistake, but stupidity which reveals a state of soul nearer adolescence than adulthood, since it denotes an absence of self-control, a love of extreme solutions, and a systematic spirit of opposition which, basically, indicates a personality which is not sure of itself.

We are not called on to sacrifice to that more or less Nietzschean outlook which recognizes spiritual strength only under strained features and a steel mask, and wants saints to have strident voices and bulging muscles. It is within that the virtue of strength, a gift of the Holy Spirit, must make us realize the balance between sweetness and strength. In Jesus Christ, manliness never proceeded from pride, nor engendered it. He who, out of love for his Father, expelled the traders from the Temple, could say in all truth: "I am meek and humble of heart." (Matt. 11 : 29)

Nothing is further from true manliness than aggressiveness, which loves arguments for their own sake, which is happy to attack without any concern for the wounds it inflicts on others, which looks eagerly for the defects and faults of others in order to spotlight them and to play the role of judge. It is childish to demand absolute perfection in others, to make hasty generalizations about the weaknesses or failings of past generations of priests, forgetting the difficult conditions in which they worked, and their devotion, sometimes heroic, and tenacity which paved the way for today's harvest.

Some years ago, a French Catholic periodical published some notes on the subject of prophecy in the Church, for the use of priests in their ministry. After recalling that in the hours of crisis false prophets can arise in the midst of the true, the genuine prophet was defined as follows: "The true prophet is disinterested; he does not preach his own ideas, his personal methods, for themselves as such, but as more effective means of promoting the salvation of humanity. He does not work for a clique, for a party or a school, but for the glory of God.

181

"The true prophet knows the requirements of charity. When he stigmatizes an error, denounces an illusion, condemns a method, he seeks to spare persons; only with regret does he deliver the criticisms that he utters.

"The true prophet avoids criticizing the hierarchy. When he thinks that he has the right and the duty to criticize particular steps or attitudes, he does so respectfully, discreetly, and never in public.

"The true prophet is mistrustful of himself, in so far as he has not received, in one way or another, and not necessarily by a juridical act, a form of appointment from the religious authority.

"The true prophet knows how to control his impatience; he bides his time, he has confidence in the Holy Spirit present in the Church and recalls that the Kingdom of God is not of this world."

True manliness does not demand a feverish activity, which, based unconsciously on Pelagianism, thinks that it can solve the problems of salvation under pressure and by intense exertion. Breathlessness never encourages the inspiration of the Holy Spirit, and the priest who, to show how much of a man he is, seeks to play the business man and practically ceases his contact with God, ends only in impotence and sterility. Our task is not purely human. We must accomplish, in dependence on God, a mission which does not come from us. We must enter a divine enterprise of which God is in control. That is why "sacerdotal effectiveness is primarily a matter of spirituality", as Cardinal Suhard told us.

"Priestly spirituality will be at once a mystique of consecration, the simple consequence of the real transformation of the person of the priest by the sacrament of holy orders. If it is true that the 'character' has marked his soul forever with the sign of God, the priest must accept the consequences which are thus imposed upon him: separation and resemblance. He is no longer an individual; he belongs to God who has set him apart to use him in his service. He must be willing, then, while fully sharing the human condition not to rely completely on human standards for his knowledge, research and outlook. He will be truly 'human', but not in the same way as others. Deeply committed to the world, he will know how to remain apart from it. He will but look on it as a sign of inferiority or as a betrayal to stop on the threshold of certain responsibilities, even legitimate ones. For one of his means of action is to abstain and to wonder. One of his duties is a mission of dissimilarity and a defence of discontinuance.

"Yet the 'character' of holy orders does more than separate: it creates a resemblance. The priest must remember that. His first effort in the order of sanctity will be to accept the marks of that image; it will be to identify himself daily and actively more and more with him of whom he should be the image.

"The interior life, the increasing intimacy with the great High Priest, by asceticism and by contemplation, under the guidance of the Holy Spirit, who forms him silently: such is the daily duty of the priest. Without this interior effort to become more like Christ, he would be a man of God by his powers and his calling, but not by his life. There would be an interior divorce, source of all pharisaisms and of all defections."

Priestly manliness is maturity, courage and loyalty to responsibilities. Maturity is a state of balance, equally far removed from old age as from adolescence. It is characterized by a perfect mastery of self, of nerves, of heart, of emotions, and by an acute sense of concrete realities. In the priest this mastery assumes a determination to record objectively the lessons gained from experience, a spiritual and an intellectual effort to view facts as far as possible in relation to God who is love and truth. The greatest danger for an apostle is to be content to live on his achievements and to cease to think ahead. "He who wishes to be raised above intelligence, passing through it runs the risk of falling below it", said Plotinus. Priestly manliness, if it is not to degenerate, requires the support of an intellectual life which ensures dauntless thought, sure of its end. What dogs all of us is the danger of using our faculties on secondary needs which do not help souls. If we wish to escape this let us concentrate on our work and be ruthless in the ordering of our tasks. Support and renewal of our spiritual life first, but also support and

183

renewal of our intellectual life, which for the priest often ensures his spiritual life.

There are still too many priests who do not make time to read and take notes. Study, however, is not sufficient. Both prayer, the contact with God, and practical experience in the ministry, are necessary to direct our activity correctly and to fulfil our role as mediators effectively. But it is meditation, whether alone in personal study, or with others in conferences and in congresses which will help us to effect a synthesis. Otherwise, after a time our prayer will be only words without soul or strength and consequently without meaning or depth. Our ministry will be liable to dry up; the tree will hide the forest, there will be routine, conformity, empty administrative activity, and we shall move in an ever narrowing circle of insipid ideas.

Today, many suitable books and periodicals are readily available. We are fortunate in this respect. For most priests it is time that is lacking, or rather the courage to organize their time according to a real scale of values. To be adult is to know how to choose. There are some who are always children, or close to second childhood; who let themselves be guided by the impulse of the moment, by caprice, by their imagination or by what is most pressing, without ever stopping to reflect. Evidently reflection often involves effort and sacrifice, but hours apparently lost in reading or in taking part in conferences, in days of study, are precious hours which will pay dividends in our apostolic work.

To cope with the modern conditions of the apostolate, we must refurbish our methods, break with ideas and procedures which no longer have any practical value, abandon a rhythm which is out of date, break out of our narrowness, enlarge our horizon, "feel with the Church", breathe in communion with her. Time wasted is never recovered. What we dedicate to prayer and study ensures the maturity of our soul and the virility of our activity.

Priestly manliness implies courage, that is strength of soul which does not fear struggles, effort, or "hard knocks". "Life on earth is a warfare", said Job. Our Lord did not cease to remind us of this basic aspect of life. Nothing is more contrary to his Spirit than a blind fatalism or a spineless resignation camouflaged as submission to the divine will. The parable of the talents is the most striking illustration of this.

For Saint Thomas, the relation of liberty to providence is one of transcendence. Under this transcendent action, what is free is free, what is spontaneous is spontaneous, what belongs to us belongs to us, even if it is dependent on grace. Whatever providence plans for us, it is we who have to accomplish it. What grace marks out for us to do, it is still we who have to achieve it. God asks us to make use of all our resources and to get the full value out of our talents and our gifts in the cause of his glory and of our brethren. In these circumstances, effort is required by God for the progress of his kingdom. Some, hoping to spare themselves trouble, have recourse to prayer. But God has not promised that what can be normally obtained by effort can be secured by prayer alone.

Finally, we must not be astonished to meet here below with misunderstanding, contradiction, opposition from those on whom we think we have most right to rely. The disciple is not above the Master, and the cross, in one form or another, is a part of our contract with our Lord. He has not misled us. Has he not declared clearly: "If any man will follow me, let him deny himself and take up his cross, and follow me"? (Mark 8:34)

There is a manly way of carrying our cross, even in the hours when it weighs heavily upon us. No complaining, no murmuring, but self-forgetfulness, imitating our Lord, who found in his great love the strength to comfort the women of Jerusalem, to ask pardon for his executioners, and to open the gates of paradise for his companion in misery.

Pius XII said: "You should be masters of courage, so that you can assert your priestly character in every contingency with a serene freedom and independence." To confuse obedience and passivity would be quite contrary to the spirit of the Church. Father Montcheuil has written: "Obedience has nothing to do with flattery or servility. The most absolute decisions of the Church are negative in character: they bar a road which leads only to error or to evil, but they do not mark out the only possible way in which measures and efforts can be fruitful.

185

They do not indicate that we must fall back simply and solely on past practice. There again, if revolt is blameworthy, it does not follow that the most perfect course will be to retire to our tents and keep silent. It is a comparatively recent attitude to regard a man who happens to have met with disapproval once as thereafter disqualified for any new assignment." And he went on to say: "To know how to proceed without waiting for prompting from authority, to know how to stop as soon as it asks us not to go further for the time being, to retrace our steps without hesitation if authority tells us that we are on the wrong trail, to be ready to resume our march on the routes that are still open without being discouraged or disgruntled, such are the dispositions which should be familiar to the Catholic, and especially to the priest."

We judge the character of a man by his fidelity, his responsibilities. Not to dare to examine problems so as to have nothing to decide, to avoid committing ourselves is unworthy of an adult. Every priest should have, with the grace of God which will never be refused him, the necessary strength of character to assume with a manly heart, the responsibilities of his ministry and the obligations of his priesthood. He is useless if he fears them, he is unworthy if he flees from them.

This loyalty to responsibilities is quite consistent with true humility, for humility is neither shirking, nor timidity before the task we are offered. Of ourselves indeed we can do nothing, but each one can adopt the advice of Saint Paul: "I can do all things in him who strengthens me." (Phil. 4:13) Our Lord has based a wonderful plan of love on us which it is our mission to carry out, a plan which takes into account our individual ability and which, while it inserts us into the plan of the redemption, is personal and unique for each of us. The good that, through laxity or through carelessness, we do not accomplish will be undone for ever.

With this plan to be achieved, God has given us gifts and talents of a natural and a supernatural order. Like Mary, we can say: "He who is mighty has done great things to me." But these gifts and talents do not belong to us; they are not ours or for us; they are from God, to be given back to God, to be used for God. We must seek to develop them to the utmost to

186

his glory and that of our brothers. "Not to us, O Lord." (Ps. 113)

This loyalty to responsibilities presupposes a complete integrity and concern for fair play with a corresponding horror of double dealings, evasive replies, soothing promises, subterfuges, and, in general, all falsehoods great or small. "I hate a mouth with a double tongue." (Prov. 8:13) What confidence can be felt in a priest who, through time-serving or fear of gossip, declares everyone right and is not ashamed, but thinks himself clever when he admits: "I bless right and left, and in this way have peace!" How far is this attitude from that of Jesus, who said: "But let your speech be, 'yes, yes; no, no.'" (Matt. 5:37)

To accept manfully the responsibilities which come to us does not mean that we must keep them for ourselves alone, without sharing them or even delegating them to some extent. On the contrary, because the "mission" commands, the priest knows very well that it is a common work: it requires, in space and time, as much appropriate collaboration as possible. It is the art of the true apostle to discover and to bring out in each one what is best in him for the service of God.

Solipsism, even in the guise of a consuming zeal, is a mistake and a danger. A mistake because whatever his good will, his health, his intelligence, the powers of the priest have limits. To want to do everything by himself, even from the finest motives, restricts the field of his influence, and after a time, deprives him of a comprehensive view of things, and above all, robs those around him of the chance of developing their religious and human personalities. Many souls have not given what they might have to the service of the Christian community, because they were not encouraged, appreciated and given the chance to exercise their talents.

It is a danger, because, worn out by his task, without adequate rest or time to refresh himself, the apostle will soon be spent and overtaken by events. A danger, also, because he has not known how to build a parish with his active laymen, and when he goes, everything will have to begin again from scratch. It is this loyalty to his responsibilities which arouses in the priest the thirst and the anxiety to share them.

187

In order to develop in ourselves the character of manliness we must practise the theological virtues in an adult spirit, we must adopt a style of life which is a little severe, and we must keep in contact with responsible men.

When we were ordained deacons, the bishop placed his hands on us and said: "Receive the strength of the Holy Spirit." But that strength must be maintained, first by prayer, and then by an effort to correspond with grace in the exercise of the theological virtues. We must struggle for this daily. As Saint Thomas says, it is this strength which assures our power to triumph over the difficulties which are opposed to the accomplishment of good.

God himself is the source of that strength. Each time that we think of it we can obtain it from him by a confident appeal to the Father, by communion with the eucharistic Christ, or by renewed obedience to the Holy Spirit who mingles strength with sweetness in the gift of his love.

Let us not forget that what constitutes manliness is the adult character of the three theological virtues which constitute the fundamental trilogy of our supernatural equipment. What we must, then, ask of God, and what we must cultivate in ourselves, is an adult faith, an adult hope, and an adult charity. Did not Saint Paul say, to emphasize the evolution of the human condition which will have its fullest maturity only in eternity: "When I was a child I spoke as a child, I felt as a child, I thought as a child. Now that I have become a man, I have put away the things of a child." (1 Cor. 13:11)

There is a life of faith which corresponds to the mentality of the child: childish faith, for the most part adaptable to the influence of its surroundings, but naïve, fresh sensitive, touching, which is just what Jesus wants and expects from little ones. There is a life of faith in keeping with the psychology of the adolescent: a more practical faith. "Christ is the great friend, he is the leader I must follow, for whose friendship I must sanctify myself, and devote myself to others."

We must pass that stage and come to a life of faith of adult dimensions, where we find a world on the march, and ourselves as part of it. "It is not only Christ in me, but it is I in Christ."

There is a life of hope which corresponds to the age of childhood: "Lord, give me your grace that I may do good"; there is a life of hope which corresponds to adolescence; "Lord, be thou my strength, to help me to become better, and my reward, if I do well." But there is the life of hope which corresponds to adulthood. This hope is not limited to me alone, but reaches out to the whole world of which I know that I am a part, to the entire body of which I am only a member, hope which is an adherence to God in the work of creation, of redemption, of unification, in the final triumph of humanity purified, regenerated by Christ resplendent in his holiness and in his praise of the Father.

There is a childlike charity: "I love whoever loves me", a charity of adolescence: "I love to love, especially anyone who pleases me." But there is a life of adult charity, in complete communion with the charity of God for all men without exception: "I love everyone with the same love with which Christ loves them, without expecting a reward other than that of being allowed to serve him more and to love all my brothers in the world." Basically, this evolution places us completely at the centre of our priesthood, making us renounce ourselves in the realization of God's eternal plan for he world.

Some years ago a review launched an inquiry under the provocative title: "Has Christianity Made Men Less Manly?" The conclusion that could be drawn from the various replies is, that if there are Catholics, and even priests, who lack virility in their behaviour, this defect must not be attributed to Christianity, but to the warping of their spirituality or to human frailty.

In itself, the Gospel is no encouragement to softness. All genuine spirituality in the Church inclines much more to the ascetic than to free-and-easy ways, to a militant life rather than to day-dreaming. Christian virtues cannot be somnolent; appeals to vigilance are too numerous for Christ's disciples to have the right to be lulled by a peaceful and easy life.

It is here that our manner of life plays its part. With his great experience, Cardinal Verdier insisted on the bad influence exerted by presbyteries that are too comfortable, on the danger, in the long run, of affected manners or speech. Apart from the physical circumstances of his life, the priest who does not know how to deny himself and who allows himself every form of indulgence, provided it is lawful, is very close to becoming unfaithful to his ideal. The façade is still intact, but the interior is crumbling.

189

When we look for the origin of particular lapses, do we not find weaknesses which appeared to be harmless but were gradually undermining the strength of resistance?

More than ever, at the present time, believers and unbelievers expect manly testimony and a spirit of disinterestedness from the priest. The era of the professional clergyman ambitious for a comfortable cure, or of the country priest looking for a peaceful life without interruptions, has gone. But it would be a mistake to think that we are immune from the dangers which, in one form or another, never cease to threaten our energy.

At one time it was a regular theme of conferences to warn priests against interesting themselves only in the spiritual welfare of women and children. Some priests even concluded a little hastily that they should deliberately give up all work with children, a procedure which soon proved to be disastrous. "It was necessary to do these things but not at the expense of other fields of action." It is, nevertheless, true that timidity with men can be the sign of a priest who has not reached spiritual maturity. Only contact with men can provide us with a real idea of the problems of life today.

The life of faith requires, as we have seen, that we consider the will of God for all humanity, even that which is profane. It was the oft-repeated thought of Pope Pius XII, who insisted on the moral and spiritual importance of social and economic questions. Contact with grown men helps us to understand, provided that we know how to observe and listen, the psychology of the different social spheres which they influence or which influence them. Problems with which they are grappling, for which we are not called on to provide a technical solution but of which we must help them to grasp the human aspects with the eyes and heart of Christ.

Through them we shall help the Church to participate in all the crises of humanity. As Cardinal Suhard advised his priests: "Let us erase from our souls every psychosis of inferiority, let us be conscious of the greatness of our mission, and of the glory of our task, let us advance with a humility which will increase with the years, with a profound respect for the great things which the Most High has done in us, and let us turn towards men with a virile mentality, created by a faith which can move mountains, with an unlimited hope in the victory of grace, and with a burning love kindled by the heart of a God who became man to save all men."

It is equally true that while manliness develops in the priest the acute and realistic sense of his task, it incites him to train and to make use of active laymen in his work, treating them not as children but as adults.

Christ speaks to his Priest

"The kingdom of heaven suffereth violence and the violent bear it away." (Matt. 11:12) I have chosen you to work for the extension of my Kingdom. I want neither weak nor tepid people in my service. "Because thou art lukewarm, I will begin to vomit thee out of my mouth." (Apoc. 3:16) You must expect to experience difficulties in yourself and opposition from those around you. When did I ever say that my Church would spread without controversy, and that my disciples would preach without contradiction? What I have promised you is that I shall be with you until the consummation of the world. What I have promised is that the powers of hell will not prevail, and that I shall have the last word. But before that, it is normal that, like me, you should know suffering, defeat and persecution. "The disciple is not above his master." (Matt. 10:24)

I have hidden nothing from you, and the warnings I have given were solemn. "If any man will follow me, let him deny himself and take up his cross and follow me." (Mark 8:34) "Blessed are ye when they shall revile you and persecute you, and speak all that is evil against you, untruly, for my sake." (Matt. 5:11)

My apostle, Paul, who knew persecution in all its forms and who was a model of apostolic manliness, stimulates and comforts you when he says: "In doing good let us not fail; for in due time we shall reap, not failing." (Gal. 6:9) "Be ye steadfast and immovable: always abounding in the work of the Lord, knowing that your labour is not in vain in the Lord." (1 Cor. 15:58) Like Saint Paul, you will find joy in suffering endured for me!

191

Like him, you will abound in joy in your trials. Like him, you will share in my strength and in my power. Listen to the advice he gives: "Labour as a good soldier of Jesus Christ." (2 Tim. 2:3) "For he also that striveth for the mastery is not crowned, except he strive lawfully. The husbandman that laboureth must first partake of the fruit." (2 Tim. 2:5, 6)

The manliness which I wish to see grow in you is born of the gift of fortitude and of the virtue of hope. It will be the fruit of the efforts and of the risks which every apostolic undertaking requires. Far from inducing inertia in you it will stimulate you to energetic and precise activity; it will ensure the sound and lasting effectiveness of your work even in the most unfavourable circumstances. I do not want to have in my service a slave, a human robot, a domestic automaton. What always pleases me, and what I seek for, is the adoration of a free man, enjoying liberty of the sons of God. It is the generous gift of a man who is at once humble and strong, strong with my very strength.

I have wanted to make of you not a servant but a friend, an associate. I place a high value on your collaboration; I want you to take the initiative. I make the granting of my grace depend not only on the intensity of your prayer, but on the manliness of your action. I deal with you as a father does with his son.

Examination of Conscience

1. Am I leading a manly sort of life from which the note of asceticism is not lacking?

2. What is my habitual reaction to difficulties? Is it discouragement, passivity, nervous irritation, or, on the contrary, patience and loyal search for a positive and effective solution?

3. Is my normal behaviour characterized by energy or indolence?

4. Do I understand that Christianity is a manly religion, the religion of martyrs and saints, whose activity was directed in struggle and effort against themselves, in the service of Christ, and of others?

5. Do I sometimes prefer an easy ministry among women and children to a ministry among men?

6. In order to work well, do I need comfort or at least testimonies of esteem and of gratitude from my superiors or from my parishioners?

7. What is my attitude when I am a victim of calumny or of unfriendly opposition?

8. If I find I am timid or suffer from an inferiority complex when dealing with some adults, is not this the result of a lack of faith, or at least a lack of personal synthesis with the gifts of faith in the greatness of my priestly mission and with the powers which have been conferred on me?

9. Am I careful in my preaching, in my conversations with adults, to speak a direct adult language, to avoid in particular obsolete, esoteric or redundant phrases? Today men expect from a priest a complete frankness, without useless roughness of course, but also without mental reservations, and soothing or obscure phrases.

10. Have I a horror of slackness, disorder, laziness, and mediocrity?

11. What is the style of my presbytery, my room, my furniture, of the pictures, status, and paintings which surround me?

12. Am I imprisoned in a soft, affected atmosphere, without character, and without strength, which denotes insipid taste, if not the total absence of good taste?

Resolutions

1. To ask God often for the gift of strength, and to associate myself with the energy of God as often as possible.

2. Not to forget that God is a God of strength.

3. To repeat often with Saint Paul: "I can do all things in him who strengtheneth me." (Phil. 4:13) "When I was a child I spoke as a child, I understood as a child, I thought as a child. But when I became a man, I put away the things of a child." (1 Cor. 13:11)

4. In all circumstances to adopt an interior and exterior behaviour that is manly and in which the goodness of the priest takes nothing away from the energy of the man.

5. With children, to avoid manners that are too affectionate.

6. Not to confound manliness with coarseness and harshness.

7. To avoid both agressive harshness, which in some priests denotes a lack of interior balance, and a certain kind of clerical affectation stigmatized by Péguy and other writers.

8. Not to confuse activity with agitation. The man who is always bustling about, rushed, and strung up is a man who has not reached psychological maturity.

9. To organize my work and my time so that I run my life and do not let it run me.

10. To measure up the effort to the result. To avoid overtaxing my strength.

11. To renounce once and for all seeking after rewards and human consolations, whatever their form. If they come, so much the better, but never let them be the motives of my activity.

12. To avoid insipidity, silly remarks, affectation, and listlessness.

13. Without pride, to become more and more conscious of my responsibilities and dignity as a man, as a priest, and as a son of God.

14. To note in the Gospels and in Saint Paul's epistles all the passages referring to strength, courage, and energy.

15. To seize every opportunity, however small, of performing acts which cost me something, and even rejoice in the effort and the pain which accompany them.

16. In little things to form the habit of deciding promptly and of carrying out the decision faithfully. "It is not by stray impulses, but with bold ones that one influences the world and saves it."

17. Without abandoning my care for little children, which is more than ever necessary, to seek to make contact with grown men, to study with them the real problems of life, to entrust to them definite tasks, with due regard for their abilities. By degrees to extend the scope of their initiative and responsibilities.

Spiritual Reading

The Church in the midst of the world is the Church in the midst of combat. Israel prefigures her a nation, led by Yaweh to claim its heritage. Her God is the God of Peace, even "a beatific vision of peace". She preaches him who "brought about peace by his blood upon the cross"; she wishes to have gentle and the peaceable in her bosom, and when she is heeded, she always exercises a pacifying influence. But she must begin by snatching us from that false peace which prevailed in the world before Christ, and in which we are always trying to settle ourselves anew. To "prepare the gospel of peace", Saint Paul tells us, we must be clothed again with "the armour of God". We are in servitude: he must deliver us. But deliverance is not accomplished without struggle. "It is only for a time that God has given peace." Before rejoicing in the Lord on account of that peace which he has finally secured, she must experience the lot of Jacob, whose name signifies struggle and labour. Before being crowned on the heights, she must combat the forces of the world, and whatever illusions may from time to time recur among her children, here below she will never be in triumph and in glory. More than persecutions, more than schisms and heresies, the irregularities of those who call themselves her children are to her a perpetual bitterness. She pursues her way in suffering and opprobrium; prosperity no longer satisfies her, adversity no longer dejects her; she withstands vainglory by humility, and reacts against misfortune by hope. But she does not compromise with the enemy. She cannot be unfaithful to him who has said: "I have not come to bring peace, but the sword", and "a man's enemies will be those of his own household". Who was in truth from the beginning to the end of his earthly existence "a sign of contradiction".

Everywhere, indeed, she seeks agreement and union, "harmony and reconciliation", as "the most efficacious way to co-operate for the good of the human race". To secure it she is ready to make any concessions which would not be interpreted as denials of Christ. She loves order, submission, respect. Indeed, she is often accused of loving them too much. In this world in which all is confused, she respects even the "peace of Babylon", which she needs in her pilgrimage to lead her children to heavenly peace. She knows that the "power comes from God", and that it is "the servant of God for our good". She prays for those who exercise it; she reminds each one of the

195

"true and solid greatness", and of "the more than human dignity" of their authority; she wants us to obey them as a matter of conscience. She herself submits to the civil laws. Following her Master, she always says: "Render to Caesar the things that are Caesar's", preaching a perfect loyalty, even to the persecuting powers. "A secular experience, an acute sense of individual and social psychology, and above all the importance of her spiritual purpose", inspire her with an habitual attitude so moderate that many are confounded by it. Yet, she adds, "render to God what belongs to God". She only wishes, as she must, to give testimony of the truth. Yet that is enough to make her opponents accuse her of "playing politics", of making a wrong use of religion, as Jesus himself was accused before Pilate. That is sufficient to put the "sword" of separation in all hearts and all strata of society.

Henri de Lubac

II

"I have overcome the world!" This exhortation of Christ on the eve of his Passion has for twenty centuries sustained the enthusiasm of the messengers of the truth on all continents. It recalls to you, Venerable Brothers and dear Sons, the value of your own sufferings for the sake of the Gospel and the privileged role which is yours in the great enterprise of the propagation of the faith. By the Passion, the faith has been strengthened in the world. By it likewise the light of the Gospel penetrates souls and even communities, by it the conclusive victories of Christ are won. All you who suffer are the first depositaries of these great hopes. With the grace of God, be worthy of the hopes the Church places in you!

Pius XII

Subjects for Discussion

1. Show how the intelligent practice of the four cardinal virtues contributes to the harmonious development of a balanced sacerdotal virility.

2. How can a priest develop strength of soul in himself?

Prayer

Our Lady, powerful Virgin, be our strength and courage in the daily struggles of our life here on earth. You who stood at the foot of the cross, obtain for us that moral strength which helps us to accept courageously all trials and sufferings, so that we may make use of them efficaciously for the salvation of the souls which are entrusted to us.

Be our support and our comfort when loneliness weighs on our heart. Develop in us the desire for responsibility, the spirit of courage, genuine virility, holy bravery in the apostolate, freedom from presumption and from rashness. Following the example of your Son, true God and true man, may we accomplish with virility the will of the heavenly Father, for the glory of his name and for the best service of our human brothers. Amen.

Thought

Men do not seek the consent of a weak authority; they rejoice to find one which is strong, one on which they can lean. Manly firmness reassures them, complacent weakness makes them suspicious, and, ultimately, disgusts them.

Lacordaire

197

11

THE PRIEST AND COMMUNISM

Meditation

Our spiritual life is lived in this world, and our priesthood, whatever its transcendence, is not exercised outside space and time. Our Lord has called us to be priests in a specific era, in an evolving society which is not that of the fourth, the fourteenth, or the nineteenth century. What characterizes our own time is that, as the result of scientific progress and the unrestricted possibilities of propaganda, ideas spread more quickly than formerly, and attitudes of mind are created and disappear according to new norms.

If there is a single fact which dominates our century, it is Communism. An inheritance from the nineteenth century, it today dominates nearly half of the globe and has dazzled men of all classes in the other half. Its strength was underestimated for a long time. Today, it has made itself felt as the central problem of social stability and international affairs.

"Communism", said Father Bigo, "aims at the transformation of man, society, and the world. It seems to surpass in power all that men have previously tried to do to influence the world. In all the realms of science and technology, the Communist works unceasingly. The very thought of the uncertainty of human life is a spur to him. He must work quickly, and do anything to find earthly solutions, for there are no others. He creates the instruments he can use to assure the development of man on every biological, psychological and economic plane. He must destroy the old concept of man and the old world to produce a new concept and a new world. What an immense and attractive enterprise, when the men who are conducting it do not know the true nature of man!"

Nothing is gained by closing our eyes and stopping up our ears. It is not a question of being a defeatist or of giving way to pessimism, but of considering the fact of Communism in all its facets, with our faith, our humility, our love of the Church and of souls. Whatever our functions are, whatever form of ministry we are assigned to, none of us has the right to remain indifferent, nor to consider himself powerless. Close to our Master, we must first reflect on what our attitude should be to Communism as men of God, as men among men, and as men of the Church.

As priests, we are first of all men of God, consecrated to the service of his glory, to proclaiming his existence and his love, to the realization of his plan, to the communication of his message, to the transmission of his life throughout the world. The more we study Communism and see it at work, the more we are forced to admit that it is in formal opposition to the idea of God. Its economic, social and even its political aspects, are less important than the fact that it is a mysticism, the philosophy of which, with inexorable logic, demands the purging of God from the mind and heart of men, and from all institutions.

In his encyclical, *Divini Redemptoris,* Pope Pius XI forcibly summarized the technique of Communist doctrine. This doctrine ". . . which Communism knows how to disguise attractively, is still based on the principles of dialectic and historic materialism originally taught by Marx. The theorists of Bolshevism claim that they have the only authentic interpretation of it. This doctrine teaches that there is only one reality, matter, with its blind forces; plants, animals, man are the result of its evolution. Human society is likewise only a form of matter which develops according to laws. Through an inescapable necessity it tends, as a result of a perpetual conflict of forces, towards the final synthesis: a classless society. It is clear that in this doctrine there is no room for the idea of God. There is no difference between mind and matter, or soul and body. There is no survival of the soul after death and consequently no hope of another life. Insisting on the dialectic aspect of their

199

materialism, the Communists claim that the conflict which brings the world towards the final synthesis, can be precipitated by human effort. That is why they try to aggravate the antagonism which arises between the various classes of society. The class struggle, with its hate and destruction, is regarded as a crusade for the progress of humanity. All the forces which are opposed to this systematic violence, whatever their nature, must be annihilated as enemies of the human race."

Marxism is materialistic. In Lenin's own words: "It is as implacably hostile to religion as the materialism of the encyclopaedists of the eighteenth century, or the materialism of Feuerbach. This is undeniable. But the dialectic materialism of Marx and of Engels goes further than the encyclopaedists and Feuerbach in applying materialistic philosophy to the fields of history and the social sciences."

The Communists are so sure of themselves that they sometimes seem to give up the direct struggle against God. They even try to fraternize with Catholics, confident that after "a little co-operation", the idea of God will be abandoned. "Come with us; we shall not talk about religion, but we know that you will abandon it . . . ." This note of implacable conviction is heard in many conversations between Christians and Communists. As one of them said: "We will never compel you . . . we will do nothing against you . . . but you will abandon religion of yourself, you will see things differently, and you will adopt scientific materialism."

For the Marxist, God is only an idea which he considers as a simple creation of society, an idea born at a given moment, under the impulse of economic conditions, an idea which must disappear when the superstructure born of these conditions has collapsed. Those who are not familiar with the Marxist vocabulary, may wish to be reminded that Marxism calls "structure" what we know as the masses. It calls "superstructure" all that is built above the structure and is subject to change. Religion is a superstructure which retards the rise of the worker towards his freedom and development. Religion is a monstrous flower which thrives on the dunghill of capitalism. It creates a complex of submission, and delays the slave-worker's longing for his deliverance.

The cynical blasphemy which underlies all Communist literature is that the twilight of God is the dawn of the new humanity. God is only an idol which transforms human energies into energies of adoration and diverts them from creative work. It is the conception of religion as opium, drugging the people, and the most insidious obstacle to the realization of earthly tasks. We can easily see the fatal consequences of this state of mind. Wherever Communism settles, there follows inevitably, sooner or later, desertion of God. The Communist methods to attain this result are as varied and as flexible as the circumstances demand. Lenin wrote that Bismarck, in his *Kulturkampf* policy, was guilty of gross stupidity because his violent and direct action provoked a corresponding reaction, a reanimation of the Catholicism he wanted to destroy.

Wherever an active Christianity prospers in the working and middle classes, anti-religious propaganda is muted, because, said Lenin, the union of the workers to conquer paradise on earth is more important than opinions about the kingdom of heaven. Also, active participation in the struggle of the classes, and acceptance of Marxist methods of achieving it, lead believers to atheism quicker than atheistic diatribes.

What should our attitude be to Communism? First of all, let us not be deluded into thinking that we shall be able to baptize it. The denial of God is in the very life of its thinking. But does not the atheism of Marx and of his disciples come, at least in part, from the fact that they never in their lives met living witnesses of the true Christian faith? If we cannot hope to baptize Communism, we ought to want to baptize Communists by revealing the true God to them. "I believe in witnesses who swoop down upon their prey", said Pascal. Are we ardent witnesses of a living, infinitely loving God? Do we make ourselves reflections of God? We know the moving words of the pilgrim who heard the Curé d'Ars: "I have seen God in a man!" Are we a "sign" of God? When we meet people do we draw them to him or estrange them from him? These are the questions we should put to ourselves in all honesty.

Is it not unhappily the case that so many men are opposed to God because such a caricature of God has been depicted to them? Many of our contemporaries, in fact many practising

201

Catholics, have only a vague and faraway romantic, sentimental idea of God: a solitary, vague, supreme being, abstract, inhabiting the cloudy summit of the pyramid of the universe, sometimes a kind Father Christmas, sometimes an angry potentate like a tyrant lying in wait for weak humanity. Whose fault is this? Let us make an objective inquiry into what children remember from our catechism lessons, into what adults have retained from the many sermons they have heard! Should we not try to re-establish the Christian religion in all its purity and in all its richness and proclaim the transcendence of a God who, out of love, makes himself more intimate with us than we are with ourselves, and the marvellous fruitfulness of his life in the Trinity which we are invited to share?

Must we not develop in our flock a spiritual religion, built on an informed and firm faith and urge them to make the Gospel a part of their life? Must we not above all form active Catholics for whom God will be a person who matters and with whom they will maintain a personal relationship and friendship? Man cannot fulfil himself without meeting the living God. In him alone can we find all our brothers and share his boundless love with them.

To do this, our life must give to contemplation the full consideration it requires in time and in intensity! There is a knowledge of God which surpasses the science of philosophy and even that of theology. We must promote among Catholics a real sense of the divine presence and life. But that again means a sharing of light and of warmth which requires the priest to have personal experience, the fruit of frequent and prolonged association with the three divine persons.

There are still too many cases – more numerous than we realize – in which the living conditions and the working conditions are inhuman (instability, insecurity, an exhausting rhythm of work, mechanization, dilapidated homes, etc.). There are still so many poor who are treated as pariahs, or as second class citizens, almost like beasts of burden! There are still so many men whose human dignity suffers because they are looked down upon, deprived of culture through no fault of their own, and denied any hope of social improvement. "The situation of the workers' world is one of congealed sin", said Monsignor Cardijn.

202

Do we appreciate that the workers may be in a state of legitimate defence against the social groups who think of them only in terms of the economic return they get from them, or as eternal children, not to mention the disdain and even scorn of those whose insolent luxury and sovereign indifference have often been denounced by the Pope as insults to human misery and suffering. It is these grave errors which are the cause of the breach between the "haves" and the "have nots".

But is Communism the solution? Is it truly in a position to ensure the true happiness of humanity? Does it not constitute one of the most terrible illusions which the world has known? Let us simply note the following facts. To assure the future liberation of humanity, Communism has sacrificed and is ready to sacrifice as long as necessary, the liberty and lives of millions of men. The class struggle is conceived not as a worker's fight for justice and honour but as a battle in which the enemy has no rights. All who do not think like the Party are criminals against humanity. Everything done against them is commendable: organized denunciations, forced confessions. Man is no more a man, but is reduced to a state of expendibility.

Among Communists you often find a highly developed community spirit, fraternity, enthusiasm, disinterestedness, ambition for social justice and a high standard of human dignity. All that is attributed to the party doctrine, which they claim, has awakened and developed these sentiments in party members. And yet, the ideological system is not the source of these qualities; on the contrary, it vitiates all of them. It distorts social justice – the justice which renders to everyone, as a common right, all that the individual is entitled to – into class justice, for the sole benefit of the proletariat. To this single class it sacrifices the rest of humanity. Communist fraternity is a class fraternity based on the ostracism of other men. It is achieved by crushing more than half of humanity, the family, religion, all values and all subjects which cannot be subordinated to the privileged class. And what a fraternity it is! Even this chosen class is born of supervision, distrust, spying, purges, and all planned to perpetuate the "purity" of the class, so that it may always be worthy to protect brotherly love! Excommunications are frequent and it is well known that the "false brother" thus rejected must become for his friends, for his parents, the scapegoat, the accursed, the being who has followed "the path of death". In practice Communism depersonalizes man in order to make him material for the service of its cause. A Russian psychologist, Serge Tchakhotine, has described the procedure of brain washing, which brings about a complete change in the character and in temperament of the individual, takes away all thought and all personal judgements, encouraging and aggravating a real collective hysteria, taking full advantage of the psychological obsession with re-education.

In the last fifteen years, Russian philosophy has conducted detailed research into human psychology and has learned with even more subtlety than Hitler, the satanic art of "brain washing", disturbing one by one the deep instincts of the human being, sublime as well as base, until it has achieved a real re-education of personalities, so clever, so powerful that even the intellectuals do not escape it. It is a kind of magic which abolishes in the human being the nerve centres of personality, removes from him all critical powers, and makes him psychically responsive to all the impulses which emanate from the central power.

In conformity with the philosophy of Hegel, the principle of identity does not exist. Things, persons, methods are valuable only in so far as they can serve the cause. Good and evil do not exist. Or rather, what can serve the cause is temporarily good; what harms it is temporarily evil. All weapons are good. Calumny, lying, theft, and murder. The great means of defense consists of shouting louder than the victim and accusing him of the crime of which you are the author. Individual life, moreover, is valuable only in so far as it enters into the collective struggle. Treaties, contracts, are only scraps of paper. There is nothing shameful about complete inconsistency. No one has the right to speak and write, or even to think differently from the party line. It is Fascism in every sense of the term.

In principle, a Communist is always sincere, but his sincerity is liable to change. His versatility, his evolution are justified by the inevitability of the transformation of man and the changing conditions of historic development. Its real cause is a philosophy of being and of truth. The gravity of

204

Communism is that it vitiates minds in the very principles of thought.

Even more serious, is the subtle sowing of hatred among men. "Men fight well only when there is hatred in their hearts. Then they go ahead, without stopping for anyone, without listening to anyone", declares the Communist. Hence their preference for those who can cause strife over those who plan reforms. They prefer to create misery and to provoke conflict, to maintain a state of crisis and to destroy peace, to discourage good intentions for reform, and to maintain a terrible state of wretchedness and injustice which provides a favourable climate for aggression and anger.

It is easy to appeal to the forces of evil and the destructive energies which are dormant in every one. But to build on violence and hatred, is to maintain humanity in a ferment of instability and discord, without any lasting benefit for the happiness of the people.

In such a situation, what should our attitude be? We ought also to want change and the renewal of the face of the earth, but under the influence of the divine Spirit which is a Spirit of love. Our message is also one of justice, but of justice in love and not justice as Communism understands it.

We must arouse the conscience of a pagan world. We must develop the idea of a fraternal society in its human and Christian aspects. We must disinfect the Church of any materialistic and pharisaical capitalism. We have only to follow the teaching of the Gospel, to act on the epistle of Saint James, to pass on the social instructions of the papal encyclicals and those of the hierarchy. In all classes of society we must enlighten those who have responsibilities on the social and on the civic plane. If the Church does not have to plan and build the city, she has to give a soul to the world which is being developed, and to the city which is being built. The plane on which this society is built will depend on whether the Church displays the spirit of fraternal and universal charity.

It is a question, then, of spiritually enlivening both employers and trade unionists, and giving them the doctrinal instruction they need to form the new world. It is important to show that to struggle out of love is more profitable in every way than to struggle out of hate. Love alone gains victories which allow building without destroying, and which repair injustice without wounding anyone. It alone permits us to advance morally and materially at the same time. For us the only true story is that of Jesus reuniting humanity from generation to generation, in communion with his Father in the midst of the terrible struggle between grace and sin. All the injustice of capitalism does not justify a single impulse of hatred in a human heart. Hatred is still more deadly to him who hates than to him who is hated. The liberation of the worker is not the final object of our efforts. We desire this change, and we must support those who have to struggle, but our action must be based on and permanently controlled by a redemptive purpose. Love alone can find new forms of associations and new communities of work towards which the minds of today must move.

Two causes, or rather two visions of the world and of history confront each other. One is a vision of a transformation of the world, in which man is his own master but really his own tyrant, and the other one a triumph of love derived from the only authentic source, which is God himself. Our responsibility to ourselves, as priests, is great, for we are, by vocation, the first teachers of the law of fraternal charity which prepares the unity of the world. We are the first distributors of that divine grace which sustains man in his effort to be united with his brothers. How do we live up to this responsibility? We have a terrifying examination of conscience before us!

As churchmen we should love the Church intensely. Jesus Christ and the Church are one. She is the trunk through which the sap passes to give life to the branches. To be cut off from her is to become sterile. She is both human and divine. Divine in her Founder, her doctrine, and her sacramental life, human in her members who have to experience the struggles, temptations, weaknesses, and infirmities inseparable from their earthly status. We love her and wish to serve her. We long to see her become, even in her members, what our divine Saviour wished her to be. He promised her storms and persecutions, but also that he would never abandon her. He guaranteed her his presence and the help of his Spirit to the end of time. "The powers of hell will not prevail against her."

206

Our hope is, therefore, certain. It does not mean that the whirlwinds of the infernal powers cannot buffet her violently. That has happened many times in history. Whole sections of humanity have been snatched from her. But never perhaps has the test been so critical, never have the enemy tactics been so insidious as today.

What makes the defence against Communism so difficult and so complex, is that it bases its propaganda, as we have seen, on genuine suffering and real social injustice. Skilfully it seeks everyone's collaboration for valid objectives – bread, peace, and liberty – but disguises its real ones. It uses all the psychological resources of the individual and collective human soul, fear, enthusiasm, solidarity, messianism until it transforms man into a real automaton.

The Catholic Church is the greatest obstacle to its expansion. And so, secretly, or openly, it carries struggle to the death against her. To attain its ends, it will try to caricature the Church and declare that it is intimately allied with all the oppressive forces of capitalism and of imperialism. But it is at the Church as a hierarchical society that it aims. And so all its efforts consist in trying to make it democratic, to make it rot from within by destroying its confidence in the hierarchy, by setting laymen at odds with their priests, priests with their bishops, and bishops, if possible, with Rome.

Behind the iron curtain, or in missionary countries, the essential effort made by Communism is to cause internal dissension in small religious communities and set them at variance. "Divide and rule" becomes "divide and destroy". Its object is to destroy completely the organizations which block its path, and to do so from within. When it is confronted by nothing more than an anarchical conglomeration of disorganized individuals, it is able to erect the framework of Marxist society in place of the old organization, and to mould men's minds as it wishes. In China, Russia, Poland or Czecho-Slovakia, the slogans may change, but the methods and the spirit are the same.

In view of these facts, our attitude is clear: to be more than ever faithful to the Church, to draw closer to her, to be united with her. Whatever casts doubt on the confidence we should have in her is definitely and finally noxious.

"Today", says Father de Lubac, "when the Church is everywhere accused, misunderstood, jeered at for her very existence, and for her holiness, every Catholic should be careful not to let others use against her what he has only said with the intention of serving her better. We must be on our guard against those with evil intentions. We should have filial delicacy which has nothing in common with prudery or hypocritical calculation."

Sometimes anxiety can take definite forms to cause pain to apostolic souls. In generous souls grief becomes more painful when it seems to indicate that in spite of all her efforts to adapt herself, the action of the Church is ineffective. The real problem is to know in what field it is important for the Church to be effective. Here we might bear in mind our Lord's advice to seek first the Kingdom of God.

If the urgent need for justice and charity summon Christians to play their part in politics and the economic field, they must not think that if they bring about social harmony and general prosperity they will thereby establish a Christian society. The example of Sweden, whose material progress coincided with its de-christianization, is particularly discouraging in this context. The spiritual apostolate is of another order, and both tasks must be pursued simultaneously.

Even if we enjoyed a perfect social system, that is to say, not a powerful economic or political machine, but an exterior order as human as possible, the work of the Church would not even have begun. For she does not wish to establish us in our life on earth, but to raise us above it. When she brings us the redemption of Jesus Christ, she wishes to take us away from the evil that is in us, and to open up another existence to us. If she made temporal efficiency her principal aim, she would not achieve it. If she waited to accomplish the work of salvation in the midst of the world, until temporal conditions were finally ideal, whatever criterion was postulated for that, she would be unfaithful to her mission, which is to pilot the whole of her human family into port, not at some faraway date, but all the time and to lead living men of each generation, not some mythical humanity.

Father de Lubac writes: "We must not judge the Church in terms of advance and retreat, success or failure, as we do in things which are only temporal." The supernatural good whose agent she is in this world can only be assessed in the next. It reaches its fullness in eternity. From generation to generation the communion of saints is enlarged. We must not again dream of a Church triumphant in this world. Her Master did not promise brilliant and cumulative successes. We are not indulging in empty phrases or romantic sentiment if we repeat what Pascal said: "Like Christ, she must be in agony until the end of the world." We must not let a dream of success, which may be illusory, blind us to the real fruitfulness of our Mother.

On the other hand, we must not be naïve in face of Communist tactics, of trying to sow confusion and to compromise us by all possible means. We must keep our clarity of vision and our self-control. Our relations with people must always have charity for their supreme rule, and the apostolate as their ultimate object. The genuine apostolate is not propaganda or even proselytizing. It means leading souls to discover, under the influence of grace, the divine light which they may possess without knowing it. We must remember what our Master said: "Smoking flax he shall not extinguish." (Matt. 12:20)

With the ordinary party member, discussion can sometimes be useful. It can bring out the contradictions and the errors of Communism. It can stress its authoritarian and totalitarian tendencies which are generally repugnant to the worker or the intellectual in Western Europe. It can dissipate errors or prejudices about religion or the Church. This work only begins to clear the ground, and even to get as far as that we need a sound knowledge of the history of the working class movement, of the psychology of Communism, and of Christian social teaching. The fact that so few of us can cover all these fields emphasizes the need for more extensive training for priests and active laymen.

With Communists who have been fully trained and indoctrinated discussion is useless. Their dialectic furnishes them with means of escape and evasion that are well nigh infinite. Whatever happens, they are always right. Whenever they are hemmed in, they always find, or think they find, a way out. The answer to them is not words or action but mere existence. Christian behaviour continually confronts them with the problem of religion

209

which they claim to ignore, and makes them, in spite of themselves, acknowledge the existence and the effect of spiritual
forces. Sooner or later, for one reason or another, Communism
will deceive them. We must strive to merit for their souls in
that hour of test, the grace to turn towards the one Saviour who
will never deceive them.

It has been said that when real Christian charity, the deep,
spiritual source of religion, penetrates Communist prejudice,
the Marxist begins to wonder and sometimes is completely
overcome.

This does not mean that we are to confine our ministry to the
workers. We must minister to all classes alike, and must bring
the truth to all in the light of a sincere love. We must be all
things to all men in order to win all of them, without exception,
for Jesus Christ, though it would not be wrong for us to favour
those who have received less in this world in order to understand and help them better.

"All things work for the good of those who love God." Our
mistakes and deficiencies provide the Communists with an ideal
excuse for waging their fight against the Church in the secular
field. They stimulate our efforts to get rid of the weakness which
make it difficult for us to sustain our role as witnesses of God.
They compel us towards a Christianity purified of human weakness. As Berdiaev wrote:

"If the working classes have been so ready to accept impiety
and militant atheism, those most responsible for this are not
those who have fomented revolutionary socialism but the Christians themselves, the old-fashioned Christians. Christianity is
not responsible, but its members, who have so often shown
themselves to be false Christians. An ambiguity has been created
which has caused grave prejudice to the cause of Christ in the
souls of the oppressed. The conversions from Marxism which I
have known, have never been a return to the past. They have
been leaps forward. The victorious opponent of Marx is Francis
of Assisi, who is not a philosopher and preaches only by his
actions. The materialist who believes only in what he touches,
needs to measure and weigh the power of the spirit."

Communism will be withstood most effectively by the testimony of a loyal and integrated priesthood, and by the example

210

of genuine and fervent Christian communities. The battle to secure justice and happiness for humanity is not a Communist monopoly. In the faith, hope, and charity they received at baptism, Christian workers have the means of changing the heart of man and renewing the face of the earth. But they are powerless if they are alone and if they work out of touch with each other. They must be organized, supported and instructed. This is the task of the Young Christian Workers who should have the full support of the clergy. It is through the lay apostolate that the evangelization of the world of the workers must progress, and we priests, who must provide the spiritual education of the workers who need our affection, our presence, and our sanctity.

Christ speaks to his Priest

If men would take the trouble to read and to meditate on my words, if they would listen receptively to the voice of my Church they would find it easy to discover the solution to many problems which are causing suffering in the world. Why are they always trying to rebuild the Tower of Babel? They are poor builders if they forget that they build in vain if they do not call on me for help.

I have spoken of the fate which awaits the rich man who is wicked. I have branded the hypocrite and the Pharisee. I have cursed those through whom scandal comes. I have denounced injustice, particularly injustice to the poor and to children. But my wisdom is foolishness in the eyes of men. It is necessary that scandal should come. Injustice will last as long as there is sin in the world. I approve efforts to struggle against injustice, or to mitigate its effects, but it is by far greater justice that injustice must be overcome. It is by a greater love that hatred must be overcome. It is by good will that evil must be conquered, and not by borrowing the methods and the weapons of evil.

I know it is sometimes hard and the temptation to do otherwise is great. But I set you an example. How did I behave during my Passion? Did I not reprimand my disciples James and John? He who uses the sword shall perish by the sword.

211

He who calls down fire from heaven will be the first victim of it.

Your mission is, indeed, to denounce injustice, but it must be through love. Your mission is to help others to conquer injustice, by your example as well as by preaching. You more than all others ought to hear and strive to make my prayer on Holy Thursday come true: "That they may be one as we are one." Everything which helps to make human unity a reality, without the conflict of class, race, or caste, is in the spirit of my Father. You must be the minister of unity and of communion. Only Christian communities which are united in the image of the Trinity and vivified by it, will be powerful enough to change the face of the earth. It is for Christians, especially for priests, to show by their lives the grandeur, beauty and goodness of God. To be effective in the social field you do not need to desert your sacred ministry. Infuse the community for which you are responsible with my Spirit of generosity and forgiveness, and it will bear unfailing witness in itself and its members to the reality of my presence, to the efficacy of my life and of my love.

Above all, let nothing discourage you. I save all of you through each other, according to hidden and mysterious laws. Community of salvation, prayer, and sacrifice have lost nothing of their secret power. Do not let gloomy appearances obscure the profound reality. Do not let the noise of storms or human discussions prevent you from hearing the silent breathing of the Church. Beneath political agitation, changing opinions, struggles, or controversies, my life, which eludes examination and inquiry, is maintained, transmitted and renewed in a way which it is almost impossible to judge from outside.

I continue on the spiritual plane what I began during my life on earth. The invisible miracles of the blind who see, of the deaf who hear, of the dead who rise again, of the poor to whom the Gospel is preached in silence, perpetuate down the ages, even in the most difficult conditions, what Isaias prophesied concerning me. It is in secret, in the intimacy of hearts, that I make my light shine, and extend my Kingdom. From time to time, in various forms, the holiness of my sons rises above the universal conscience and creates institutions which bring about the happiness and the prosperity of the people. But it is from Christians, and above all among those of my priests who seek first my Kingdom and my justice that the rest benefit.

Examination of Conscience

1. Have I not, in spite of the definite and repeated warnings of the Church, minimized the danger which Communism presents for so many souls?

2. Do I give way to defeatism by accepting Marxism as fatal, and yield to the fear that I am powerless against it?

3. Do I understand that the strength of Communism is often built both on an inaccurate and distorted presentation of Christianity, and on an illogical attitude towards justice and charity?

4. Do I appreciate that the Communist will never be impressed by discussion but rather by living deeds, numerous enough and convincing enough to confound him?

5. Do I realize the importance of Catholic Action for the formation of lay apostles who will regulate their lives according to faith, and will so be able, in their respective fields, to be genuine witnesses of the Gospel?

6. Do I understand the ineffectiveness, and even the risk involved in an anti-Communism which is purely theoretical? What is negative is sterile. It increases our differences, and creates psychoses which, by reaction, increase the importance of what we are anxious to struggle against.

7. Am I careful to avoid all violence, even verbal, and any partisan attitude, even when I have to denounce social injustice?

8. In what way would I have to change my behaviour to appear in the eyes of all as the loyal witness of Jesus Christ?

9. In my parish am I truly an element of union and of mutual understanding? Am I careful not to let myself be monopolized by any group or by any class, so that I may be in all truth at the service of all to increase the growth of Jesus Christ in each of them?

Resolutions

1. To re-read the encyclical of Pius XI, *Divini Redemptoris,* and the decree of the Holy Office, published in 1949, concerning Communism and its evil effects.

2. To extend and to make known by every means in my power the true social teaching of the Church.

3. To point out tactfully but fearlessly to Christians who have social responsibilities how serious their obligations are.

4. To assist Catholic Action movements to carry out their responsibilities.

5. To try to make the middle classes undertsand the true conditions of working class life. How much ignorance, how many prejudices, illusions, even among the best of them. To make them uneasy, if not repentent.

6. To denounce categorically the errors and faults that are rampant, but always to preserve charity for all.

7. To hold on to the two ends of the chain at all costs. Never compromise with error, deceit, selfishness, injustice, whatever its source, but not to reject anyone from the human community if I can avoid it.

8. To reflect more often on the millions of men, who, all over the earth, live in inhuman conditions, sometimes in degrading situations.

9. To reflect often on the millions of men, many priests among them, who have undergone mental if not physical torture and subtle interrogations to obtain so-called confessions and suffer so distressingly in concentration camps.

10. To pray and to get others to pray that God may raise up and multiply real saints who will ask the world today not to lose its soul.

Spiritual Reading

Without leaving the field of moral law and of religion, the Church has condemned atheistic materialism, as it is displayed in Marxist Communism, on the grounds that it inevitably leads to the

214

suppression of the human person and of the family by absorbing them into the State machine.

The Church has always refused to be associated with political opposition to Communism, which denies social injustices, the true cause of Communism. She remembers that "every error has some truth in it: to desire the amelioration of the working classes, to suppress the real abuses caused by a free economy, and to obtain a more equitable distribution of wealth are clearly perfectly legitimate objectives." (*Divini Redemptoris*)

To generous Christians, who are attracted by the immediate objectives of Communism, the hierarchy suggests that they should look further and understand the true dimensions of the problem and its implications. The Church has condemned Marxist Communism for three reasons: because of its atheistic materialism, which influences not only its philosophy, but its economic-social principles, its tactics, its propaganda and its operations; because of the religious persecution that it inaugurates wherever it is in power; and because of its effect, particularly on the human person and the family.

The Marxist conception of the class struggle represents a particular danger. For a Marxist, it is not only a struggle to free the workers, nor simply a wish to secure them better conditions. It is the surest means of inducing those who are caught up in it gradually to accept the whole Marxist philosophy. The Communist thinkers have never concealed this.

Christians who have not discovered this fraud are liable to be taken in, in all good faith. They reassure themselves by saying that the class struggle is an inescapable fact, imposed by capitalism itself, and practised by both sides. But war is also a fact. What Christians who really loves peace would willingly resign himself to war? They add that they put all hatred out of their heart in this struggle, as if they could resist the incessant appeals to violence and hatred. Gradually they are affected by the pernicious influence, and if they were perfectly free in their judgement they could perceive the signs of their growing dependence on Marxism.

They think that they can amputate from Communism the atheism of which they disapprove, when it is an integral part of it. They seem to forget that the triumph of Communism will be

215

the certain annihilation of the Catholic religion to which they profess to be attached. They deny or attribute to political motives – on exactly the same lines as Communist propaganda – the reality of religious persecution in the Church of silence. They are ready to take part in every campaign organized by the Communist party for political ends. But they show little concern for the sufferings and for the martyrdom of their brothers in the faith, for the imprisonment of the spiritual leaders of the Church, or for the deportation of many disciples of Jesus Christ.

They are opposed to social reforms, which could bring about the better conditions, because their primary object is to destroy the capitalistic system, and, for the final struggle, they must maintain the spirit of aggression and revolt, even if it causes increased suffering for those they are claiming to help. They extol the improvements brought about by Communism in a country in which social development had previously been neglected, but they say nothing about the totalitarianism of the régime, the suppression of personal liberty under the tyranny of its propaganda and its police machinery, the absence of any genuine moral obligation, and its overriding and universal requirement of absolute submission to the superior interests of the party.

Next they come to accept the false messianism of Communist propaganda, which promises happiness, peace and liberty as the fruits of the Communist revolution. They adopt the Marxist conception of the mythical symbolism of the proletariat and give it Christian values. They confuse evangelical poverty with working class conditions. They declare with the Communists that the Church is allied with the bourgeoisie and capitalism. They certainly add that they are faithful to the Church, but, because, as they say, the Church is no longer just the Pope, or the hierarchy, but each of us individually. Thus they try to introduce anarchical individualism into the Church. The objective underlying the Marxist appeal to Christians is then attained.

It is no longer enough for the Gospel to be announced to everyone and for the Church to put the means of salvation at the disposition of those most distant from her. It is also necessary for those to whom the message is carried to find around them, in the parishes, the visible sign of charity in the existence and life of real Christian communities. If these communities keep aloof and remain insensible to the drama of the salvation of humanity, all missionary activity will be paralysed. That is why the hierarchy wishes to make the faithful aware of missionary perspectives, and bring home to them the implications of belonging to a Church which is missionary in its very essence. They ask Christian communities to become centres of life and fraternal charity, to participate to the full in prayer, the sacraments and the Mass, to realize that they are responsible for their unbelieving brothers, with whom they are in constant contact, and to welcome Christians wherever they come from. (Extract from the declaration issued by the plenary assembly of the French hierarchy, April 1954.)

II

The following extract was written by a priest, who managed to escape from a concentration camp, and make his way across the Iron Curtain.

After the deportation and imprisonment of all regular clergy in 1950, we began to reflect on and analyse together our religious activities in the past, the current religious situation in our country, and the outlook for the future. We asked ourselves particularly what were the causes of our disaster and what we ought to do today and tomorrow. It was a real communal examination of conscience. We had plenty of time for that. We were left more than six months without regular occupation, in the hope of bringing us to a better frame of mind, and making us sign a declaration announcing our decision to leave our Order. I am now venturing to indicate the dominant ideas and the most important conclusions to which we came.

1. The bishops are interned or imprisoned. Many priests have met with the same fate. All Orders and Congregations are liquidated. Relations with the Holy See are severed and any contact with it is almost impossible. The Catholic press is suppressed, so are the Church schools. All Church organizations are dissolved. Every aspect of religious life is controlled by the State. The régime is fully associated with the internal affairs of the Church through a department for ecclesiastical affairs. Intensive

217

propaganda for atheistic materialism is being carried on. It is taught officially in all schools. The activity of the Church is very restricted, since it is paralysed or rendered impossible by the régime.

2. The moral unity – unanimity and harmony – of the hierarchy and clergy is undermined.

3. The confidence of the faithful in the clergy is shaken, partly by the influence of Communist propaganda, partly because the attitude of collaborating priests scandalizes the faithful.

4. Instruction and religious life are made increasingly difficult. Communist propaganda reports increasing success, especially among the young, at first on the social and ideological plane.

We are to blame. We were not ready. Communism has come to power by means of violence and external assistance which was too great for us to prevent. Given the international situation, on which we had no influence, our geographical position and the international agreements dividing the world into "zones of influence", our fate was settled in advance, without our opinion being asked. But if we had made the necessary preparation, we would have been able to slow up and to render less effective the action of Communism against the Church.

We were not sufficiently acquainted with the Communist technique. We expected violent persecution, the closing of churches, formal forbidding of belief in God and in prayer, a mass assassination of priests. Nothing like that happened. We understood too late that the Communists wish to destroy our faith by more subtle means. They believe that the day will come when we shall leave our churches voluntarily and ask the authorities to close them. We did not realize that they would want to penetrate into our very midst, that they would first want to divide us on the political plane in order to subdue us on the religious one later. We underestimated Communism. We counted on its speedy defeat. That is why we were not ready. We thought that the Communist system was so stupid that it was not worth taking it seriously. That is one of the principal reasons for our defeat.

Our struggle against Communism mostly took the form of global condemnation. We represented it to the faithful as one of the greatest moral and social evils, as the greatest plague of our time. Even if that is true, we forget that Communism, like every erroneous system which meets with success, must also have its attractive aspects and its moments of truth. When the faithful, particularly students, educated people, intellectuals, came to us with their doubts and their problems about Communism, many of us gave them the reply: "It is not worth taking seriously. It must be shunned as a diabolical temptation."

That was the line we took, while the Communists sent their agents into every factory, made contact with people of all classes, spread their ideas everywhere, discussed the most vital current problems, gave comprehensive answers to the questions put to them.

Against such tactics, formal arguments and summary condemnations were not sufficient. When Communism was installed among us and won successes in the social field, the negative attitude of the laity and some priests was shaken to the core. They had no real knowledge of Communism. They expected only negative things from it, they believed it would meet with prompt and total defeat. And Communism did not come in the way we had explained it to the faithful. Because of our own ignorance, there are people who now believe more in Communism than in our words. They have been brought over to Communist ideas, or no longer believe that Communism is the enemy of religion.

Many priests, after courses in re-education organized by the Communists, in which they were forced to take part, declared: it is only now that we know Communism, the danger it represents to us and can defend ourselves against it. That is why one of the first things we did in the concentration camp was to make a profound study of Communism.

It is evident that the most fundamental reason for the success of the Communists is the social injustices which exist in the world. Since we have not fought these injustices, we have facilitated the success of the Communists. Every measure against Communism will be useless as long as flagrant social injustices persist.

We were not united enough. In the past we were divided on the political and national plane. Religious Orders were rivals.

219

Each had its own methods and its field of activity, but they did little to co-ordinate their work or to direct it towards a common end. So, in some places and for some tasks there were too many priests, while in other fields of the apostolate, which may have been more urgent, the labourers were lacking.

In the monastery where we were all confined, we very much regretted that we had not met from time to time, when we were still at liberty, to find out how to co-ordinate our efforts, how to organize our apostolate, how to collaborate, how to help one another. We lived near one another, we worked side by side, and yet we remained strangers, as if we did not belong to the same army of Christ.

It was both ironical and tragic that the Communists taught us how to discuss and work in common, by confining us all together in a single monastery. Only then did we learn how much we had lost through failing to collaborate and to co-ordinate our work. If we had worked together fraternally, we could have been more united now. Today, when Communism is sowing discord among us, this lack of unity is cruelly felt. It is now that the clergy should act unanimously. It would be preferable to sacrifice even the legitimate freedom which moral theology permits, because of the benefit which the Communists derive when the clergy react differently to identical cases of conscience provoked by the Communist régime. These different reactions would be proper in themselves provided they were not excessive. But because the Communists exploit them for their own purposes, they represent a tactical error with particularly annoying consequences.

It is true that unity of practice is virtually impossible without meetings and consultation. Today, freedom to meet no longer exists in this country. Our clergy face a very delicate situation. Each of them is almost completely isolated by the régime from his superiors and his brethren. In this almost complete isolation he must act in circumstances which are still quite unprecedented and resolve for himself and for the faithful, cases of conscience of which he has no theoretical or practical experience, but which involve very serious problems.

Because the régime does not ask for direct action against the faith, but for things which seem rather to belong to the social, economic, political, or civil order, the priest can easily get the impression that if he resists requests of this kind, he will not suffer for God or for religion, but for profane things. He does not feel that he is a martyr for the faith, but has a sensation of civic guilt. When propaganda has succeeded in infusing a priest with this sensation, he no longer has the strength or heroism which the circumstances demand. This is particularly true of priests who previously held an important political or economic post and cannot therefore say that they are suffering solely because of the discharge of their priestly duties.

Equally to blame are those who take up a very extreme and uncompromising attitude at first, and then, when the pressure by the régime increases, give way abruptly. It would be much wiser to choose a middle path, to which they can adhere. To do this, however, we must first know Communism and its methods thoroughly, and above all, we must be ready to sacrifice everything, even life, rather than serve two masters.

We have neglected our duty to our flock. We have not educated them properly. Our parishioners always went to church and the sacraments, but their faith was not deep or sufficiently spiritual. Their faith was adequate in times of peace, but not when put to the test. We did not preach the Gospel in a way that all could understand. Our public and private life and our institutions, were not sufficiently permeated by the spirit of the Gospel.

We did not train our laity to a full and complete conception of life, as the Communists are now doing. The religious training of our parishioners has so often never gone beyond what they knew as children, whilst their scientific knowledge deepens unceasingly. That is why they do not know how to solve the apparent conflict between faith and science. This is particularly serious at the present time when priests do not enjoy free access to the faithful and when a well organized propaganda is systematically spreading false ideas about religion and the Church.

We often preached on the moral requirements of Christianity, but we did not explain sufficiently what Christianity is and what it gives us. That is why our religion may have seemed to many of the faithful simply a code of laws rather than a vital attachment of Jesus Christ. Today, when the very fact that we

221

are Christians demands great sacrifices, it is difficult for men to remain faithful when they have not understood and appreciated the interior splendour of Christianity, and have equated their Christianity with going to Mass on Sunday, receiving the sacraments from time to time, and to giving a little spare cash in the collections.

Our method of educating our Christian people has not been adequate. This was confirmed when we saw enthusiastic and indefatigable Communist agents going from village to village, from house to house to spread their "gospel". They seek men wherever they are to be found at work, at leisure, at home. They know how to find the right approach and to talk in a comprehensible and interesting manner to the worker, the intellectual, the child, and the aged. We were often content to wait for the faithful to come to churches and to school, and paid little attention to those who did not come. Those who do not come to church may never meet a priest face to face in their whole life. We have forgotten that it is the sick who need a doctor.

We have neglected the lay apostolate. Communist propaganda is always repeating that each Communist is a pioneer. We ought to be reiterating that each Christian should be an apostle. Catholic Action should be the realization of this idea. But Catholic Action is not sufficiently developed because the clergy, secular and regular, have not understood it properly.

The priest's strength is limited. He hasn't enough time to go everywhere, and he finds certain circles are closed to him. If there are no lay apostles who can make contact with those who are unwilling to see a priest they will be lost to the Church. There are older priests who do not know enough about modern apostolic methods and the necessity for them. In our monastery we regretted that we did not train lay apostles to replace the priests to some extent. Today, when priests are becoming more and more rare, and their freedom of movement and activity is more restricted, the role of the lay apostle is more and more indispensable and essential.

We neglected charity. Communist propaganda classes us among the bourgeois. In our prison we frankly acknowledged that the accusation was not without foundation. We forgot that Christ came to serve and not to be served. We took advan-

222

tage of our spiritual dignity to put ourselves among those who are served. Our material life may not always have been based on evangelical poverty. We have often overeaten and lived in well heated houses, without thinking of Christ who suffered from hunger and shivered from cold in our brothers, under our very windows. If we gave something to them, it was only the crumbs which could no longer be put on our table. Ought not our houses to have been living centres of the charity of Christ?

Even institutions such as hospitals and schools, which had been founded to serve the poor gratuitiously, for the love of God, were often accessible only to the wealthy who could pay fees.

"Show us the charity which you preach, and of which your books speak", the Communists say to us. Communism sees in religion only a money-making business. One of the arguments which they use to support their claim is based on the fees which are required for certain church ceremonies – the fact that the way in which a marriage or funeral is performed reflects the amount paid to the priest. The Communists tell the faithful that the rich are favoured by the Church, and that they will have priority even in heaven. Everything depends not on your Christian life but on your money. This propaganda has its effect on those who judge the value of a religious ceremony by its external solemnity.

In social conflicts of our time we often, morally at least, upheld the rich. Or, at least, we dared not protest against social injustice for fear of losing the contribution of our benefactors who were not the most fervent Christians. All this gave the poor and the working class the impression that we did belong to the ruling class. So they believe in the Communist propaganda which puts us in the same category as the capitalists. Thus all the hatred that Communism stirs up in the hearts of the workers against the bourgeoisie and the capitalists, whom they make responsible for all the sufferings of the proletariat, is also felt against priests. That is why so many workers, even if they are believers, distrust priests. They see in them their social enemies or at least the accomplices of their enemies. This prejudice against priests is easily transformed into prejudice against the Church and religion.

223

Communism is a reaction. It is a reaction against social injustice – and against our lack of charity towards the poor. We have neglected Christ and the poor, his friends. Now Communism calls them to testify against us. In places where there were priests who did not only speak of charity but practised it, where priests fostered an intense social apostolate, Communism has found it difficult to secure an entry, and Communist accusations against priests as enemies of the people are ineffectual.

This chapter may seem severe. It is meant to be. But in criticizing our former religious life we have no wish to underestimate it. For the religious life of our country, in some parts particularly, was intense and alive. And it is still. Much has been done among us for the Kingdom of God, and of this we are very conscious. But what we regretted after our deportation – when we saw how the wolves were ravaging our sheep and we were powerless to defend them effectively, was that we had not prepared the faithful for the heroic times which require real saints.

Father Michel

Subjects for Discussion

1. Comment on the statement of Lenin: "Truth, for us, is always subjectively objective. Facts exist only as far as they express the Marxist conception of the world."

2. What problems are created for the priestly conscience by the existence of Communism?

Prayer

O Lord, who desirest above all things the unity of mankind, who art the substantial bond of that unity, look upon this poor blind world, which gropes after its salvation. Under the influence of your Spirit of Love, let men understand that salvation is in you alone, and that the only unity is what is based on you.

Have pity on those who in various ways suffer persecution for justice's sake. As you laid Saul low on the way to Damascus, convert those who persecute the Church and make them your missionaries and apostles.

Raise up the saints whom we need so badly today, but above all, grant that all Christians, sharing your great love for their brothers, may become real witnesses of the Gospel in the various fields in which you have placed them. Enlighten those who have social responsibilities. Help them in their efforts towards loyalty and justice.

Grant that our search for the common good may be allied with respect for the human person, and that, faithful to the social teaching of the Church, men may discover the way which enables those in peril to recover their equilibrium, harmony and peace. Amen.

Thought

The existence of Communism can help us to see that human weakness is always obscuring the light of the divine message. If we wish to check Communism effectively and regain the ground that has been lost, we must first reform our personal life and our behaviour according to the purity of the Christian message.

Dufay

12

THE SPIRIT OF PEACE

Meditation

Let us adore our Lord who greets us as he loved to greet his disciples with the words: "Peace be to you! It is I, fear not." (Luke 24:36) Let us hear him say to us as in Saint John's Gospel: "Peace I leave with you: my peace I give unto you: not as the world giveth, do I give unto you. Let not your heart be troubled, nor let it be afraid." (John 14:27) "These things I have spoken to you, that in me you may have peace." (John 16:33) And in Saint Mark: "Have salt in you and have peace among you." (Mark 9:49)

Let us listen to his promise: "Blessed are the peacemakers, for they shall be called the children of God." (Matt. 5:9) Let us recall the repeated appeals of Saint Paul: ". . . be of one mind, have peace. And the God of peace and of love shall be with you." (2 Cor. 13:11) "Follow peace with all men, and holiness: without which no man shall see God. Looking diligently, lest any man be wanting to the grace of God: lest any root of bitterness springing up do hinder and by it many be defiled." (Heb. 12:14, 15) "To no man rendering evil for evil. Providing good things, not only in the sight of God but also in the sight of all men. If it be possible as much as is in you, have peace with all men." (Rom. 12:17, 18)

"I therefore beseech you that you walk worthy of the vocation in which you are called: with all humility and mildness, with patience, supporting one another in charity. Careful to keep the unity of the Spirit in the bond of peace." (Eph. 4:1-3) "And the peace of God, which surpasseth all understanding, keep your hearts and minds in Christ Jesus." (Phil. 4:7) "Let the peace of Christ rejoice in your hearts, wherein also you are called in one body." (Col. 3:15) "Now the Lord of peace himself give you everlasting peace in every place." (2 Thess. 3:16)

While celebrating Mass, we have all noticed how often the word "peace" recurs as a dominant idea from the beginning of the Canon onwards. "That it may please thee to grant peace . . . throughout the world." "We beseech thee to order our days in thy peace." "Mercifully grant peace in our days . . . that we may be free from all sin and secure from all disturbance." "The peace of the Lord be always with you." "Lamb of God . . . grant us peace." The first of the three prayers before Communion is entirely devoted to peace: "vouchsafe to grant her peace and unity according to thy will."

Today, after so many cruel wars, we never cease to talk about peace. But we must remember that the word does not have the same meaning for everyone. If all men long for peace, few work effectively to achieve it. Some make use of the word to camouflage a partisan spirit and work to secure the domination of one class or party. Others use it to dispense themselves from effort or to escape from action. "They call it peace, and there is no peace", declared Ezechiel and Jeremias. The peace which we seek, the peace which it is our mission to procure for men, is the peace which comes from Christ, which the world cannot give, and which always eludes us if we seek it elsewhere than in God, his justice and his love. Let us try, then, to share this divine peace and, under its influence, let us analyze what it means.

The spirit of peace is not the spirit of tranquillity. The definition of peace given by Saint Thomas has become a classic. "Peace is tranquillity in order", but he never claimed that order is the fruit of tranquillity. As long as we are on this earth, order, the fruit of justice, will always be threatened. That is a consequence of original sin, of weakness, and of human limitations. To stand by unperturbed when unjust assaults are made on justice is to make ourselves for all intents and purposes accessory to them. In his *Mystère de la Charité de Jeanne d'Arc*, Péguy refers to this opposition between the spirit of peace and the spirit of tranquillity. Madame Gervaise does not hesitate to say: "From the moment God calls you, you will never find tranquillity."

Sometimes there are individuals who place their tranquillity above everything else. To have a tranquil life, without cares, is an ideal unworthy of a noble soul, and is moreover an illusory ideal, for life takes care to ruffle those who strive to avoid struggle and effort. How can a priestly soul be indifferent to the miseries of the world, to the spiritual and moral distress of souls, to the sufferings of so many men?

The spirit of peace has nothing in common with quietism, which is the fruit of a false mysticism, and soon ends in a completely self-centred life, and in a false conscience, forgetful of the wishes of God and of the requirements of the mission he has given, for fear of the difficulties action may bring in its train.

Hinduism, which in fashionable circles tends to haunt some currents of spirituality, is no stranger to that false conception of peace, a real migration to things of the spirit. For the Brahmin, existence is an evil; activity is the great obstacle to happiness and salvation. Did not the quietism of the eighteenth century tend, in the name of absorption in God, to suppress personal activity and moral responsibility? It is so tempting, in a difficult period, to bypass responsibility. A priest, even when he is a contemplative, should be a fighter, even if only against the infernal powers which prowl about us so craftily. "The kingdom of heaven has been enduring violent assault, and the violent have been seizing it by force."

The spirit of peace is not simply the love of exterior order. A priest should indeed love order; the word forms part of the name of the sacrament which made him a priest. His motto is; "To serve God first." To have order in his ideas, in his business, in the employment of his time, is a very praiseworthy quality. But he must beware of a distortion which would make him judge the value of a society by the order which exists there, the worth of a group, and even of a ceremony, by its external order. There is an order created by fear which can be only false. Let us recall the famous phrase of Sebastiani, at the moment when the Polish insurrection of 1831 was being drowned in waves of blood by the Russians: "Order reigns in Warsaw."

Order is no longer the collective privilege of one class. Of what value is a "moral order" which is paid for by the misery and the suffering of a great number of men? We are not required to make the distress of the world weigh on our nerves; but to bear it in our hearts and to contribute, through our faith, our hope, and our effective charity, to the renewal of the face of the earth.

Pontius Pilate is not dead. Shirking is still the permanent temptation of all those who hold authority; fear of complications, fear of being compromised, fear of being committed. It is certainly not a question of binding ourselves without due consideration. But when we have the honour and responsibility of leading, we must know how, without acting "quixotically", to cover our subordinates, to stand by whatever we have signed, to consider that our word is our bond, to defend those who are accused unjustly. It is easy to wash our hands, to get out of a venture without a loss, but it is cowardly, and cowardice can be fatal. Until the end of the world, humanity will associate the name of Pontius Pilate with the sufferings and death of Jesus Christ.

It is not pacifism, swallowing everything and condoning everything, surrendering before the least opposition, going so far as to forego the responsibilities imposed by our duties and the mission we have been given. "Peace is not a matter of sentiment", said Cardinal Feltin. "We do not want a sentimental peace. It has made too many tears and too much blood flow; it has reassured too many hypocrisies, favoured too many illusions. Let us not lead peace into the mire of utopian pacifists."

"Peace is a great good. Yes, a great good, but not the greatest good", said Father Lebbe, who paid with his blood for that declaration. "There is a good more precious still and more absolutely necessary to man. This is justice: a peace which is not based on justice is false, deceptive, and ephemeral. A peace bought at the price of slavery is a disgrace; life purchased at the price of this disgrace is not worth living; it is nothing more than a slow death. This choice would be for a Christian the worst

229

of downfalls. It is the vile sin of cowardice, of running away from duty to save our skin."

The spirit of peace is a spirit of communion with God. He is infinite peace because he is infinite love. Peace is in fact the fruit of love. It is in love that the three Persons are distinguished infinitely and are united intimately: the Father who gives himself to the Son, the Son who never ceases receiving everything from the Father, and who offers himself to the Father unceasingly, the Spirit who is the substantial fruit of this actual gift. Far from being opposed to each other, the three divine Persons, having only one nature, live in harmony, the utmost harmony. God is peace because he is love and love tends to unity.

Each soul created in the image of God receives with his nature, his place in the world and all the graces needed to realize the plan God has made for him, the principles of his individual peace, and, because he is placed in the midst of others, the principle of peace with those around him. Men can have peace only if they agree to collaborate, with a filial and fraternal love, in the plan of God for each individual and for all. In other words, the more the heart of men desire to love God and to accomplish his will, the greater will be the possibility of harmony which will bring the peace of the world.

Peace is the desire to know better in order to understand better; to understand better in order to love better; in order to help more all our brothers near and far. It is sometimes easier to achieve this in respect of those who are far away than of those who are close at hand. But how will it benefit a man to try to agree with the whole world if he is not capable of living in harmony with those around him?

Finally, peace is the habitual disposition to reduce to just proportions the conflicts which cannot fail to spring up among men; it is the will to resolve them in an atmosphere of loyalty, justice, understanding, and if necessary, firmness.

How can we develop the spirit of peace? In this world peace is always precarious. It is the drama of humanity, for man is a finite being, subject to error and to sin. The ransom of sin is death and illness – it is also war. On all sides, as Saint Peter warned us, the enemy prowls around. Force grounded in our faith will be the best means of resistance, but in this world there is never permanent peace, never perfect peace. We should not, however, take the line "all or nothing". A degree of peace can be achieved. It is the only possible peace, the peace of Christ himself which we have to weave into the weft of humanity by our communion with his Spirit of peace.

Peace is one of those treasures which depend on an atmosphere created by everyone's efforts. It is not a simple problem, but its solution, at least relatively, can be furthered by an attitude of soul which is penetrated by love. Even if peace can never be a complete and universal conquest, we can at least contribute to the creation of a breathable atmosphere, and further mutual esteem by developing sentiments of solidarity, by making reasons of mistrust disappear, by demonstrating in all circumstances a sincere will for justice and respect for the equal dignity of all men, with consideration for the strength, needs and merits which will differ in each individual. Is not this what being a pacifist means?

We must, of course, pray for peace, for peace is a gift of God, but as Cardinal Feltin has said: "If peace needs God, God needs men. The world will belong to those who love God more." All the Christian virtues contribute in varying degree to peace in our own consciences, in our homes, in society, in the world. The spirit of justice is a source of peace. On the first Christmas night, the Angels sang: "Glory to God in the highest and peace on earth to men of good will." The two parts of the sentence are connected. The more men work for the glory of God, the more they find peace for themselves. The more they obey the commandments of God, the more they suppress the principal causes of disunion among themselves. A peace based on injustice is a false peace. A peace imposed by constraint is not peace. There is peace only where no legitimate right is voluntarily damaged. If the number of those who, on all planes, are concerned about justice grows, we can hope for the safety of peace. Partisan spirit, sectarian spirit, the spirit of vengeance are opposed to the spirit of peace.

You will find true peace only in humility. Abase yourself sincerely before God more and more. Try at least to do so: you will see results. If you can come to love (in your will) humiliation and contradiction, you will have gone a long way towards

231

God. Accept frankly and without interior or exterior discussion the little humiliations of each day. Try; it is only the first step which is difficult. Habit can take deep root. And then, what joy and peace! Accept with humility your inability to please everyone: to want it to be otherwise would be to wish for the impossible.

Discretion is a source of peace. The priest, trustee of so many secrets, acquainted with so many things, even outside the confessional, should contribute more than any one else to the avoidance of all that can set men against one another. An imprudent word can make sparks fly in homes; indiscretion can upset lives. "A soul at peace is a soul which does not gossip, which does not get mixed up in gossip, which does not listen to gossip", said Mother Marie-Thérèse. She added: "Someone has hurt me; I will not repeat it to anyone, not even to myself."

Obedience is also a source of peace. Those who live in a state of obedience have a guarantee that they are in order, since they are sure of doing the will of God. Those who resist, suffer and exhaust themselves in their resistance without profit to anyone. Their suffering, unlike those who expiate and produce an increase of love, is likely to be sterile.

Moderation is a condition of peace. Many priests wear themselves out in efforts which leave their souls bruised and impoverished because they strive for an ideal of virtue and sanctity which God does not ask of them. God indeed gives them credit for their generosity. Their ill-considered efforts do not, however, produce the fruits which they would have produced if they had been more attentive to what God expects of them than to their own desires. As Saint Paul says: "Let no one rate himself more than he ought, but let him rate himself according to moderation, and according as God has apportioned to each one the measure of faith." Commenting on this, Father Roguet said: "We should not pursue perfection by means more perfect in themselves than those which are appropriate to our measure of faith and of grace. Good works are the nourishment of the life of our soul. Works more perfect in themselves are not always more perfect for us. Let us be obedient to the Holy Spirit, and not try to forestall him."

"Prayer is the first of all the duties of man. Neither empires, nor wealth, nor the show of power, nor wars, nor family or national interests, must outweigh the question put to each of us: 'What do you think of prayer? What progress are you making in your prayer life?'"

"The more contemplatives there are, the less will efforts be squandered in empty searching after peace. Society will obtain not the peace of men which is basically only animal, but the peace of God which surpasses all understanding." This is the enlightened faith, which allows us to see Christ in every man, a living cell of his mystical Body, and to consider as done to Christ whatever we do to one another, and so facilitates the development of the spirit of peace.

Above all, it is charity that is the basis of every effective effort for true peace. Only charity allows us to understand the point of view of others, to respect their rights, and to facilitate harmony by creating an atmosphere of confidence, understanding, and union. It is charity which smoothes off the edges which rough justice might make hurtful. Charity alone allows us to discover points of agreement and to resolve discord. We shall be workers for peace if we are messengers, real charity, which pardons, which gives, which asks nothing in return.

Christ speaks to his Priest

I am there within you, the source of peace. Drink from this source, taste of this water, let yourself be penetrated to the very depths of your being. I am peace. I give you my peace. I leave you my peace. Peace be with you. In saying that I give myself to you. Breathe me in. Greet me. Receive me. Guard me and hold me in your soul. Then you will know the secret of interior calmness. You will receive the grace of deep stability.

Why are you troubled? Are you afraid of me? Am I not near you, with you, in you? Your sins, your resistance, your frequent carelessness? Humble yourself, accuse yourself honestly, but do not lose your peace, or, if you have lost it, come to me to find it again. Am I not in you, the one who sees you, the one who, as soon as you regret a fault, excuses it, pardons it, and takes it on

233

himself? Am I not in you, the one who sees the efforts, the trials, the choices of love, the one who assesses them at their true value?

I am much more concerned with your good qualities than with your faults. I see your faults only to apply my virtues to them, so as to cure them if you consent. Your good qualities are for me positive advances of your will in reply to my gifts which have traced out paths of grace in your soul. Many lose joy because they do no longer feel they are receiving any more sympathy, confidence, or affection. Do not do this. Of course, sympathy, confidence and affection are a great comfort. I do not ask you to despise or reject them, but to value your peace more highly. If some one attacks you, leave your defence to me, give me the joy of defending you when I wish, when it seems opportune. If you find your suffering hard to bear, thank me for letting you have a share in the work of redemption, and you will find peace again.

Do not worry about the future. It is only the present moment that you can sanctify. Sufficient for each day is the evil thereof. For each difficulty there is sufficient grace. Do your work well today through love. That will be the best way to prepare for tomorrow's task. Spread union and peace wherever you go. Peace should emanate from your whole being and from every action. There is a manner of acting and of speaking which agitates and which troubles. There is a manner of acting and of speaking which calms and creates an atmosphere of serenity. Ask me for the secret. It is a secret of confidence and love. So little is necessary sometimes to change an atmosphere: calmness, a little gentleness, much humility, the remembrance of my presence.

The spirit of peace is contagious. It is like a perfumed oil which lubricates and perfumes everything. But it is the heart which distills it and secretes it drop by drop. When all the thoughts, all the feelings, all the desires are impregnated by it, it pours out and by degrees wins over all human groups. A handful of souls who are steeped in it would be sufficient to transform the world. Divine peace is found in the bosom of God. As a little child gradually develops, so do you grow in the bosom of God. Grow in me, move in me, breathe in me; be nourished by

234

my thought, my sanctity, my desires, in order to live in me. Then you will acquire unalterable peace, the peace which the world cannot give, but which through you, and through all souls united to me I shall give to the world.

Examination of Conscience

1. Am I at peace with God . . . with my conscience, with those around me . . . with authority?

2. Do I live in an atmosphere of calm or of unrest?

3. Do I accomplish everything diligently but without unnecessary haste?

4. Am I more impatient than formerly? Do I not see that this impatience lessens my prestige and brings no good result? Men soon feel that a priest who is incapable of controlling his nerves has lost his right to advise them.

5. Am I convinced that a priest should never give the impression of being rushed, and still less say he is? For he will end by believing it and that would cripple him.

6. Everyone makes mistakes, everyone blunders. The only people who make no mistakes are those who do nothing. Do I understand that the surest way of putting things right is precisely not to lose my calmness?

7. Have I been impressed by the fact that there is no fruitful activity in feverish agitation? It is better to do a little less, very well, than to do a lot badly. If the task to which I am assigned upsets me, it is either not willed for me by God or I do not know how to tackle it the right way.

8. Am I not tempted to look upon calmness as a simple question of temperament, forgetting that every temperament can be improved?

9. Have I been able to observe in what circumstances I lack serenity? Is it not above all when my self-love is at stake, when my weak points are exposed to view?

10. If I become irritable, is it not because I have taken on too many things, more than I can manage, and because I am unable to succeed in them and then become a victim of an inferiority complex?

11. Am I in the habit of seeing things and events from a supernatural point of view? Nothing so facilitates return to calmness as re-establishing our scale of values, and focusing the light of eternity or even of a few years ahead on our weariness. In two or three years I shall have forgotten this unpleasant episode. In any case it will appear but of little importance, and the shock that I feel today will be lost in the past.

12. Do I force myself, wherever I am, not only to be peaceful but pacific?

13. Many divisions between men, classes, nations, result from a fundamental misunderstanding of differing points of view. Truth and justice are never totally on one side. Can I not, in many circumstances, bring light and peace to souls? It requires much tact and love. As Saint Thérèse of Lisieux said: "We should be, not judges, but angels of peace."

14. Do I appreciate the danger of leaving to non-Christians the monopoly of the struggle for peace? Have I not observed that there are many people unbalanced by a deceitful propaganda which represents the Church as having allied itself with armaments, manufacturers, and warmongers?

15. Am I capable of explaining what the Church has done and is doing unceasingly for peace?

16. Do I myself pray and do I get other souls to pray for the peace of Christ, which is the fruit of justice and of love?

17. Do I realize that there is, among children as well as among adults, a real need for the re-education of souls in the understanding of peace?

Below the surface of much antagonism is religious fanaticism. Anyone who believes that he is defending a just cause identifies it freely with that of God. "There is no other way to the peace we all wish for", said Pius XII, "than that which proceeds from the re-education of humanity in the spirit of fraternal fellowship."

Resolutions

1. To share often in the peace of Christ, in the calmness and the serenity which emanate from his divine Person.

236

2. True peace is a gift of God. To ask it humbly, every day, for myself, for others, for the world.

3. To get to know, to study thoroughly, and to assimilate the messages of the Pope about peace.

4. To note and to meditate on the places in the Mass in which peace is mentioned.

5. Not to make a tragedy of the little difficulties inherent in human society. To force myself to minimize the knocks, the misunderstanding, the opposition I experience. There is no opposition so complete that there is no point of agreement. To bring out these points which are often basic elements, before defining calmly the points of disagreement which are often only problems of method or procedure. To try then to resolve them one by one in an atmosphere of conciliation and calmness. To invoke the Holy Spirit, asking him to inspire all reasonable concessions for the good of peace.

6. Never to transfer opposition which arises from facts and things to the personal plane. To make it my duty to appeal to the love of Christ if I feel antipathy developing for the person with whom I find myself in disagreement, to list his good qualities and to offer them frequently to our Lord, without forgetting to mention those "qualities and merits of which I am unaware". To do him all the kindness in my power.

7. To be careful about putting things on paper, remembering that: "Words fly off, what has been written remains." The word spoken too hotly can escape quickly; it is easy to apologize and put things right. But what is written is lasting, and a bitter pen can inflict wounds which fester. Never to write when I am angry, and if I do so to "relieve my nerves", not to post my letter without letting a night pass. In all probability I shall then decide to write a note which is calmer and more effective.

8. If my lack of calmness results from over-exertion, to make a list of the tasks which I have to carry out and put them in the order of urgency. Specify the approximate amount of time needed for each of them, and do not think about the second until I have calmly done the first.

9. If my lack of calmness comes from fatigue, from a passing indisposition, to arrange some periods of rest, however short they may be, to practise relaxing.

10. If my lack of calmness comes from a tendency to place too much emphasis on exterior things, to make myself take a few minutes for interior silence, several times a day.

11. If my lack of calmness is the result of unexpected mishaps, to recall that everything is a grace, and that everything can serve for the glory of God and the good of souls.

12. To develop among the faithful an understanding and a respect for others. To make them understand that nothing is more contrary to the Christian spirit than generalized criticisms and ostracism of other social groups or other races.

13. To publicize the Pax Christi movement, a movement of prayer, thought, and action for peace, warmly encouraged by the hierarchy.

Spiritual Reading

Mary is a source of peace, the hope of peace for our feverish, sinful world. Mary is a source of peace, the hope of peace for each of our feverish and sinful souls. To have peace among ourselves, it is necessary to have peace in ourselves. Since sin is the root of all disorders, of all wars, and grace is the only principle of the peace of God, we should uproot sin wherever it is to be found, that is, in our heart.

In sin, in the satisfaction of disordered desires, our heart is never at peace. It finds only disquiet. It is only in God that it finds true peace. The experience and the confessions of Saint Augustine are sufficient confirmation of this. Only the soul which is freed from sin and living in God rests in serenity. Injustice or persecution cannot alter his peace. We can understand how much the Immaculate Virgin enjoyed interior peace, and what must be her power to obtain it for us.

The man who, without offending God, "is burdened, nevertheless, with strange worries and tries to spread them around him", cannot know peace. On the contrary, recollection, silence, the hidden life, are powerful factors towards interior peace. How truly, then, by the circumstances of her life, the Blessed Virgin was and is an example and a source of interior peace.

Father Dusserre

Subjects for Discussion

1. Is peace on earth a supreme good to which all other benefits should be sacrificed?

2. Comment on the Beatitude: "Blessed are the peacemakers, for they shall be called children of God."

3. What line of demarcation can one establish between a pacific person and a pacifist?

Prayer

Heavenly Father, from whom proceeds every gift in this world, keep my soul always in that peace which comes from you. Grant me the grace never to be troubled by passing difficulties, present or future.

Our Father, who loves neither agitation, nor noise, let me find in contemplation the serenity which I need to accomplish my duty according to your will and in your Spirit.

Our Father, who loves union among your children, grant that good understanding, based on the loyal search for justice and charity may rule my relations with those around me, for the greater good of all. Have pity on this poor world which gropes after peace, without being able to find it. May men recognize your Son and find, with your grace, in the realization of their fundamental brotherhood, the secret of lasting peace promised to men of good will. Amen.

Thought

The peaceful man is more useful than the learned man. Ask all men: Do you want peace? With one voice the human race will reply: I want it, I long for it, I love it. Then love justice as well: for they are two friends, justice and peace: they embrace each other.

Saint Augustine

13

PARISH VISITING

The problem of parish visiting is very topical. Pope Pius XII often stressed it as one of the most pressing duties of the clergy. A priest cannot really know his parishioners unless he is aware of all the social influences which affect their lives; that is to say, the psychological and moral consequences of their professions or their studies; whether they live in misery, modest comfort or luxury; the trade union to which they belong; the laws or regulations which restrain or assist them. We cannot reach souls through the abstract. Each man has a personal destiny, but groups depend on the behaviour of the individuals in them.

Research, surveys and actual visiting give priests an opportunity to obtain a fuller knowledge of those in their care. It is as part of this practical knowledge that priests must make their plans for evangelization, organize the liturgical life of their parish, prepare parochial or general missions, distribute tasks, choose sites for churches and halls.

Meditation

At the beginning of this meditation let us adore our Lord, who is asking us to imitate him in his role of Good Shepherd: "I know mine, and they know me." Every priest ought to be a missionary: "As the Father has sent me, I also send you." Sometimes into the midst of a faithful flock, sometimes "like sheep in the midst of wolves".

If God's grace urges us to it, during a few minutes we can review some of the aspects of our mission, which our Lord himself has emphasized. "I came to give testimony to the truth." (John 18:37) "The truth shall make you free." (John 8:32) "I am come that they may have life and may have it more abundantly." (John 10:10) "Now this is eternal life: that they may know thee, the only true God, and Jesus Christ, whom thou hast sent." (John 17:3) "I am come to cast fire on the earth. And what will I, but that it be kindled?" (Luke 12:49)

The more we reflect, the more we shall understand that parish visiting is one of the key actions of our priestly ministry. How, therefore, should we regard it, and in what disposition of soul should it be undertaken?

Whether we like it or not, we are not entirely "like other men". Even to those who do not practise any religion we pose a problem. To some people we are even incomprehensible. In any case, our sacred character is subject to many misconceptions. Where there is not open hostility our mere presence causes a kind of psychological release of memories and feelings favourable to religion.

If, moreover, we pay this visit with simplicity, putting people at their ease quickly; if we do not appear superior; if we show ourselves to be true, human, understanding, we make religion estimable, desirable, sympathetic. There are so many homes which a priest has never visited! And sometimes so little is needed to dissipate prejudices, to dispel hostility! The fact of becoming friendly with the parish priest is not tantamount to a conversion, but it is a first step which can lead farther. "Before Christianizing, we must first make friends", said Father de Foucauld.

On the other hand the priest should not be looked upon as a technician, a doctor whom people call only in case of need. When a priest has already crossed the threshold of a home, those who live there are less embarrassed to ask him to come again.

Finally, the influence of the priest on the children is likely to be much deeper when the parents are seen to be collaborating with him in a positive way. Instead of hearing his parents declare that religion is out-of-date, the child sees that the priest is welcome in his home and that he is looked upon as a family friend. This bond between the family and the priest is very effective in encouraging the faith of the child.

The stranger who sees a herd passing by sees only a confused mass and would be hard put to distinguish the individual beasts; he finds that all the animals look alike. The shepherd, who knows the sheep individually, knows that no one is exactly like another. "And he calleth his own sheep by name and leadeth them out." (John 10:3)

"It is the duty of the priest" said Pius XII, "to provide himself with a clear and detailed picture of his parish. We suggest a street map showing the homes of all the faithful and in particular of outstanding parishioners capable of organizing Catholic Action; secondly, of the areas which have abandoned Christianity. These areas are also full of sheep belonging to the parish: strayed sheep. If you are good priests, you must spare neither work nor trouble to seek them out, to reclaim them; you must allow yourself no rest until all have been brought back to shelter, to life and joy in the fold of Jesus Christ."

Every home presents a different case. There are homes completely Christian, homes where only one member is Christian, homes where there is only a vague idea of religion, indifferent homes, hostile homes. There are homes where union prevails, there are homes where lives are disrupted, with every shade of difference. There are homes where parents take great care of the education of their children, and others where the children get along the best way they can.

We have many things to learn in our contacts with our parishioners: not only the knowledge of various situations, but also sociological difficulties and problems which characterize the texture of their lives. We shall grasp more readily their prejudices, their ignorance, and the origin of the trains of thought which influence their psychology. Perhaps we shall be able to find out the hidden aspirations which each one has towards a more beautiful, if not a better, life. There are so many Christians who are ignorant! It is always for us to develop the yearnings for redemption in each heart.

These contacts gradually help us to discover those who have a gift for leadership, those who mould the opinion of the district, those who exercise a real influence in one sense or another. It is quite feasible to discover potential leaders who would not of themselves have approached us. The pride they feel in knowing the parish priest personally, of having received him into their homes, makes people more interested in when he says in the pulpit if they come to church on a feast day or for a funeral, and makes them more willing to read what he has written, in a parish magazine, for example. These points of contact bring us in touch with the sufferings, the difficulties, the miseries, the deficiencies of our people and so give more realism to our preaching, and to the organization of our work in the parish.

Finally, do they not spur us on to give ourselves to the priest for all our parishioners and to try and make Christ grow in each one of them?

If we ensure that the first thought in our mind when we make a visit is not to discuss our own concerns, even parish problems, but to show an interest in the concerns of those we are visiting, the true problems of their lives will be put before us. For many parishioners a meeting with a priest can be a chance to expose the depth of their souls, the long unhappiness of their personal history, their protest against what they believe to be the injustice of fate. It is for us to express a Christian view on these happenings or facts. It is for us to inject real hope into their hearts and to lead them gradually to faith and true charity.

Many do not know how to think, and often the exchange of views opens up perspectives hitherto overlooked, which can make a deep impression on their minds. It is not impossible for such discussions, in which all the problems of their married, social, and professional life can be examined from a Christian point of view, to give birth to local groups which will form a basis for real Catholic Action movements.

What should be our disposition in undertaking this work? Certainly with a great spirit of faith. When Father Michonneau was explaining his method of paying parish visits at a conference, he insisted that every priest should adopt the habit of spending some time before the Blessed Sacrament before going out among the parishioners.

A parish visit is not a simple neighbourly visit, on a purely human plane. The priest is literally sent by God. He brings God

243

with him. It is not necessary, and in all probability not opportune, to say so; but we must act accordingly. So much the better
then, if it is felt.

The spirit of faith will doubtless bring us the inspiration of
the Holy Spirit and will suggest to us, at the right moment, what
we should say. The spirit of faith will also give us the intuition
which will enable us to understand souls better, to sense what is
best in each one, and to help them to accomplish, in their own
environment, with the grace and light they enjoy, whatever God
expects of them.

We must be discreet and disinterested. Discretion as to the
choice of time, the duration, and the frequency of our visits. It is
a question of tact, of delicacy, and of environment. There is a
happy medium which varies with the place and the person.

It is clear that a priest must know how to adapt his life to the
conditions of the people of his parish. There is a difference between the time that will suit a working man's family, and the
time that will suit a family in the country or a professional
family. Let us not forget that we must adapt ourselves to our
parishioners; the parishioners should not have to suit our con-
venience. And if, as a result, we have to change a mealtime, let us
look upon this sacrifice as part of our mission.

Above all, let us not think that we are wasting time if we do
not see immediate results. We must act on the principle that we
will not neglect anyone. We are to bring the message of our
Lord to everyone. Our personal disinterestedness must be manifest to all. Nothing would be more harmful than visits in which
questions of money came up: an offering for a good work, a
subscription, alms for charity. Putting such requests in the home
is liable to be misunderstood by many of our parishioners and to
earn us the reputation of beggars.

We cannot imagine how much "the clink of money around
the altar" has harmed our reputation and our moral authority.
Some prudent priests even refuse Mass stipends offered during a
visit, and explain that they should be given in at the sacristy.
Similarly, nothing would be more inconsistent with the spirit of
parish visiting than to take advantage of it to discuss financial
difficulties over upkeep of the church or of the school. The less
we speak of money, the more good we will do.

244

This disinterestedness should go still further. Zeal can make us thoughtless and lead us to profit by these visits to invite our host to particular meetings or functions. Experience proves that it is better not to do this. Anything that can be interpreted as proselytism or recruiting spoils the atmosphere of our approach. Those we visit will examine their conscience of their own accord; they will admit to us that they do not go to church often. Let us try to understand what our Lord asks of them. We must not minimize Sunday obligations. But we should insist more on the fact that we look on them as adults who are old enough to know what they are expected to do, and on the elementary truth that we do not want to bring pressure on anyone. Our Lord wants souls to come to him freely. The idea that God wants volunteers, that he wants men to be free to love him and to serve him, will do more to make practical religion esteemed than reproaches or pressing invitations, which are liable to be inappropriate and untimely.

There are equally elementary rules of discretion which the priest should always observe in the questions he asks and in the remarks he makes. For example, he should never make an observation to the parents in presence of the children, and he should be careful not to repeat in one house what he has learned in another.

A priest should have sympathy for all the people in his parish, no matter who they are, or what may be their faults; not a forced sympathy, but a genuine one, which springs from the heart. That attitude of soul is not acquired in a few days. It is the fruit of a charity drawn from the heart of Christ, and at the same time of an intelligence awake to all miseries and moral or material suffering. This active sympathy will be at once a tender and respectful affection for all our people burdened by material problems, as victims more often than guilty, whom God calls and waits for.

This sympathy should extend to all, even to great sinners or to those who are unfriendly, for all have their portion of sufferings and they may have excuses of which we are not aware. Our Lord loves them, not only in spite of their misery, but in their very misery. They should feel that they are loved as they are, without any ulterior motive, without a dread that we may try to

245

force their liberty in order to bring them over to our ideas and to our practices. That will call for great patience on our part. Elizabeth Lesseur used to say: "It is not a question of approving of everything, but of understanding everything."

This deep and sincere love will bear fruit. For we will earn the right to speak of true love and disinterested charity. We will not teach others to love if we do not love intensely ourselves. Then we will be messengers of peace while appearing as a man among men, the friend of all, because we are men of God who love them all and suffer in their suffering. Basically, the result of these pastoral visits shouldbe to reveal, by our conduct as well as by our words, the true image of Christ and the authentic spirit of the Church. In this way we shall accomplish one of the aspects of our mission of mediation between God and man.

Christ speaks to his Priest

If I have given you so much power and so many talents, it is not for yourself, as you well know, but for all the men whom I have committed to your care. There are those who come to you; so, too, there are those who do not come. All are in your care; you must have an interest in them all; you must go to them all.

I have chosen you and put you where you are, not for you to remain shut up in your presbytery or sacristy, but for you to go everywhere, to all homes, to harvest fruit in them, the fruit which lasts. That demands much love and zeal, as well as a deep interior life, for he who abides in me, and I in him, bears much fruit.

Wherever you go, there should be a little more light and the will to do more. Sometimes you will have the comforting feeling that you have done much good. As my disciple, you will see how far your intervention has been providential in keeping Satan at a distance and in preparing the way for my love. At other times you will ask yourself if you have not wasted your time. Be reassured: I am in your very soul; through you I act; the essential thing for me is to be allowed to work through you; nothing that you do when united with me is sterile. And so, if on days when you are tired out, these visits pall on you, and in spite of that, you go ahead and do your best, it is then, perhaps, that they will be most effectual.

You are my envoy, my delegate; do not forget that. I accompany you in a mysterious way, and I want to be the kindness in your face, the smile on your lips, the tone of your voice, the graciousness of your approach. Address yourself deliberately to what is best in each individual; thus you will join me in that corner of heaven which each man has within him. In many I am paralyzed, misunderstood; your appeal will free me and perhaps it will allow me to reveal myself. There are so many souls in whom I sleep, and so little is necessary to reawaken me. There are so many, too, who have not given what they might have to the service of my glory, for lack of someone who, at the right time could have opened up perspectives large enough to stir up their generosity.

Have confidence in your power and in the very virtue of your presence, if your loyalty is faultless and your goodness undarkened. Base your confidence on my mercy and not on your gifts or talents. In you I am; in you I speak; in you I sanctify. Believe this and let me act.

Examination of Conscience

1. Do I consider parish visiting one of the essential tasks of my ministry?

2. Am I concerned to bring the message of Christ in a spirit of faith, light, and love, to every house in my parish, without exception?

3. Before going to visit the families in my parish, do I habitually pay a visit to the Blessed Sacrament and draw from it that interior light which ought to shine through my poor person to share Christ with all those whom I approach?

4. Am I alert to choose the most suitable time so that I can meet the whole family together, and to give each of them an appropriate share of my attention?

5. Aware as I am of the evil which comes from talk of money by the priest, am I careful to avoid money topics in my visits?

6. Am I careful to observe the elementary rule which forbids repeating in one house what I may have learned in another?

7. In my visits do I take great care not to talk the whole time? Do I try to make others talk and listen myself? I have as many things to learn from others as I have to teach them, and what I have to teach them will be more effective if they feel that I have understood them.

Resolutions

1. To draw up for myself a definite programme of visits providing for all my parishioners to be visited within a given time.

2. In these visits, to show that I am first and foremost a priest, forgetting my own concerns to concentrate on those whom I visit.

3. To be very simple and very natural, neither stiff nor listless, neither proud nor off-handed; but at the same time to be deeply supernatural, trying to make my hosts realize the deep concern of God for them.

4. To be discreet and disinterested, avoiding all personal confidences about the difficulties of the diocese, in my presbytery, or my sacristy. Every criticism, every negative judgement is liable to be repeated, and often amplified and distorted. If I am new in the parish, I must avoid at any cost giving the impression of taking the opposite view to that of my predecessor, and I must be careful, if the parish is divided, not to be drawn into any clique or coterie.

An obstacle which often occurs upon the arrival of a new parish priest is division among the parishioners, whether it be caused by family or political reasons, or, what is more shameful still, religious ones. It is not unusual to find that the division was caused by changing the preceding pastor. In this case sometimes there exists a deep hatred between two camps.

The whole success of the new priest will depend on his attitude. The most prudent and the most apostolic attitude will be to keep himself above and outside all that has taken place before his arrival. That is not easy. It requires much self-control on the part of the new priest if he is going to *want* to ignore the different attitudes, to avoid the least word, the least step which would imply an appreciation or a criticism of either side. The least gesture will be noticed by both parties, spread abroad, and distorted. The priest will be classified from then on; he will collect noisy and compromising sympathy from some and he will attract the animosity of the others. He will do no good. To every attempt of either side to tell him what is happening and to draw him to their side he must invariably reply that he is ignorant and that he wants to remain ignorant of all that may have happened, that he has been sent to be a man of peace and of reconciliation, that he suffers in finding himself thrown into the middle of a battle instead of seeing the realization of the ideal of peace and of family life that has been his dream.

Soon the parishioners will be silent around him, and they will gradually forget. During this time the priest will show himself everywhere, in church, visiting the sick, with the children, the man of God, and he will attract hearts to him. He will have pacified their minds, and he will be able to exercise a fruitful ministry.

5. An atmosphere of cordiality and of wholesome gaiety is often appropriate, but we must avoid teasing or ill-timed pleasantries to which the speakers cannot reply and which sometimes leave a bitter memory.

6. To take care not to make negative and sterile reproaches. To try to bring out what is best in each individual, and always to end all my visits with words of encouragement.

7. As far as possible, to extend the benefit of these pastoral visits by organizing family retreats, and by the formation of Catholic Action groups.

8. To keep a notebook with the personal information I have obtained outside the confessional to assist my memory and to help my eventual successor to continue the work I have begun. But organization and administration must not obstruct inspiration and apostolic spontaneity.

"In the accomplishment of these duties, your zeal must not be diverted or hindered by administrative tasks. Perhaps many

among you have had to sustain a daily struggle not to be submerged by administrative tasks and to find the means and the time to devote to souls. If organization and administration are, undoubtedly, valuable means of carrying on the apostolate, they must be adapted and subordinated to the spiritual ministry and to our true, active pastoral responsibilities."
(Pius XII)

Spiritual Reading

Every soul contains the elements which could coalesce to make it a truly Christian soul. They are only waiting for the necessary spark. That spark is love. Love, and then your life as a priest, your sermons, your visits, your smile, your reprimands, and your silence, will all be wonderfully effective. Love means being kind, charitable, obliging, ready, night and day, to answer every appeal, sympathizing with every grief, relieving every suffering. Love means doing everything amiably, for we can be good and yet disagreeable, and that is why Saint Paul, in his famous passage on charity does not only say that charity is good but that it is benign, and Saint Thomas defines benignity as adding affability to goodness.

Be good but discreet, be master of yourself, be understanding, be good as your heavenly Father is good. Your meeting with them will not only make others happy, but better. They will become good as their priest is good, because they have felt the effect of his goodness – in the same way as a body struck by the rays of the sun first experiences the beneficent effect of their warmth, then reflects the rays around it. If you say severely to a little child, "Smile!" it is very likely that he will begin to cry. But without saying anything to him, look at him kindly, and let your lips gradually break into a smile. The child only learns to smile under the gentle influence of its mother's smile. No one knows how to smile until someone has smiled at him. Christ only loved us so much in order that we should love one another as he has loved us.

Peter Lippert, S.J.

250

II

The priest who comes into a rural parish should begin by following the advice of Christ himself and getting to know the flock entrusted to him. He must, accordingly, visit his parishioners without delay. By this means he will be able to find out the state of the souls in his parish and the qualities or defects which it is important for him to discover as soon as possible. If this visit is to produce the happy results we hope for, the priest must not lay himself open to hostile criticism. This will certainly happen if he does not visit everyone, if he shows any preferences or if he allows himself to ask indiscreet questions.

During his first parish visits, the priest should try to see all his parishioners, even those of bad repute. Later he can decide if it will be consistent with the dignity of his priestly character to pay a further visit to houses in which he has been received rudely, or in which the people showed they did not want to receive him. In order not to hurt anyone, he should be careful to visit houses in the order in which they occur. If the parish is spread out, and if there are long distances between the houses, he will announce from the pulpit that he will go to a particular district on particular days. He will take care to remain for about the same length of time with each parishioner; if he stays five minutes in one house and an hour in another, the result will be disastrous. Generally a visit of a quarter of an hour to a half an hour should be sufficient, for the farmer has his work to do and it inconveniences him if you stay for a long time. Next, what should you talk about, particularly on your first visit? Ask the questions which will give you the facts you need to know: the members of the family, the location or the occupation of the children, the health of the family, and be careful not to monopolize the conversation. Try to get the parishioners to talk while you listen attentively to all that is said. In this way by the end of your itinerary, you will not only have found the exterior features of your parish, but also something about its moral condition, the degree of charity which reigns there, the family quarrels which cause divisions. You will have learned all that while you have been talking about the rain and the

251

fine weather, by storing in your memory what you have heard in the course of your first visits.

After this initial contact, which must be made as soon as possible, the exercise of your ministry will give you the opportunity of returning to the homes of your parishioners: you will not neglect any of them. This work is now so deeply established in our parishes that the approach of the priest going from house to house, far from being misinterpreted, is normally very much appreciated. They are happy to welcome their priest, particularly if he takes advantage of this opportunity to show his people the interest he has in them.

The priest must beware of entering the homes of his parish only as a beggar. He has more to give than to receive. His visits should be regarded as a benefit, and they are truly that when he knows how to conquer the hearts of his flock by his kindness. He should take a deep interest in their problems. He should not be too proud to visit the stables or the fields; if a cow is sick, he should inquire about it. Is he not the representative in his parish of him who is concerned with all his creatures, with the birds which fly in the air, as well as with the grass which grows in the meadows?

One good way for a country priest to learn to know his parish thoroughly and to reach the parts which appear to be inaccessible to religious action in the ordinary sense of the term, is to search for the old popular customs, which are liable to disappear today when we are so disdainful of the past. Folklore, that science of local traditions, is now held in honour. It constitutes an object of entrancing study. It consists in observing the facts of daily life, the occupations, the tools used at work, the homes, the furniture, the clothing, the types of harness, etc.; in collecting the tales and legends, the traditions, the songs, in short all that goes to make up the complete life of the farmer in every sphere, including that of religion.

This research gives the priest the opportunity of a valuable contact with the country people. It enables him to go everywhere and to be accepted by the most indifferent, for when it is a question of talking about his village, its traditions, and its local customs, the countryman is much more willing to enter into conversation than when it is a question of discussing his personal life. By means of such conversations the ice is broken, contact is established, the priest is no longer a stranger, a man apart. He becomes a part of the familiar life of the village, and if he is truly priestly, eager to profit by all the opportunities he is offered, he will often be able to say something, for the good of their souls, and sometimes even discreetly to exercise a true apostolate. How can we think that such a method which has become more and more necessary with the spread of religious indifference, is not pleasing to our divine Master who loved to talk to the Jews, his fellow countrymen, to discuss their occupations and their material cares?

Monsignor Dubourg

Subjects for Discussion

1. Where parish visiting is concerned, how shall we overcome the obstacle of lack of time?

2. What are the advantages and the limitations of a notebook about our parishioners?

Prayer

Holy Virgin Mary, who in the mystery of your Visitation are again the model of the priest, deign to bless my visits to my parishioners. Because you bore Jesus within you, your presence alone was sufficient to bring joy to Elizabeth and to sanctify John the Baptist in the womb of his mother. By your maternal influence may my visits bring rays of peace, rays of light, rays of joy to all. Teach me to be a good listener. Help me to understand people. Inspire me with what you want me to say. Let me, above all, love as you wish me to love. And so may my visits be for a little like those of your divine Son. Amen.

Thought

A minister of God and father of a community which, through him, must render to our Lord the worship that is due to him, the priest must take care of all the souls entrusted to him, whether they are practising their religion or not.

Cardinal Suhard

253

14

THE PRIEST IN THE CONFESSIONAL

Since my ordination, there have been two things which, above all, make me realize that I became another man, that I could no longer be as I was before: the power to consecrate hosts, and the power to absolve sins." All of us can confirm this young priest's claim. More even than our first baptism, our first visits to the sick, our first sermons, or our first catechism classes, our first Masses and our first confessions were what made us conscious of the extraordinary "change" which our new state represented.

But in time we grow accustomed to everything. With age, above all with the disturbed, demanding, wearing life most of us live, we are only too likely to let the marvel of our early years get blurred. The progress of liturgical studies has made it easier for a priest to prepare his soul for the eucharistic offering and to rediscover the God of his youth, when he goes up every morning to the altar of God. The development and brilliance of the national and international Eucharistic Congresses have also played their part.

The sacrament of penance, by its very nature, prefers obscurity or at least the half-light. We must make an effort to realize, through the obscure light of the confessional, the splendour of this sacrament which we administer in the name of Christ and of the Church. May this meditation revive our first fervour for this astonishing power which drew from Father Badillon the cry of anguish and admiration: "To me, in my folly, loaded down with worldliness and sin, God has given ministry over men and angels. It is to these stained hands that he has given the power to bind and to loose."

Meditation

In this meditation let us consider two main points. Firstly the greatness of our mission, and secondly the practical consequences which follow.

The sacrament of penance is the sacrament in which we are most closely identified with Christ our Saviour, to cure sinners while reconciling them with the Church. When Jesus wished to define his mission, he spoke especially of life, light, resurrection, and healing: "I came that they may have life, and have it more abundantly." "I am the Light of the World." "He who follows me does not walk in darkness." "The blind see, the lame walk, the lepers are cleansed, the deaf hear, the dead rise, the poor have the Gospel preached to them." "The Father has sent me to heal repentent sinners." (John 8:12, 10:10. Luke 4:18; 7:22)

Let us recollect the words in which Jesus pardons sins: "Son, take courage, thy sins are forgiven thee." (Matt. 9:2; Luke 5:20) "Neither will I condemn thee." (John 8:11) "And he said to her: thy sins are forgiven thee." (Luke 7:48)

We can also recall the vivid parables of the lost sheep, of the lost drachma, and of the prodigal son.

It is to continue this work of forgiveness that our Saviour has chosen us and sent us forth. "As the Father hath sent me, I also send you. Receive ye the Holy Ghost. Whose sins you shall forgive, they are forgiven them: and whose sins you shall retain, they are retained." (John 20:21–23)

Let us reflect for a moment on the extraordinary power which has been conferred on us: "Who can forgive sins, but God only?" (Mark 2:7) "He hath given to us the ministry of reconciliation." (2 Cor. 5:18) We are truly his deputies, his plenipotentiaries. "For Christ, therefore, we are ambassadors." (2 Cor. 5:20) God has placed in our hands a little of his omnipotence, by virtue of which we can apply to ourselves the words of God in Isaias: "I have blotted out thy iniquities as a cloud, and thy sins as a mist: return to me for I have redeemed thee." (Isa. 44:22)

Saint Augustine does not hesitate to proclaim it: "We accomplish therein a work more important than the creation. It is a greater work to make the sinner a just man again than to create heaven and earth." In reconciling with the Church the sinner who has broken away from God, we insert him again into the Mystical Body, and we give divine life back to him. By reuniting to the Church the links which have been broken by venial sin, we restore the penitent into fuller communion with Christ. Let us try in silence to understand more profoundly the great mystery which takes place in us and through us.

The sacrament of penance is the sacrament in which we struggle most directly against the devil, sin, and all the powers of evil, and all that is, basically, the cause of suffering and unhappiness for humanity. Have we not sometimes experienced the feeling that it is there, in the confessional, that we struggle at close quarters with the devil? Our powers as exorcists are involved, at least so far as their solemn exercise is concerned. Are we not driving out devils when we are dealing with a poor man who is the victim of, as well as responsible for, his vices? Is it not in the confessional that we feel how important God regards the part we play, in collaboration with him, as deliverers and physicians so that in this sacrament more than in any other, he leaves a tremendous amount to our human initiative inspired and made fruitful by the grace of our ministerial office? Every absolution is a defeat for the kingdom of Satan, and shuts a door against his activity in this world. Do we reflect enough on the personal as well as on the social consequences of sin? Humanity is a single body; we are all jointly involved. Every sin, even if it is secret, has sociological consequences in the sense that it increases the burden of expiation which humanity must achieve before it can fulfill in its flesh what the Passion of Christ requires to complete the application of the fruits of the redemption.

Sin is not a simple transgression of a law imposed by God on humanity. Let us distrust such a legal interpretation. Sin is an opposition to the divine law by which God rules the world with love. In the same way sin strives to ruin the equilibrium, the

256

development, in a word, the happiness of humanity. It is from within that the world, once it refuses the love of God, acquires the seeds of corruption, damage and decay and drifts towards distress. This requires a great penitential generosity by the parts that have been least affected so as to counteract the poison and allow the gradual cure of the whole body.

It is within souls that the great drama of the redemption is played at the stage of its fruitful application. Souls dedicated by baptism, and even more by ordination, or by religious profession, should be the salt of the earth. If the salt no longer has its savour, if it loses its strength, what use is it? It is fit only for the dungheap. That is why the history of peace or of war, of prosperity or of human misery, is only the projection on the terrestrial globe of the state of conscience of Christian souls.

"For the wages of sin is death." (Rom. 6:23) Sin does not pay its own debts. Death is its ransom. It is one more door open to Satan, with his train of hatred and evil. "Sin no more, lest some worse thing happen to thee." (John 5:14) To take only the problem of peace, experience has taught us that the efforts of the most intelligent men are doomed to failure. It is the Tower of Babel. "Saying: peace, peace, and there was no peace." (Jer. 6:14) The problem is extremely difficult. "Peace", said Saint Thomas, "is the tranquillity of order". And everything which contributes to the re-establishment of the order of justice and of love, contributes more than all the speeches and all the diplomatic conferences to the establishment of peace in the largest sense of the word, both on the social and on the international plane.

What the angels sang to the shepherds of Bethlehem is ever true: "Glory to God and peace to men!" There is a substantial bond between the two. The man who gives or restores divine life glorifies God and ensures the peace of the world.

The sacrament of penance is the sacrament in which we contribute most of the formation of conscience, to the strengthening of character, and to the spiritualizing of humanity. Let us take the sacraments in order. Each has its unique value, but in none of them does our role as teachers appear with so much force as in that of penance. In none of them is our responsibility, by virtue of *ex opere operantis,* so involved.

Saint Pius V said: "Give me true and worthy confessors, and the reform of the Christian world is assured." The immediate effect would be to turn all humanity towards God. If all Christians who go to confession were inspired to act according to the spirit of the Gospel, as true sons of God and of the Church, would not the face of the earth be changed? As Mauriac says, "Spiritual progress is the only human progress which is not misleading", and it is only for spiritual progress that we are necessary. In the name of Christ and of the Church, which are one, we have not only to purify the sinner, but to awaken his conscience, not by casuistic subtleties, but by showing him how God's plan effects his daily life. We must help him not only to correct his weaknesses, but to reply by positive personal effort to the call God and the Church are making to him.

It is by the light of Christ and of the Church that we discover sinners, and we recognize the true gravity of sin which opposes itself to the wisdom and holiness of God's plan and destroys or reduces Christ's presence in us.

The important thing is that the loyal soul should recognize his faults and renew his intention of following Christ with all his might, and be willing to do whatever God wants of him. That is true moral progress, in the Christian sense of the word.

There is no need for psychotherapy or Pelmanism, although practical measures can be useful. We are on the plane of faith and love. We need to renew the promises we made at baptism and to decide by our behaviour and in our daily life to say "No" to Satan, and "Yes" to Christ. It is in this mysterious way that the Church, through us, renews or tightens the bonds which unite men to Christ and sharpens the moral conscience of humanity. It is in this way that, in so far as we, his representatives, enter fully into his Spirit, the Church helps humanity, through us, to become God's people and to move with hesitant and stumbling steps but nevertheless surely towards its divine transfiguration.

There are, of course, more brilliant and outwardly impressive tasks than sitting in the confessional. Besides, the long period of sitting still, the lack of air, the close attention of mind that this ministry requires, can often make it very difficult. As Saint Francis de Sales said with humour: "As they call martyrs those who confess God before men, we have some right also to call martyrs those who confess men before God." All the same, the exercise of the sacrament of penance is so intimately a part of our priesthood that we should pity a priest who deliberately, or through force of circumstances, seldom hears confessions. Often, nothing is more successful in restoring his ideals about the priesthood to a priest who has grown slack or disheartened than some long sessions in the confessional during a pilgrimage. Many priests have been sanctified by their devotion to the practice of hearing confessions: the Curé d'Ars, and, more recently, Father Léopold de Castel Nuovo, a Capuchin who died in Padua in 1942, used to spend ten or twelve hours a day in the confessional.

"A priest who does not love the confessional", said Saint Alphonsus Liguori, "is a priest who does not love souls." A priest who detects in himself a distaste for the sacrament of penance, whether for himself or in ministering to others, must recognize that this represents an aberration from our Lord, and from his priesthood.

The way in which the laity regard this sacrament largely reflects their parish priest's belief in the importance of confession and of frequent confession. Where young people are concerned, research has confirmed that whether particular age groups, even in the same parish and with the same background, appreciated how to take advantage of the sacrament or not, depended on the particular priests who had instructed them and had been their confessors.

The position is more complicated with adults, but it is still apparent that the way in which the priest speaks of confession in his sermons, and his understanding of different types of penitents, determines whether the confessional is valued or ignored by his flock. Joseph Folliet has written: "If the confessor regards his work as an imposition, how can he prevent his parishioners from doing the same?"

We fully appreciate how difficult and even discouraging this ministry can be, but it is a question of faith and of love. We must not consider our own comfort, but the highest service to the

259

Church and our brethren. Perhaps we might spend a few minutes thinking about the following suggestion. The laity have not yet discovered the relationship between the sacrament of penance and the Church because priests themselves have not yet appreciated it. They look upon confession as cleansing the soul and re-establishing its good intentions, but not as an action which restores them to full communion with Christ and their brethren. It is in this sense we must interpret the words of the confessor of Charles de Foucauld: "I cannot look at anyone without wanting to give him absolution. I think that other priests feel the same." Pope Pius XII issued a grave warning in his encyclical *Mystici Corporis:* "Those who try to temper the zeal of young priests for frequent confession should realize that they are doing something contrary to the Spirit of Christ, and are damaging the Mystical Body of our Saviour."

This love of the confessional and this desire to make the reception of the sacrament easy for all must be accompanied by a complete absence of self-interest. Souls do not belong to us. We must respect their freedom. And if some day they leave us, we must not show any surprise or resentment. If our confessional is crowded we must never boast of the number of our penitents, nor of the hours we spend in the tribunal of penance. That would be childish vanity, which our Master would not bless. Nor must we be offended if our colleagues hear more confessions than we do. There is nothing less apostolic than jealousy, even though we try to call it zeal.

If we are to carry out our mission adequately, love and devotion will not be enough. In this ministry so many problems are brought to us, and we come into contact with age, every variety of temperament, and personal circumstances. We must continually revise and develop our technical efficiency in theology, psychology, and sociology. While we learned the essentials of moral theology in the seminary, we must continue to study, both because memory is a faculty which forgets and because problems and mentalities develop. The Church advises us when this has happened and we must study her warnings.

It is the height of folly for us to trust our personal intuition or experience. Superficial impressions are no substitute for solid arguments. The grace of our state is not a revelation arranged

260

for the benefit of the negligent or the lazy. It demands conscientious and regular effort on our part to keep ourselves up to date. All of us have been told in confidence about rulings on important matters which were completely misguided and had disastrous consequences. If a conscience has been misdirected, it is not easy to correct this. Nothing can take the place of keeping our knowledge up to date with the current teachings of moral theology. Without this, the confessor is a fatal victim of his own temperament; his judgement does not rest on any solid base. He is liable to deviate into undue laxity or severity.

Remember the words of our Lord: "If the blind lead the blind, both fall into the pit." (Matt. 15:14) May we never deserve God's curse: "Because thou hast rejected knowledge, I will reject thee; thou shalt not do the office of priesthood to me." (Osee 4:6)

There is another skill that is equally necessary, psychological skill. We must not apply abstract principles automatically without allowing for the *terminus ad quem,* that is to say of the penitent kneeling before us. Every case of conscience is a specific case, and as Cardinal Suhard loved to repeat, "a battlefield of principles". Tact and experience are important. But they are not powerfully reinforced by the knowledge of the considerable progress modern psychology has made.

Nevertheless, the primary requirement for this psychological skill is that we should be able to forget ourselves and put ourselves in the place of others. And it is at this point that true charity, which is both merciful and demanding will make perspicacity grow in the soul of the confessor, and help him to see the essential, and develop the supernatural tact which enables him to enlighten without blinding, to stimulate without inflating and to win the confidence of souls without constraining them. We must love souls very much if we are to help them to enter into the plan which God's love and the Church have for them.

Our psychological skill ought to be increased by sociological skill. Our penitents do not live outside space or time. It is in a concrete reality that they must lead Christian lives. It is in their allotted social and professional milieu that they have to bear witness to their faith. It is often ignorance of their real

261

conditions of life that makes our advice ineffective or completely unacceptable.

It is often our inadequacy, in our penitents' view, which leaves the most important problems of their life unrevealed, so that they seldom accuse themselves of shortcomings in their social obligations, of injustice, or failure to honour their family responsibilities. It would seem that apart from the sixth commandment and the faults of which they accused themselves when they were children, none of them show a sense of responsibility about their family, their work, their citizenship, and their religion. Whose fault is it if our penitents do not feel impelled to get away from their egotism and if they do not recognize the extent of their obligations in the Church and in civic life?

All our priestly functions require a faithful effort on our part to become holy. That is true especially in the confessional, where we are personally committed "in the name of God" more than in any other sacrament. As Monsignor Guyot has said: "The absolution given by a lukewarm priest has the same efficacy *ex opere operato* as that given by a saint, but the welcome, the prayer, the inspired counsel, the supernatural irradiation which emanates from the holy priest, help a soul to get the full benefit of the sacramental grace. It certainly makes a difference to have our confession heard by a Curé d'Ars or a Don Bosco!"

This effort to attain sanctity of life which is required by the ministry of the confessional must primarily be based on hatred of sin and love of the sinner, purity of heart and a spirit of penance, deep union with God.

In these last few years, much stress has been laid on the weakening of the sense of sin. Joseph Folliet has indicated the various reasons for this: a progressive suppression of the moral distinction between good and evil; sociological determinism replacing all the complexities of guilt by irresponsibility under the influence of social pressure; the lessening of the spirit of faith, and the loss of the sense of the divine transcendence.

We must not be misled by a legalistic approach to sin which limits our outlook and makes us see it as a breach of a code, a moral infraction. We must not deplore in sin the damage that it causes to a person or to society. We must go further, and view it ontologically as the refusal of love to a God of Love.

The mystery of sin is the mystery of infinite love scorned, rejected by the dust which we call man, and which has the dangerous power to use the free gifts of God to say "no" to that God. There lies the essential malice of every sin, the malice which caused all the sufferings of Christ and, in him, all the sufferings of men, which are added to his Passion in the fullness of the Mystical Body.

For a priest accustomed to hear the most varied accusations in the confessional, the great danger is that such recitals become a matter of routine. He must react against this so that he never becomes blasé. Hatred and horror of sin can be combined with kindness and mercy for the sinner and even produce it. If we love God deeply, if we suffer when we realize that evil means a refusal to love, how happy we should be when we hear the sinner submits to that love which he had mocked. It is in this sense that there is more joy in heaven when one sinner does penance than for ninety-nine just who remain faithful.

As we learn to understand the wretchedness of man without God, so we feel the need to give thanks when the prodigal son returns, and we share the merciful tenderness of the Father. This kindness for the sinner will be shown by the graciousness with which we receive him, by the effort we make to understand him, by the patience with which we listen to him, and by the trouble we take to help his soul to respond confidently and generously to the desires God has for him.

The sanctity of the confessor will manifest itself by a complete purity of heart. In the confessional we must consider neither our sympathies nor our antipathies. We are there at the service of everyone without distinction. We must love each penitent for himself, without any thought of ourselves. Conscious of the dignity of the sacrament and of the greatness of him whom we represent, we must take the greatest care how we behave and what we say. Our questions must be put tactfully and discreetly. We must never ask questions out of mere curiosity.

We must go further still. When we deal with our penitents, the spiritual paternity which is conferred on us by our priesthood urges us to take on ourselves some of the expiation of their faults and to sanctify ourselves so that we may help them more in their amendment and in their progress in virtue. How can we ask

263

souls to make sacrifices if we do not impose some on ourselves? How can we urge humility effectively or counsel charity and justice, if we ourselves do not make any effort towards these virtues? Not otherwise our penitents could justly retort: "Physician, heal thyself", and we may well incur the condemnation our Master uttered against the Pharisees: "All things, therefore, whatever they shall say to you, observe and do: but according to their works do ye not. For they say and do not." (Matt. 23:3)

If we are going to snatch sinners from the devil, he must have the least possible hold on us. If we are going to lead fervent and generous souls to prayer and self-dedication, we must have become familiar with the path ourselves. By a sort of interior logic, the regular administration of confession forces the priest to climb towards God. "To climb" is a metaphor. We must be filled with God, since it is in his name that we are in the confessional. It is he who greets the soul in our greeting, it is he who speaks by our voice, it is he who loves through our heart, it is he who absolves through our word. The more we try to be united to him and to merge ourselves in him, the more we will be able to help souls to meet him. May our penitents say of us what the pilgrim who visited Ars said: "I have seen God in a man!"

Christ speaks to his Priest

I know your disappointments as I know the weariness that assails you from time to time. Do you forget that I experienced all that? Does it never occur to you that I am near you and that I feel in my heart all that you experience? Come nearer to me, and listen to me. What I make you do, what I achieve through you is infinitely greater than the visible results. When will you understand that it is of another order? To understand, you must humbly accept the mystery which surrounds you on every side: the mystery of your being on earth, in a particular country, in a particular year; the mystery of your vocation; the mystery of your spiritual fatherhood; the mystery of the scope I have left to your initiative; the mystery of your unique role in the

264

history of the redemption, since you are only dust, ashes, negation.

What you must know is that this mystery is a mystery of love, and it is love alone that will give you an appreciation of the wealth of grace which will keep you tranquil in the face of doubt and contradictions. Do not waste time acting without love. The more you grow in love, that is, in forgetfulness of yourself in the service of other souls, the more surely you will find balance, peace, and fruitfulness. What I expect of you is an immense respect for the souls whom I attract to you. They do not belong to you. If I have made you their judge it is in a spirit of love. You are their physician as well. Still more are you their servant. Do not be content with pardoning them, but encourage them to take full advantage of the grace hidden in that pardon which you grant them in my name. Those souls cost me my blood. Love them with the same love with which I have loved them, that is to say for themselves. Help them to realize the plan of love that my Father has for each of them.

Your mission is not to think for them, but to help them to think; not to act for them, but to help them to act. If sessions in the confessional weigh you down, remember that it is natural for you to take upon yourself part of the expiation of the sins on which they accused themselves. I pardoned sinners, but at the same time I made superabundant reparation for them. The disciple is not above his Master.

Be confident. I speak and make expiation in you just as I listen and profit by your offering in the penitent. Be so united to me that they can discover me in you, and that you in your turn can easily discover me in every soul, or at least discover my desire for that soul.

I know the interior of the soul. You know that I am he who sees within. I grant a lucidity, a perspicacity, an astonishing intuition to the priest who has grounded his will in mine and who has rid himself of every personal desire, in order that my Spirit may take possession of him. Have a strong and persistent faith in the efficacy of your ministry in the confessional. Trust more in what you do there, and for that purpose trust in what you are, that is to say, in what I have done for you, in what I want to do for you, if you are united with me.

265

Examination of Conscience

1. Do I take care to be in the confessional on the days and at the times that have been announced?

2. Apart from the regular times, am I always available when someone wishes to go to confession?

3. Do I get out of temper, and even a little abrupt, when a penitent is badly prepared, has difficulty in explaining himself, or is too long in giving details of his sins?

4. Am I careful to recommend or make available to my penitents ways of examining their conscience which suit their practical problems, and help them in judging their life?

5. Do I take care to follow the advice of Saint Paul not to discriminate between individuals, and to receive every soul with the same paternal affection?

6. Am I faithful to the rule of wisdom which consists in letting the penitents accuse themselves of their sins without interrupting them, intervening only to help them if they seem embarrassed, or to encourage them if they are nervous?

7. Am I not inclined, from habit or weariness, to let grave faults pass without trying to advise the penitent that he should make an effort to avoid them?

8. Without lapsing into superficial conversation, do I try to establish a discussion which will lead my penitent to make positive decisions to strive and make progress on particular points?

9. Am I tactful in the questions I put? It is better to keep quiet than to risk a question which could do harm or be misinterpreted.

10. Instead of advice that is general and anonymous, do I try to give to each soul the counsel its circumstances require?

11. Do I know how to vary my sacramental penances, adapting them to the strength, the possibilities, and the fervour of each soul?

12. Even though I am as available and devoted as I can be, am I always detached from my penitents? Can I accept without disappointment or resentment the fact that they choose another confessor?

13. Do I take care to go to confession regularly? Have I not observed that the less frequently we go to confession the less we want to?

14. Have I thought about what is required for children's confessions: regularity, careful preparation, sufficient time given to each one?

15. No matter how many penitents are waiting their turn, am I careful to give to each one the time to which they are entitled to explain themselves normally and receive, in the name of the Church, the advice they need? Nothing is more opposed to the Spirit of Christ than "mass production". Without giving to anyone more time than is necessary, it would be better to hear a few confessions properly than many badly.

Resolutions

1. At least every ten years, to go over my moral theology again, using a good, up to date text-book.

2. To heep abreast, through the appropriate periodicals, of the decisions or directives of the Holy See.

3. To create in my parish, or in the groups on whom I can exert an influence, a favourable attitude towards frequent confession. To watch over myself whenever there is a crowd waiting to make last-minute confessions, especially on the day before a holiday of obligation or on Sunday morning.

4. From time to time to base my sermons on the sacrament of penance, its benefits, the means we should use to benefit by it, and its position in the life of the Church.

5. To observe perfect propriety in the confessional and ensure that those who are waiting cannot hear what is said by me as confessor or by the penitent.

6. Always, before I enter the confessional, to invoke the Holy Spirit, and to renew my union with our Lord as each penitent enters.

7. To be gracious and paternal, which does not imply being easy-going. The kind Father, like the careful doctor, knows how to be firm and insistent when necessary.

8. To hear confession in the spirit of the Church and according to the spirit of the Church, avoiding both laxity and undue severity.

9. Not to detain my penitents any longer than is strictly necessary, but to give plenty of time to each individual.

10. To seek, with the collaboration of the penitent, for possible ways of improvement which are suited to his practical problems.

11. To make it easy for all those under my care to choose a confessor, by inviting other priests to hear confessions in my parish and encouraging my parishioners to take advantage of their presence.

12. To renew my resolution to be fanatically prudent about everything that relates, directly or indirectly, to the secret of the confessional.

Spiritual Reading

The Church, in the sacrament of penance, is not only the messenger who transmits the divine pardon to us; not only the strength which supports our efforts and helps us to return to God. She is more than that: she is the object of our progress. Salvation means belonging to the Church to that visible and hierarchic society, which is truly the body of Christ. The sinner, if he is separated from God, is also like a rebellious son in relation to the Church. He does not come only to find the Church so that she may intercede for him; he comes to be reconciled with her. The sacrament, the efficacious sign, the guarantee of a re-conciliation with our Lord, is our official and liturgical reconciliation with the Church. The proof of the reality of the invisible order which is called the pardon of God, is that visible, practical, humanly efficacious scene between the Christian and the Church.

People often say that penance has all the grief and pain of a second baptism. It certainly has. By baptism we became children of the Church, her members. We were taken into her bosom. We were re-born in her. By the same act we became "holy in the holiness of our Saviour". It is because we are more closely

268

attached to Christ and the Church, that we reflect their sanctity. But this second baptism is said to be hard and painful. That does not imply that we can command grace by our efforts. We do not command grace, it is given to us. The actions to which our Lord has linked the assurance of it are not just ritual movements. They are human acts which, even if they did not signify meeting with God, would have a meaning and a lasting effect on our life.

In calling the actions which make up the sacrament of baptism simple ritual gestures, I do not want to imply that baptism, or any of the other sacraments, are magic acts. They fall into the category of symbolic acts, the direct result of which is not important, because their purpose is to express an idea, an intention. The ablution in baptism is a simple rite because it does not involve real washing. The anointing in confirmation is a simple rite because it does not involve giving the person who is confirming the treatment which wrestlers were given in bygone days when they were rubbed with oil.

For two sacraments, penance and matrimony, the effective sign of the invisible grace is already true and effective on the simple human plane. Marriage is a true contract and, if our Lord had not made it a source of grace, it would still be a binding ceremony, heavy with consequences. So, too, with penance. If the Church were not a society careful of the education of its members, Catholic confession would still be useful, beneficial and expensive. Nevertheless, what it brings pays for what it costs. But penance is a sacrament, and what it bestows far outweighs what it costs. What it bestows in the order of grace far outweighs its psychological benefits. Yet the grace that it guarantees transfigures the demands it makes and its visible results in such a way that both become the work of the Love which makes all things visible and invisible, to his own image.

We must, therefore, note that our sanctity is not the result of our moral effort: the sacrament of penance is not an accidental, or even supernatural, help which will remove the obstacles to moral progress. Like baptism, it "sanctifies" us because it makes us a member of the body of Christ. On the other hand, the visible element in this mystery is a very effective stage in moral progress, the fruitful dialogue of a Christian with his Church.

Sin is a betrayal of the Church as well as a betrayal of God. It seems to me that we must show the penitential character of every effort required of Christians today in working "in the Church": to surrender our individualism, and co-operate loyally in the work of the community presided over by its leaders. That is a realistic way of living in the spirit of penance which the Church requires of those who confess, in addition to the short penance which is now imposed. We remain throughout our whole life in the "Order of Penitents", and our desire to be better sons of the Church should be impregnated with a deep desire to make reparation.

When the Church, by the voice of its appointed representative, has given peace, and provided the penitent has tried to carry out faithfully what has been required of him, all is complete. The peace of the Church is the peace of God. And this peace the priest gives with a recognized authority. He must try unceasingly to enter more into the spirit of the Church and to ignore his personal reactions.

In canonical legislation, in all the directives which refer to the priest in the twentieth century, the confessor must not only look for restrictions and prohibitions, but for an outlook of mind, an ambition to be the kind of confessor the Church desires. But he is not a simple official, a subordinate concerned not to exceed his commission. The Church does not ask him to apply a code rigidly, she entrusts to him a soul whom he must treat with an indulgence and understanding modelled on the heart of Christ. He must long for this soul to reflect the sanctity of Christ in his whole life. He must behave without weakness and without harshness, as he would if the whole effect of his action was on the psychological plane. He must be a real teacher. His role is not only to give or refuse absolution. He has to receive a soul of good will and to adapt his approach to the capacity of that soul. Christ has truly entrusted to him the keys of the kingdom of heaven.

It ought to be impossible for one of the faithful, whatever the moral difficulties which he discusses, ever to say when thinking of the sacrament of penance: "What good is it? I know in advance what he will say to me." The confessor may not be able always to give the peace of the Church, but there is no reason why the penitent's contact with the Church should be sterile.

Father Sauvage

II

The faithful want good confessors whose teaching is firm and considered, who show them clearly the limits of what is lawful or unlawful; who do not impose burdens or unnecessary obligations on them, but come to their aid when justice requires it and when charity counsels it; confessors who are prudent, in whom their penitents may confide everything without any risk of spiritual wounds; confessors filled with the spirit of God, who know how to lead them to a perfection corresponding to their circumstances. Dear sons, show yourselves worthy of so exalted a ministry.

Pius XII

Subjects for Discussion

1. Why can we say that the love of the confessional is the test of sacerdotal zeal?

2. Why and how can one hear confessions in the spirit of the Church?

Prayer

Lord Jesus, who, in spite of my unworthiness, has chosen me to exercise the ministry of your mercy, deign to infuse my heart with your feelings for all souls who come to me in the confessional. Help me to understand them. Be in me to guide their conscience and to answer their problems in the light of your Spirit.

Grant that I may become the instrument of your pardon and of your gifts, that all may find when they receive this sacrament,

271

the grace of a true amendment, and of a new fervour in the service of your love, for the good of their brothers and of the whole Church. Amen.

Thought

The greatest sin is that men have lost the sense of sin.

Pius XII

15

HELL, THE GUARANTEE AND GUARDIAN OF LOVE

Meditation

Every year Pope Pius XII used to address the priests and Lenten preachers of Rome. Here is an extract from the sermon he gave in 1949. "In our era, the preaching of the faith has lost nothing of its timeliness, but it has become even more necessary and urgent. Even preaching on hell. We must, of course, treat this subject with dignity and wisdom. But it is the sacred duty of the Church to preach and teach it just as Christ revealed it, and there is no circumstance of time that can lessen this obligation. It binds in conscience each priest who is entrusted with the work of instructing, warning and guiding the faithful. The desire for heaven is in itself a more perfect motive than the fear of eternal suffering. But it does not follow that it is also the most effective influence in keeping everyone away from sin and turning them to God."

It is a fact that there is less and less reference to sin in sermons, and even in retreats. It has even been claimed that if the world is dying it is because it does not believe in hell any more. The extravagance of preachers, in the last century, who addressed themselves to the imagination rather than to faith, may well have had the result of putting their successors off this topic. It is the law of the pendulum: excesses lead to the opposite extreme until a point of balance is achieved.

During the Middle Ages, paintings of the Last Judgement were commissioned in order to frighten a world which had scarcely emerged from barbarism. They had to speak forcefully,

273

without any nuances. But today, when faith is less simple, and the scientific spirit makes legitimate demands, if we invent a spiritual chamber of horrors to impress the masses, we are likely to terrify some and amuse others, without converting anyone.

Dogma is remarkable for moderation. If we add to it inventions of the imagination, and try to exaggerate it to arouse the emotions more easily, we are likely to diminish respect for a mysterious and sacred reality. Is it wise, for example, to produce an illustrated catechism for children, in which there is a large page showing devils with horns torturing with pitch-forks wretched souls who have been consigned to the avenging flames, whilst a clock beats out its eternal rhythm: "Always, forever! Always, forever!"?

Besides, hell is not the central truth of Christianity, demanding everything on earth to be organized in fear and trembling. It is an element which can be understood only in a synthesis of which the love of God is the centre.

If we do not balance the reality of hell with the truths of faith based on divine love, we end by distorting the dogma and by presenting God as a sort of bogey-man. Such impressions will remain in the mind of the child when he becomes a man, and will incite him to shed a religion with such unnatural memories for him.

Another reason why we do not speak more often of hell, is that preaching about it is not easy. We are apt to say too much or too little. If too little, the priest makes people complacent. If we err in the other direction, we distress unstable souls and cause them to have scruples which can lead to neuroses.

"All the eschatologies which profane the mystery are deluding", said Berdjaer. There are today so many people who, because of war and the noise and stress of modern life, are on the verge of mental breakdown, that it takes very little to capsize them. But that is another reason for setting this dogma in the context of the Christian truth, and to do that, we ourselves must have clear and deep convictions about it. Then we shall be in a position to avoid troubling anthropomorphisms and violent images, as well as the silence which deprives souls of necessary enlightenment.

274

If we hesitate to speak of hell, it is, perhaps, precisely because we priests have not meditated enough on this mystery, nor plumbed the exact teachings of revelation about it. It is clearly a subject which is not attractive, particularly in isolation. Gazing into the abyss soon makes us dizzy. But just as the Christianity which would banish the cross would be only a lie, so an eschatology which ignores the dogma of hell would be mutilated.

A Christian, and even more so a priest, should not be afraid to face the truth, and it must be the whole truth, and not the parts which suit us. Truth, even in its formidable aspects, sets us free.

The first reason why we should meditate on hell is that it is a reality which we must take into account. It is a truth of faith which, at our peril, we cannot neglect. If Jesus referred so many times to the existence of an eternal hell, it was not without reason.

The dogma of hell, clarified by the light which other dogmas throw upon it, can nourish our living faith. If it is freed from anthropomorphism, purified from morbid weakness, grounded in the understanding of the lawful requirements of infinite love, in the full perspectives of theology, preaching on hell, can emerge from its eclipse to become again, as in the time of Saint Francis Xavier, one of the best spurs to a spiritual and apostolic life.

Hell is the amazing proof of the value God attaches to our free and personal love. He so loved man that he created him free and immortal. He gave him the power to say "no" to his immense love and in a manner of speaking to frustrate his omnipotence. "God wants all men to be saved", says Saint Paul, but, out of respect for his creation he wants a free and voluntary ratification of his plan of love. He is prepared to take a risk. Some may refuse him and persist in doing so freely and deliberately.

How can a person deliberately refuse the love of his Creator? That is a mystery, but it is the very mystery of our liberty. To wish that God had made creatures incapable of sinning, is to ask him to make creatures either irresponsible or gods by nature. To want to prevent God from creating them because they might

275

make bad use of their freedom, would be to ask him to renounce his love. In his infinite goodness, God has done all that was humanly and divinely possible to facilitate the loyalty of men, without trespassing upon their free will, God took the risk. Damnation is a possible solution for every being in the moral world. If the being really deserves a choice God never ceases to multiply the help. He offers the possibility of damnation thereby confirming the sacred character of our earthly existence. Without the real possibility of eternal death, neither the freedom of man loving God, nor the liberty of God sacrificing himself to save man, would have their true meaning. Of course we should walk in the ways of love, but who can boast that he has never been tempted? As long as we are here on earth, we are not confirmed in grace. "Therefore let him who thinks he stands take heed lest he fall." (1 Cor. 10:12)

There are times of trouble when only fear can stop us. It is, says the psalmist, the beginning of wisdom. Saint Augustine calls it the guardian of love. "Fear hell", said Saint Basil, "the fear of hell is a bridle which prevents the soul from being led into committing sin". We must remember that there are those who receive more than others and who abuse the grace and mercy they have been given. Those who have been favoured with a special love and who have misused for their own satis-faction the gifts, talents and powers which God granted them are most likely to lapse into blindness of mind and hardness of heart which are the beginning of hell here on earth.

The sculptor of one of the porches at Chartres appreciated that when he placed a bishop and a monk in the first ranks of the damned. There is nothing like a sermon on hell to rouse us from our torpor. "Always remember thy last end, and thou wilt never sin!" says Ecclesiasticus.

Half-heartedness, slackness, inaction are the primrose path down which we travel imperceptibly to the abyss. Do not forget that our Lord may come for us like "a thief in the night". He has warned us of this. We may comfort ourselves by reflecting that it is our final choice which determines our eternity, and that God in his mercy increases his appeals up to that time. But will not this final option be largely determined by our previous preparation? Our acts follow us, our choice each day shapes our last choice, and it is the last act of a man's will which is ratified for eternity.

Men are always liable to grow obdurate in their sin, and to prefer their egoism to the God who invites them to strip themselves of self. They will be strongly tempted towards a rebellion which pride will prolong, and which will foster, to the very last, a perverse determination to refuse God and to repel his advances.

The thought of hell should normally arouse our generosity. All the saints who were particularly moved by the horror of eternal punishment have found it a great stimulus to acts of generosity. The accounts of the martyrdom of Saint Polycarp, who was put to death in A.D. 156, speak of the courage the witnesses of the faith derived from the comparison between the fire of the stake and the fire of hell. We must aim at the reactions of the children of Fatima when the police threatened to throw them into boiling oil: "That does not frighten us as much as the punishments of hell – and it will not last as long."

The writings of Saint Catherine of Sienna and of Saint Teresa of Avila brought one nun to declare: "Although I am so afraid of suffering, I do not know what I would not endure to avoid hell. I see so well that all the sufferings of the world are nothing in comparison with the grief of not being able to love any more, for in hell they breathe only hatred and thirst for the loss of their souls."

There are souls who rebel against effort, who need salutary punishment, in the face of this frightful danger with its eternal consequences, to restore their self-control and equilibrium. Meditation on hell can stir up apostolic zeal. All souls receive sufficient grace for salvation. But if they fail to take advantage of it, they need help to restore the position and it is our responsibility, *ex officio,* to obtain this for them.

If there were more saints, more souls would be helped. Our apostolic activity can help to create a psychological and sociological atmosphere which makes the return and the ascent to God easier. The Curé d'Ars, who thought a great deal about hell, willingly accepted the fatigue of an exhausting ministry for the very purpose of enabling himself to work for the conversion of sinners and to bar the way to the abyss for thousands of souls, by his sacrifices as well as by his exhortations. It was that which consoled him for having to remain longer on this earth when his whole soul longed for the happiness of heaven.

Every one knows of the vision of hell which Saint Teresa of Avila describes, and which she herself says constituted one of the most remarkable graces which our Lord granted her. She ends the account by saying: "In spite of the six years which have elapsed since then, I am so terrified when I write these lines that my blood seems to run cold in my veins . . .." But the conclusion of the reformer of Carmel is essentially apostolic: "That vision inspired me with an immense sorrow for the loss of so many souls. It also inspired me with an ardent desire to help other souls. It seems to me that to free even one soul from such terrible torments I would suffer death willingly a thousand times. I do not know how we can live in peace when we see so many souls whom the devil is dragging with him into hell."

A final reason for meditating on hell is that only the illumination which we receive from the Holy Spirit in prayer can help us to speak with full knowledge of the facts, with suitable conviction, but also with the wisdom, prudence, and discretion which Pius XII recommended.

The first thing to do is to listen *submissively* to Jesus, when he expresses himself so clearly and forcibly in Scripture about eternity. For his words to be "spirit and light" in us, we must receive them with the intense desire to be taught by him who is light and life. Let us consider some of the essential words of Christ. Everyone can add to this anthology.

"For what doth it profit a man, if he gain the whole world and suffer the loss of his own soul?" (Matt. 16:26) "And fear ye not them that kill the body and are not able to kill the soul: but rather fear him that can destroy both soul and body in hell." (Matt. 10:28) "But he that shall deny me before men, I will also deny him before my Father who is in heaven." (Matt. 10:33) "You serpents, generation of vipers, how will you flee from the judgement of hell." (Matt. 23:33) "And the unprofitable servant, cast ye out into the exterior darkness. There shall be weeping and gnashing of teeth." (Matt. 25:30) "Depart from me, you

278

cursed, into everlasting fire, which was prepared for the devil and his angels." (Matt. 25:41)

"If thy hand scandalize thee, cut it off: it is better for thee to enter into life maimed, than having two hands to go into hell, into unquenchable fire: where their worm dieth not, and the fire is not extinguished." (Mark 9:42–3)

"Seeing it is a just thing with God to repay tribulation to them that trouble you: and to you who are troubled, rest with us, when the Lord Jesus shall be revealed from heaven with the angels of his power: in a flame of fire, giving vengeance to them who know not God and who obey not the Gospel of our Lord Jesus Christ, who shall suffer eternal punishment in destruction, from the face of the Lord and from the glory of his power." (2 Thess. 1:6–9)

"A man making void the law of Moses dieth without any mercy under two or three witnesses: how much more, do you think he deserveth worse punishments, who has trodden under foot the Son of God and hath esteemed the blood of the testament unclean, by which he was sanctified, and hath offered an affront to the Spirit of grace?" (Heb. 10:28–9)

"But according to thy hardness and impenitent heart, thou treasurest up to thyself wrath, against the day of wrath and revelation of the last judgement of God: who will render to every man according to his works. To them indeed who, according to patience in good work, seek glory and honour and incorruption, eternal life: but to them that are contentious and who obey not the truth but give credit to iniquity, wrath and indignation." (Rom. 2:5–8)

Finally, let us remember that the severity of the punishment reflects the greatness of the graces received. "Because being ministers of his kingdom you have not judged rightly, nor kept the law of justice, nor walked according to the will of God. Horribly and speedily will he appear to you, for a most severe judgement shall be for them that rule. For to him that is little, mercy is granted; but the mighty shall be mightily tormented." (Wis. 6:5–7)

Without appealing to our imagination, let us make an act of faith in the mysterious truth of hell, that is, in its possibility, and its reality. The challenging paradoxes of Marcel Jouhandeau

279

convey an essential lesson, stemming from the maxim: "If man does not understand hell, it is because he has not understood his own heart."

"To understand his own heart", said Michel Carrouges, commenting on this remark, "requires more than a knowledge of the mysteries of psychology. We must penetrate the central domain, the axis of all destiny, where human liberty operates in its inscrutable way. This liberty confers an amazing grandeur on man, but also represents an appalling danger which God has left in man's hands. Just as man is free to love God, so is he free to hate him. Just as he is free to undertake the great pilgrimage to the heavenly Jerusalem, he is no less free to run away from it for ever. Where I am, there is my free will, and there where my will is free, absolute and eternal hell holds sway."

God created paradise, but a rebellious creature created hell. God created liberty, but creatures can use it freely to bring hell about. Hell is only the horrible guarantee of human liberty. Men are free in relation to their Creator only if God has granted them the power to refuse him their love for ever. If the odyssey of angelic and human creatures must inevitably be achieved by a final and complete reconciliation between God and them, then the liberty of these created beings is only a sham. Hell must at least be a possibility.

For reality we must keep unreservedly to the authentic teaching of the Church, the depositary of faith. She has always taught that hell is a painful reality, irrevocable, characterized by the three elements of physical pain, eternal pain, and the pain of the damned. The pain of the damned, we know, is separation from God. The damned soul deprives himself voluntarily of the joy of God, although he feels in his whole being that he was created to possess him and that in him is perfect happiness.

It is difficult to conceive this pain which Saint Thomas and all the theologians tell us is so severe. Damnation is only the realization of the state of revolt the soul has freely chosen. The damned soul rejects of his own free will him towards whom he cannot help being drawn from the very depths of his being. Intense suffering here below gives us a faint idea of that separation of being and of will: "Oh! what an atrocious thing it is to love and hate at the same time . . .", cried out Anna Karenina when she had to flee from the man for whose love she had sacrificed the affection of her husband and the presence of her child.

The faithful are much more impressed by what the Scriptures say about the fire of hell than by efforts to describe eternal damnation. Tradition is unanimous in speaking of physical pain, and identifies it with the pain of fire. We know that this fire is real: the common opinion of theologians does not authorize us to think otherwise. They call it fire not because it resembles earthly fire, but because it has some analogy with it, an analogy which is difficult to define, except in the sense that it causes in the damned soul acute sufferings which we can compare only to the burning produced by fire on our human frame.

It does not follow that the fire of hell is a fire identical with the fire that we know. We know simply that the fire is real. "Why have the sources of our faith given the name of fire to this mysterious infernal agent? Why do they not speak of it as frost and ice? It is", a German theologian tells us, "because the most acute suffering that we can imagine on earth is that caused by a burn."

Everyone knows the cruel comment of Sartre: "There is no need of a gridiron, hell is other people." That is perhaps one of the functions of the fire, infinitely more terrifying than the material flames with which preachers have frightened the faithful.

"The uttermost depth of hell" said Dostojevski, "is the realization that we can no longer love". The damned soul has chosen this fundamental suffering, which dominates life inexorably in hell. Death crystallizes forever in hatred the soul which has rejected love. That is the source of the unsuppressible universal hatred. Hell was founded by Lucifer and his angels at the very moment when they rebelled against God. The whole of hell flows from that flaming source. The damned are associated in this accursed work to their own ruin and to the suffering of others.

The eternity of hell is declared in scripture. The Gospel leaves no place for doubt. Doubt is not possible. Our Lord presents the next life as a tragic alternative: on the one side eternal life, on the other eternal death. There is absolute parity between the duration of the punishment and of the reward.

At the moment when it enters eternity, the soul adheres irrevocably to the choice it has made in this life. It is a fixed and immutable state. God, once again, does all that is divinely possible before the last hour, to attract, to stir up the desire to return in the prodigal without interfering with his freedom, but the moment must come when rejected mercy must respect human liberty, leave the sinner to his obstinacy, and withdraw from him forever.

This word, eternity, which surpasses human understanding, can only make us dizzy. But the irrevocable character of the choice made by man during the earthly phase of his existence shows how seriously God deals with us. We are all sinners whether we are preserved from sin, or purified from it. And if God has preserved us or has purified us, it is none the less necessary that we watch and pray that we may not yield to temptation. As Monsignor Benson said: "Each of us has on his lips the kiss of Judas."

Remember the prayer of Saint Philip Neri: "My God, do not trust me, give me your grace, for there are no crimes of which I do not feel capable today, if your grace is lacking to me." The best antidote to presumption is precisely the loyal *humility* which relies on grace rather than our own efforts. At one of the most solemn moments of the Mass the Church puts on our lips a humble prayer to beg our Lord to preserve us from eternal damnation. "We beseech Thee, O Lord, graciously to accept, and to order our days in thy peace and bid us to be delivered from eternal damnation and numbered among the flock of the elect."

Life on earth is a warfare and the devil is used by God to test men. For those who are humble of heart, who pray, and are vigilant, the test will not result in failure but in victory.

A priest will always benefit from re-reading in the account of the Passion, the story of Saint Peter's denial. We cannot accuse Saint Peter of lacking generosity. He was all fire, all flame to protect Jesus. He had taken even unexpected precautions. Has he not procured a sword? And when the moment comes, he will make use of it to cut off the ear of Malchus. "Even though all shall be scandalized because of thee, I will never be scandalized." But his vanity and his presumption made him neglect the warnings of our Lord: "Amen, I say to thee, today, this very night, before the cock crows twice thou wilt deny me thrice." He did not want to understand that the true arms with which we conquer the devil do not consist of human means but of prayer and vigilance. "Watch and pray that you enter not into temptation. The spirit is willing indeed, but the flesh is weak." Instead of praying, Peter slept. We know the result.

Each of us can easily apply this to our own state of soul, without forgetting the conclusion of the episode on the shore of the lake: "Peter, dost thou love me more than the others? Lord, Thou knowest all things. Thou knowest that I love thee!" The mystery of the next world surrounds us on all sides and God alone can measure each soul's guilt. But if a soul is humble and does not reject divine help, his misery attracts divine mercy.

God has more power to pardon in his heart, than the whole world has to sin. The *Dies Irae* places on our lips our claim to the indulgence of the sovereign Judge:

> Quaerens me, sedisti lassus;
> Redemisti crucem passus;
> Tantus labor non sit cassus.

> To seek me thou didst not disdain,
> And on the Cross died with much pain,
> Let not such anguish be in vain.

The Church, which has canonized thousands of saints, has never defined the names or the number of the damned. The Curé d'Ars consoled the widow of a suicide by declaring to her that between the parapet and the river her husband had had time to repent. How much time is there between a parapet and the flowing stream!

Alas, there are real and manifest monsters. The revelation of the atrocities committed during the last war leads us to suppose the existence of human consciences that are truly devilish. But as long as they are on earth we must never despair. One of the grandeurs of our mission is to help, by our repeated prayers and the celebration of Mass, to enlarge, while there is still time, the little corner of blue sky which every man, even though he is a criminal, carries in his heart. "Deliver our souls, and those of our brethren, relations, and benefactors, from eternal damnation."

We should end this meditation by offering the hour of our death, in union with the death of our divine redeemer, so that none of those whom it has been our mission to save may fail the eternal rendez-vous!

Christ speaks to his Priest

Come to me with my infinite mercy, and hear what I say. Hell is a terrible and appalling reality. It is the unchallengeable witness of the seriousness with which I respect the will of man. My Father wishes all men to be saved. I myself came on earth and suffered so much that all might have life and eternal happiness. Unceasingly our spirit seeks to penetrate men's hearts to diffuse the divine light in them. But the contest between infinite love and human liberty is not a laughing matter. Each man judges himself by his own works and determines for ever the state which he has chosen freely. We do all that is divinely possible to be done to enlighten, help, guide, sustain, attract, call and urge, without restricting man's free will, a fundamental requirement for his merit as well as his greatness.

In scripture I remind men so often and in so many ways: "What does it profit a man if he gain the whole world, but suffer the loss of his own soul?" My warnings are clear. My Church by its teaching, its liturgy, and its sacraments never ceases to recall the importance of the choice men make. All my life on earth, my labours, my sufferings, my merits, my words, my miracles, had but one end: to enlighten you, to make you watchful, to heal you, to purify you, and to urge you to help one another in order to enter one day into the splendour of the life of our Trinity.

I have poured out on every human soul appeal on appeal out of my mercy: graces of every kind, striking miracles, interior joy, punishments, sicknesses, and war. How easily man could understand if he wished. I ask my saints to contribute their sacrifices in order to touch hardened hearts, to enlighten rebellious minds, and to help to rouse fatal sluggishness. To the very last moment, until man is on the brink of the abyss, I strive and watch; as long as the soul retains a touch of grace it can heed the last appeal of merciful love.

If man, through pride, hate, love of money or the flesh, persists in refusing, he places himself in the way of damnation, and we respect his freedom to the extent of being willing to withdraw ourselves from him. What significance would a liberty which was finally determined against free choice, have for the dignity of man, made in our image and likeness?

The existence of hell shows the sacred character of the earthly phase of our existence. Without the real risk of eternal damnation, neither the freedom of man when he chooses God, nor the love of our Saviour when he proceeded to the supreme sacrifice would have their true significance.

Heed the warning of my apostle Peter, which you will repeat every evening until your last day on earth. "Brethren, be sober, be watchful. Your adversary, the devil, as a roaring lion, goes about seeking someone to devour." Watch and pray that you enter not into temptation. Your life is a succession of choices. To err is human. You may take the wrong road. Have the humility to retrace your steps and to find the right road again. For to persist on the wrong path is to follow the devil.

Mercy is never wanting to the weak soul who has failed, but acknowledges its guilt. But the man who abuses my grace openly and who closes his heart to my voice, plunges along the dark road which leads to the abyss. Hardness of heart follows close upon blindness of mind. Woe to him who makes use of my gifts and of the authority which I have conferred upon him, to mislead the souls whom I have entrusted to him and who leads them to their destruction. When a blind man leads a blind man, both fall into the ditch. Woe to him who, chosen from among thousands of others to worship my Father in spirit and in truth, worships the idols of money, pleasure, and vanity.

285

Remember that you have not only to keep yourself from hell, but you must keep from it all the souls whom I have united to yours. Remember your spiritual paternity. You have charge of so many spiritual sons and daughters, whom you must help by your exterior ministrations, and even more, by your interior activity.

As long as you are on earth, you can acquire merit, you can expiate, you can implore. Later, it will be eternally too late. Trust, then, in your power. Throw yourself into your great work as co-redeemer. At your Mass, when you read your breviary, when you say your rosary, or when you are meditating, always take care to recount all the spiritual needs of the children of your soul.

Be zealous. Help souls to absorb me, and you will raise the moral level of humanity. You will also keep from perdition many unfortunate souls who are blind to my light and deaf to my voice. Do not be content to be a correct priest. When will you decide to become a holy priest, that is, to refuse me nothing, in little things and in great, and so to put all the love of which you are capable into doing what I ask you to do and suffering what I ask you to suffer? I so long to find, among my consecrated souls, hearts which love me without limit, without reserve, without any reservations; wills which have no other ambition except mine, souls completely empty of self, so that I may be served by them as my zeal desires! A holy priest, docile to the motions of my Spirit, blocks the road to hell for thousands of souls.

Examination of Conscience

1. Do I sometimes preach on hell? If I do not, is it not through lack of conviction and through fear of running counter to contemporary thinking? If I do preach, do I avoid falling into the excess of certain preachers of times past who addressed themselves more to the imagination than to the faith, and sought to stir up their congregation to servile fear rather than generous love?

2. Do I understand the danger to faith, especially with children, of an over-dramatic presentation of hell, in words or pictures?

3. Do I know how to show that the dogma of hell, without being the central truth of Christianity, is part of the synthesis of divine love?

4. Does the thought of hell stimulate me to humility and vigilance in my own life and to a more ardent zeal for the salvation and sanctification of others?

Resolutions

1. From time to time to read the warnings given by the Pope about our duty to preach on hell. The subject must be treated with dignity and wisdom. But the Church has a sacred duty to proclaim this truth without any palliation, just as Christ revealed it. It is a matter of conscience for each priest whose duty it is to instruct, warn, or guide the faithful.

2. From time to time to meditate on hell, asking our Lord to enlighten and deepen my faith, and so enable me to proclaim the truth worthily and competently in all its detail.

3. To inspire the reverential fear necessary to ensure resistance to temptation but to avoid falsifying perspectives and causing morbid psychoses. To put the accent on divine mercy which never abandons a humble and loyal soul, however weak it be, as long as it does not give up the struggle and the effort.

4. In the spiritual education of souls, to insist on the charity which covers a multitude of sins, on forgiving the trespasses of others, and on the duty of helping our brethren.

5. To remember that there are on earth many hardened sinners who have withdrawn obstinately from God and live under the sway of Satan. To recall sometimes that as long as they are on earth the last word has not been said and that one of my missions is to help them, by the invisible net of the communion of saints, to say the "yes" that will save them to the final appeal of their redeemer.

6. To treasure, and repeat, in the name of all, the liturgical texts which imply the preservation of eternal punishment.

Spiritual Reading

I want you to know, my daughter, that although they have been regenerated in the blood of my only Son, and have received the grace which has restored the human race, men have failed to recognize the favour which I have shown them. Amen, I say to you, they will become more hardened and they will deserve a greater punishment, now that they have received the redemption of the blood of my Son, which they did not have before the redemption, when the blemish of Adam's sin had not been effaced. It is only just that those who have received more should give more in return, and we are under a greater obligation to those from whom we have received most.

A lapsed Christian incurs a greater punishment than a pagan. By divine justice, he is burned more severely by the fire which never consumes, that is to say, he is more tortured, and in that torture he feels that he is devoured by the worm of conscience. The fire does not consume, because the damned, whatever the torment they endure, never lose their being. I say to you: they ask for death but they cannot obtain it, because they cannot lose their being. They lose their supernatural life of grace, but never their natural life.

The more they received from me, and the more their soul was enlightened through scripture, the more obligations they had, and, in consequence, the more unbearable is their shame. The more they have known scripture in their lifetime, the more clearly do they see at the moment of death the great faults they have committed. Furthermore they will be condemned to torments more severe than others, as the good will be more exalted in glory. The lapsed Christian will be more tortured than a pagan, because he has possessed the faith, and did not want the light, while the pagan has never had it.

So, too, unhappy priests, for the same reason, will be punished more severely than other Christians, because of the ministry I entrusted to them of distributing the eucharistic sun, and because they possessed the light of knowledge which enabled them to see the truth for themselves and for others, if they wished to. It is just that they should be given a more terrible punishment.

They do not think, unfortunate men! If they only reflected on their state, they would not fall into these misfortunes. They would be what they should be, and what they are not. Through them the whole world is corrupted, because they are worse than the laity. It is not only their own souls that they defile with their impurities, but they poison those who have been entrusted to them. They suck the blood of my spouse, Holy Church, until she becomes pale and enfeebled. The love and attention which they owe to my spouse they have expended on themselves. They are zealous only for her destruction. There are souls whom they should be eager to help, but their ambition is only for livings and large incomes.

Saint Catherine of Siena

II

After our Lord had given me great graces, of which I have already spoken, and others still greater, while I was at prayer one day, I found myself in an instant, without knowing how, as though transported to hell. I understood that our Lord wished me to see the place which the devil had prepared for me, and which I had merited by my sins.

This experience lasted only a short time, but now after many years, it seems as if I can never forget it. The entrance to the place seemed to me like a very long and narrow lane, or a very low, dark, and narrow furnace. The earth under my feet seemed to me soaked with a horrible mud, very dirty, with a pestilential odour, and with venomous reptiles in it. At the bottom there was a hollowed out cavity in the wall somewhat like a niche, where I was put in a very cramped position. The worst place on earth would be attractive in comparison with that spot. Anything I could say about it would be incoherent. Word just cannot give any idea of it at all. I felt in my soul a fire that I do not know how to describe. All the physical sufferings I have endured in my lifetime, and doctors have told me are the most terrible to which humans can be subject, all the other kinds of suffering, some of them caused by the devil, are nothing in comparison with what I experienced in that place, and especially with the realization that they would be endless.

But those bodily tortures were nothing compared with the agony of soul, the pressure, the anguish, the hopelessness which I experienced, and which I cannot describe. To say that it was all like perpetual death is understating it, for in death there is some external cause, but in hell the soul torments itself. The truth is that I do not know how to describe that interior fire and the despair, under the torments and atrocious suffering. I did not see who inflicted those tortures but I felt myself burned and mangled, and I say that the interior fire and the despair were the worst sufferings. I was in a place utterly pestilential, without any hope of the least consolation, with no means of sitting down, or of lying down, or of escaping. The walls themselves were terrifying and seemed to be closing in on me and crushing me. There was no light. Everything was plunged in darkness. I do not understand how it was possible, when there was no light, for me to see so much that was horrible to behold.

It was not our Lord's will that I should see more of hell. Since that experience I have seen frightening punishments imposed on vices. But as I did not suffer the pain, it did not terrify me as much as the vision in which our Lord wanted me to experience spiritual torments of spirit, as if my body had experienced them. I do not know how it was possible, but I appreciate that it was a great grace and that our Lord wished me to see for myself the punishments from which his hand had delivered me. For there is nothing said nor written about the various torments of hell, which the devil inflicts on the damned that can be compared with the reality. The difference between fire on earth and fire in hell is the same as the difference between an image and a living person. I was so horrified by this experience that I am still frightened, as I write this, although it is six years since it happened.

Saint Teresa of Avila

Subjects for Discussion

1. How to develop in our parishioners unreserved faith in the existence of hell and a complete confidence in God's infinite mercy?

2. In what circumstances and in what way should we preach about hell?

Prayer

Lord Jesus, God of mercy, increase and enlighten our faith in the formidable reality of hell eternal. Make us understand in its tragic light the importance of our choice here below, and gravity of the abuse of graces by those to whom you have given so much. Preserve us above all from blindness of mind and hardness of heart.

By the blood of your Passion, by the tears of your Mother, by the merits of all your saints, have pity on all those, our brothers, who are in danger of perdition. In their name we cry out to you: "Help! Lord Jesus, we perish!" Say but one word and their soul will be cured. You have loved them, O Lord, infinitely more than they have loved their sins. O Lord, for them, for us, for your glory, pity! pity! pity! Amen.

Thoughts

The only irreparable evil is to find oneself some day unrepentant before him who forgives.

Bernanos

Hell does not come from God. It comes from the sinner who puts an obstacle in the way of God.

Paul Claudel